Thinking
About
FAITH

Thinking About FAITH

AN INTRODUCTORY GUIDE TO PHILOSOPHY & RELIGION

DAVID COOK

Academie Books Grand Rapids, Michigan
Zondervan Publishing House

THINKING ABOUT FAITH:
An Introductory Guide to Philosophy and Religion
Copyright © 1986 by David E. Cook

Published by special arrangement with Inter-Varsity Press,
Leicester, Great Britain.

ACADEMIE BOOKS is an imprint of Zondervan Publishing House,
1415 Lake Drive, S.E., Grand Rapids, Michigan 49506

Library of Congress Cataloging in Publication Data

Cook, David, 1947-
    Thinking about faith.

    Bibliography: p.
    Includes indexes.
    1. Apologetics—20th century. 2. Christianity—Philosophy.
3. Faith. I. Title.
BT1102.C59 1986   201   86-15965
ISBN 0-310-44131-5

Printed in the United States of America

86 87 88 89 90 91 92 93 / 10 9 8 7 6 5 4 3 2 1

In memory of Margaret Falconer Cook

Contents

Acknowledgments

Every book owes much to others. There are many who have helped in the ideas and the production of this book. I am grateful to them all from Professor R. Hepburn, who taught me philosophy, to Angela Booth, Stuart Dobson, Maggie Gibbon, Mike Harris, Dorothy Johnson, Gwynneth Roberts, and Tim Yates. Kathleen, Simon and Kenneth have put up with a great deal so that this book appeared. Thanks are due to them.

This book is dedicated to the memory of my mother, who first taught me to think, and who worked hard to give me every opportunity in life.

Introduction:
why this book is needed

It is not difficult for me to kill a conversation. If I am on a train or a bus and someone asks me, 'What do you do for a living?' I can end the conversation there and then by replying, 'I am a philosopher.' In a nutshell, philosophy terrifies people. This seems silly. After all, philosophy is literally the love of wisdom. We are all keen on acquiring wisdom and being thought of as wise, so where is the problem? Perhaps it is that philosophy seems to make things more difficult. Philosophers ask questions that no-one else seems to ask. They raise doubts where there are no real doubts as far as most people are concerned. Philosophy is a nit-picking kind of exercise. It seems to be about words and the meaning of words. It has the feel of an intellectual exercise with little or nothing to do with reality.

Yet philosophy is here to stay. Its roots go far back into the history of humankind and every ancient culture worthy of the name seems to have had its thinkers and sages who indulged in philosophical speculation. As long as people have the capacity to think, it seems that they will philosophize and speculate. But such speculation and thinking can create problems and doubts. What we all take for granted can be questioned by the philosopher. What we have always believed to be the case comes under fresh scrutiny from the philosopher. What is accepted as beyond all possible and reasonable doubt is put on the chopping-board, dissected, and perhaps not put together again. An example may help.

One of the very first lessons people learn in doing philosophy is to define their terms. This is much more complicated than might be expected. For example, if we try to define what a 'game' is, we may begin by giving examples of games. If we list football, squash, tennis, bowls, scrabble and monopoly we may start to have some idea of games, but the list does not in itself tell us what is common to each and every game. What makes a game a game? It sounds as if we should try to find some essence or core of what constitutes a game. It might be that a game is played by different numbers of people, or it is something done for fun, or it is a rule-following activity. The problem is that if we think about each of these attempts at defining an 'essence of game', we soon realize that none of them is exhaustive and it is all too easy to give counter-examples. Some games are played by just one person. Some are played for money. In some, part of the 'game' is not following the rules. Such an examination of examples and searching for definitions soon end up in a feeling of disgust.

If we cannot arrive at an understanding of 'game' by a positive means, we might try to get there by a negative route. One way we often describe something to someone else is by making clear that it is not the same as some other things and does not have the same kinds of qualities as these things. Thus by a kind of process of elimination we may approach a better understanding of what something is, though this will be far short of a crisp, easy and tight definition. Again this is part of what disturbs people about philosophy. It does not seem to lead to greater certainty and understanding, or to general agreement about anything.

WHAT THIS BOOK IS

If it is difficult to define what a game is, it is equally difficult to say exactly what this book will be trying to do! It is about philosophy and its impact on religion and theology. It is about the kinds of questions and problems that philosophy raises for theology and the Christian faith, and the ways in which we can respond to these questions and enter into the debates on these issues. If you want to understand philosophy, its impact on Christianity and some ways of responding to that impact, then this book should help you. It is *not*, however, *a* or *the* Christian answer to all philosophical problems. It is *not* a philosophy book which seeks to propound one main philosophical view and then tries to fit all the questions and answers into that view (though the critics will probably complain otherwise). It is not an attempt to write the last word about the relationship of philosophy and religion. Rather, it is an attempt to write a first word. It is a beginner's book. It is an attempt to introduce people who know little or nothing about philosophy to some of the ways and ideas that philosophers use when they approach the study of religion. It is a general overview, which seeks to give a feeling of the main lines of thinking and general sweep of the debate rather than to indulge in the detail of 'jot and tittle'. This will not satisfy the pure philosophers, who will complain that there is not enough depth to the treatment of each theme and too little detailed philosophical argument. They will feel that there are too many issues dealt with in too brisk a fashion. In other words, they will complain that I have not done or said everything, or even enough. I confess that both these judgments are true. In my defence, I can only say that I feel it is better to say *something* rather than *nothing*. I have not gone deeply into each issue because I want to give ordinary people the flavour of the problems and to show the width that philosophy and theology cover when they are brought together.

This book is for the far too many people who are afraid of philosophy. It is also for those who imagine that philosophy is a huge waste of time and gets people nowhere. Both these judgments are false and need to be refuted. People fear that philosophy is too difficult because it is highly complicated and technical. Of course it is and can be, but it can also be approached in a simple way. This makes writing about philosophy dangerous. If you are not true to all the complications then you will be charged with cheating and making things seem easier than they really are. If you are true to all the complications, then you will end up writing a book that only philosophers will be able to read. That would be no help to all those who are afraid of philosophy. So this book simplifies and may well over-simplify.

My book is meant as a starter. It is meant to help people to begin to do philosophy and therefore it must, if it is to do its job well, lead people on to read philosophical books for themselves without fear. To help that, I have included, at the end of each chapter, a glossary which is nothing more than a 'Noddy-guide' to philosophical terms, and a small reading list of books that will take people on to the next stage of philosophical thinking. I have also included a who's who of leading and representative philosophers.

This all sounds rather apologetic and defensive. But there is still one more fear in my mind. Many Christians and other believers think that philosophy does terrible things to faith. I do not believe that this is, or needs to be, true. I do not believe that Christians have anything more to fear from philosophy than anyone else. Thus the aim of this book is to encourage students, thinking Christians, and anyone interested in Christianity and philosophy to begin to face up to the philosophical questions which challenge faith in Christ. This book suggests some ways of thinking about the challenges, responding to the questions, and trying to clarify the presuppositions which lie behind the questions and the challenges. The material has been tried and tested in schools, universities, theological colleges and adult education settings in the teaching of philosophy, philosophy of religion and theology.

My aim is to clear the ground and to equip people for evangelism and ministry. It is to give people more confidence in the classroom and sitting-room as they discuss Christianity with all and sundry.

Inevitably there has to be selection and I have tried not to be too idiosyncratic and to look for key texts and people in the debates. I have tried to analyse the nature and extent of the problems posed and the kinds of answers given as well as trying to suggest the kinds of ways forward in discussion and thought. Naturally there are all too many questions left unanswered. Each of these is an invitation for you to find the answer yourself. The validity of the Christian position is assumed, yet argued for in relation to what I hope is a fair account of alternative views.

1 Can faith be proved?

Any distinction between faith and reason depends on the distinction between knowledge and belief. Philosophers have long disputed the connection between these two things. Knowledge seems to afford absolute certainty. When we are less sure, it is a case of belief. I can say that I know that 2 + 2 = 4. But I only believe that the sun will rise tomorrow, for I cannot know that it will. The world may come to an end overnight, so the best I can claim is that I believe that the sun will rise.

FRIENDS OR ENEMIES?

How do belief and knowledge relate? The classic account suggests that knowledge is justified, true belief. If I discover that my belief is in fact true and that the reasons for believing were fully adequate to justify that belief, then many philosophers would argue that it is therefore proper to claim knowledge. They are saying that I reduce my claims for my view to that of a belief if I do not have certainty. Such a situation might occur where the evidence for my view was insufficient. This is less than satisfactory, for very few indeed would be happy to accept that their beliefs were either false or unjustified. If I say that I believe something, then I am claiming to have some grounds for that belief and am happy to try to justify it.

Christian believers, despite their name, often claim that they know. They know God. They know that Christ is the Son of God. They know that 'in everything God works for good with those who love him' (Romans 8:28). These kinds of claims suggest that something more than mere 'belief' is at work here. Knowledge is being asserted. Indeed, rational arguments have often been propounded in support of the claim to know. These rational arguments have taken the form of various proofs. For example, if I said that I knew God, then I might go on to offer various proofs of God's existence and reality. Other Christians preferred to argue that knowing God was a true knowing based on intuition. Intuition is a direct awareness of the reality of something. Here, when one experienced the living God, then one knew it was God beyond all shadow of doubt. This was no mere belief, but so certain that one was willing to die for it.

We are immediately faced, however, with a danger and a difficulty. Knowing God must be a different kind of knowing from that of knowing objects in the world, or knowing gained through experience of things within the world. God is not an object in the world and does not operate totally within our world. This is why Christians argue that to know God depends not so much on our capacity to experience God, nor on our ability to prove his existence, but rather on God's revelation of himself to humankind. This means that if we are to come to any conclusions about the relationship of faith and reason we shall need to understand the nature of reason, of faith and of revelation.

WHAT IS REASON?

Reason is a human faculty of interpretation, organization and explanation. It is a function of humanity which is exercised in relation to everything round about a person. As we shall see, the rationalist and empiricist philosophers differed over their attitudes towards reason. The rationalist upheld a high view of reason, while the empiricist tended to belittle it in favour of sense-experience. The rationalist favoured a deductive approach, working out everything on the basis of first agreed principles. The empiricist believed in an inductive approach, learning by experience and modifying views as new knowledge and insight were acquired.

Reason seeks to understand the way things are and how they function. It seeks to offer a description and interpretation of reality which is true to the facts. It seeks objectivity, which means that no subjective factors influence what is known. That is more difficult than it sounds, for the knower affects what is known. Some suggest that therefore we cannot rely on our knowledge. They are saying that, when we state the meaning or understanding of something, it is not so much the meaning or understanding of the thing in itself. Rather the statement is a function of the way we see it or of our own subjective prejudices.

There is a crucial shift in the senses of 'subjective' here. The first sense is that of 'real to a subject or person'. A subjective judgment in this sense is one which is experienced by a thinking subject. In other words it is a human judgment, which, to be a judgment at all, must be performed by a human being. There is no threat to objectivity in this sense of subjective. The danger arises in the second sense, where we mean 'as a result of personal prejudice'. Here the threat is one of cheating and begging the question in our own favour by allowing personal assumptions to lead us to a conclusion which is not strictly the case. This is a useful warning to us to check that we do not cheat when we make judgments, especially when they concern matters of importance. Other people are the normal and proper checks against such prejudice and cheating.

Reason ultimately relies on rationality. The presence and value of rationality with standards and power over and against emotion and will is assumed, as is the sufficiency of such rationality. These assumptions may be queried.

CONTEXTS AND LIMITS

Perhaps it is helpful to draw a distinction between two senses of 'rationality'. The first one is a basic sense which distinguishes people from animals. People are rational beings. Thus to be 'rational' in this sense is to be sane. It is to recognize the need for and the value of thought, consistency, argument, justification and all that goes with these. There is a second sense of 'rationality' which refers to what is counted as reasonable within a particular philosophy or system of thought. Each philosophy may have a set of standards which define *what is reasonable on that particular view*. Such standards of rationality may vary then from object to object and setting to setting. In this sense, to be rational is to be rational within a particular context, with reference to a set of assumptions, whether these be the axioms of Euclid, the notational system of propositional logic, or those of the Christian faith. When people attack others with the charge of 'irrationality', we need to be clear which sense of 'rationality' is at work. Many charges of irrationality are not suggesting insanity, but are rather expressions of the clash of presuppositional frameworks. The effect of this kind of clash has been to modify some of the more sweeping claims made for reason and to call in question the absolute certainty of knowledge.

If you asked an ancient Egyptian how the world worked, he would have described the earth as the centre of the universe with the sun moving round it. As a convincing proof, he would have pointed to our experience of the sun rising in the east, moving across the sky and setting in the west. As far as he was concerned, he knew this meant that the earth was the centre of the universe. In the end, this judgment was mistaken. Copernicus, Galileo and Newton proved that the sun was the centre of the universe and that the earth was in orbit round the sun. This was claimed to be known. But was it? With the coming of Einstein and his theory of relativity, it now seems that what is claimed to be known for certain may not be as straightforward as was once thought.

Science shows us that knowledge changes and develops. Today's knowledge becomes tomorrow's old wives' tale. Before we hold up our hands in horror and moan that we cannot therefore know anything, it is important to see that all that is being implied is the need for care. We need to recognize that reason, and its application to various areas of life, has its limits. We cannot stop using our rational capacities, nor need we despair totally about their efficacy.

Theologians·have sought for a rational basis for Christianity in terms of natural theology, proofs of God, miracles and basic doctrines. They have developed a whole series of arguments to propound and defend the Christian case. They rightly feared that if there was no rational content to Christianity, then there would be nothing to communicate and no means of communication. Many of the ways in which this search has happened form much of the content of this book. There has been in Christian theology a serious attempt to satisfy the standard of reason. Two comments may be made. We need to recognize some variation in the sense of 'reason' and the standards of rationality people propose as standards by which to judge truth or falsity, adequacy or inadequacy. This has been partly hinted at in our reference to the different meanings of 'rationality'. For some, what is reasonable is defined as what fits in with their contextual presuppositions. It is also important to remember that reason has its limits. When we are faced with some issue that is too difficult for our minds, then our language and thought processes tend to break down. We shall see something of these limits in practice.

Reason tries to give an explanation for something. Sometimes the explanation is inadequate. Part of the problem may be that a variety of explanations is possible. It then becomes necessary to judge between explanations. To do that is to move back to the first sense of 'rationality', the value that humans put on thinking and judging. We may not be able to overcome the differences at that level, for the content is so simple and basic that it tells us very little other than what is nonsense and what is sense. It may thus be difficult to arrive at some absolutely certain knowledge which will satisfy all of us. This is not quite the same thing as sense two, what is reasonable within a particular philosophy or system of thought. What satisfies may be more a matter of psychology according to some people. They have applied this analysis to religion and sought for some psychological explanation for all religion. They suggest that it is purely a matter of self-illusion or wish-fulfilment.

Such an attempt at an explanation is open to question. Can their view escape from their own attack that only people of a particular psychological outlook or with certain psychological need could believe those kinds of things? Psychological explanations, if carried to extreme, destroy not only reason but argument, proof, justification and the need for any of these. Even from the necessity to pass judgment on psychological explanations, it is clear that reason has an important role. How, then, does reason relate to faith?

THE NATURAL AND THE SUPERNATURAL

Living and working in the realm of nature, we are familiar with how reason operates and the kind of evidence, argument and normal processes followed by rational people. That does not mean that we can have absolute certainty by using reason. There is not some magic certainty which we know in the natural realm which is impossible in the supernatural. Reason has its limits. Even acknowledging this it is not clear how human reason can or should operate with reference to a transcendent, supernatural realm. Reason seeks to give explanations. These explanations are usually in terms of something else.

This creates a problem when dealing with the transcendent, for reason may try to give an explanation of the supernatural in terms of something else in the natural realm. This might reduce the supernatural to the natural and mean that it was no longer the supernatural. An alternative course of action might be for reason to suggest that at the moment it was not able to offer an explanation. Rather, rational processes are set in motion, but as yet have come up with no solution. Reason might even try washing its hands of religion altogether. The supernatural might be seen as mysterious, inexplicable and contradictory. Reason might resign and call religion the business of faith alone.

FAITH

'Faith is the assurance of things hoped for, the conviction of things not seen' according to the writer to the Hebrews (Hebrews 11:1). It is neither knowledge nor sight, but goes beyond the kind of evidence they deal with and their responses to that evidence. Faith is the essence of Christianity. It is expressed in two major forms. There is belief *that* certain things are true, such as dogma, doctrine and propositions. Faith is thus assent to certain propositions. The belief expressed in these assertions may be claimed, justified, attacked or defended. The other form of expression sees faith as *believing in* a personal God and in Christ. Faith is thus a response to God and to the life and example of Christ. Faith, in this sense, is trust and obedience. Such faith is vindicated by the inner certainty it offers and in the consequences it leads to, in contrast with other beliefs. Faith is about passionate commitment. The truth of the matter is that before one believes *in* someone or something, then there must be a certain amount of believing *that* things are true. There is a close interaction between these two aspects of belief.

Within the context of Christianity, various attitudes towards faith have been expressed. Brief pen-portraits will sketch some of the key kinds of attitudes expressed concerning the relation of faith and reason.

ANSELM

The phrase that sums up Anselm's view is *fides quaerens intellectum* (faith seeking understanding). This type of approach stresses that one must begin the Christian life by a step of faith. Beginning from the standpoint of faith one is enabled to understand both faith itself and the grounds for faith. If there is no belief, there will be no understanding. In a sense, therefore, it is only the believer who can fully understand the content of faith. For the believer, faith fits together and makes sense because he or she has entered into the experience of and context in which religious reality is known. The criticism of this kind of view is that it assumes what it wants to prove and begs the question in its own favour. This is a little unfair, for the believer is only explaining and describing his or her experience of coming to know God and is expressing what knowledge has been gained through that initial step of faith.

PASCAL'S WAGER

Blaise Pascal suggested that faith was a kind of hedging one's bets. There might be a God or there might not. You could live a good life or an evil one. If you lived a good life and there was a God, then you would be richly rewarded in the hereafter. If you lived a good life and there was no God, then you would still have lived a worth-while existence. If, however, you lived a bad life and there was a God, you would be in serious trouble. If you lived a bad life and there was no God, then it made no difference in the end. Thus Pascal argued that the best way to hedge your bets was to live a good life, just in case there was a God to be faced. In this way, faith was a kind of sensible and reasonable bet, in case Christianity were true!

SØREN KIERKEGAARD

The phrase that sums up Kierkegaard's view is the 'leap of faith'. Reason has no useful role in relation to Christianity. Faith enables us to go beyond reason; yet it is like a leap in the dark. We do not and cannot know what such a leap will entail. Faith is thus a total risk and can have no reasonable basis. If it is reasonable, it is no longer faith. Christian faith is essentially about commitment. This is a commitment which goes beyond reasons and which radically affects the way one lives. One cannot and does not give reasons for one's faith. One simply lives it.

KARL BARTH

The early Barth is pictured as a *fideist* (one who stresses faith alone). He suggested that belief cannot argue with unbelief. It can only preach to it. Barth cast doubt on the history of Christian apologetics and theology's attempt to come to terms with reason. God was so other, so transcendent, and Christianity so foreign, to sinful people's minds, that only God's gift of faith can enable people properly to hear the Word of God. The only human grasping of God comes from the faith that God gives to people in and through Jesus Christ. Thus reason, in theory, has no real role on the fideist account. Yet Barth followed Anselm who emphasized that faith seeks to understand. One only needs to read a little of Barth's voluminous work to see how reason was very much at work in his theology.

RUDOLF BULTMANN

Bultmann, a leading German theologian, was deeply concerned that Christianity seemed foreign to modern people and was for them literally unbelievable and unreasonable. Talk of angels and demons at work in the setting of a three-decker universe with heaven above, earth below, and hell at the lowest level made it impossible for twentieth-century people to believe in the gospel. Bultmann believed that there was an essential kernel, the *kerygma*, contained in the Scriptures. This *kerygma* (God's good news) was obscured by once meaningful 'myths'. If we could translate these 'myths' into modern guise, then the reality behind them could be grasped and believed. The task of reason was to help us strip away the mythical layers to uncover the core reality. This core was apprehended by the passionate commitment of faith so typical of Kierkegaard and the related philosophies of existentialism. Bultmann allied himself with an existentialist outlook, which stressed the importance of a whole-hearted commitment of oneself in light of the past, open to the future and yet facing up to the present. By doing so he, as he saw it, 'demythologized' the Gospel accounts in order to enable modern people to come to faith. Faith is thus our existential, personal response to the *kerygma*. It is our escape from living an inauthentic life, hiding in the past, the present or the future. To live by faith is to live an authentic existence. Reason cannot provide this authenticity. Faith alone can.

JOHN HICK

John Hick suggests that faith is a kind of perception. It is a way of interpreting or seeing the world in light of God and in relation to him. Faith is a *seeing as*. It is to see what happens as the work of God. The hymn-writer expresses the point as

> Something lives in every hue,
> Christless eyes have never seen.

Hick's view stresses that while there may be a natural explanation for some event, that is not the only level of explanation possible. If I miss a flight and the aeroplane crashes, my escape from death is not just the result of a traffic jam. God's care and protection may have been at work. The eye of faith sees what appears to be a coincidence as the direct result of God at work in the world. Faith is a way of looking at the world.

There are, however, problems with this account, if this is all that there is to the nature of faith. Such a view presupposes that there is an organ of perception of faith. The presence of unbelief suggests that only a few possess this organ. But why these few, and what is this organ like and how does it operate? The view assumes that there is an object there and that the object can and does affect us. The view is supposed to prove the object's existence, but must assume what it seeks to prove in order to present its proof. If one tries to take the perceptual model seriously, it is also hard to see how one can re-identify the object perceived by the organ of faith. Such re-identification would require a different and second perception. But how then could the one be compared with the other? How could one test for misperceptions, for another seeing would be required which might produce different results? In the end, Hick seems to be offering to substitute the idea of 'experiencing as' for 'experiencing', but if this is done consistently, there is then no difference at all between 'experience' and 'experiencing as'.

THE TIGHTROPE OF FAITH

Faith is different from reason. Faith implies that there is an element which is not totally certain. Some try to characterize that element as subjectivity. But as we have already seen, all knowledge and belief are subjective in the sense that they belong to us as human beings. The charge of subjectivity is, however, meant to imply a lack of evidence and/or a certain psychological predisposition towards things. The one tends to go with the other, for the absence of any adequate grounds for faith makes it seem a totally irrational matter. Yet there is nothing to be feared from admitting that faith occurs in a setting where doubt is possible. Christianity knows only too well that the revelation of God is not unambiguous. There is room for doubt. There is no *overwhelming evidence* for God's existence or for much else in Christian doctrine. If there were, then faith would disappear, for all people would be forced to assent to the truth, by the irrationality of unbelief. All would know beyond all possible doubt. If faith were totally reasonable, it would no longer be faith. Theology has known that there was room for doubt. Indeed it has often grappled with doubt and sought to set limits to what become unacceptable levels of doubt. Heresy and credal formulation are testimonials to the lack of certain, indisputable evidence. The key issue is what is to count as sufficient evidence.

For many this has led to an emphasis on decision and an act of will as the gateway to faith. This cannot be called a 'leap' and nothing else. If it were, there would be no basis for one decision rather than another, no reason for one leap rather than another. To justify the risk of faith there must be a 'fit', a sense of coherence, and evidence to support the risk-taking. Nevertheless, the element of risk remains. Many Christians are hesitant to admit that such a risk carries with it the possibility that they are wrong. Such an unease is part of the motive behind Bultmann's reduction of faith to the more 'believable' propositions of existentialism for modern people. The aim is immunity from criticism. It is to arrive at an irreducible core which cannot be doubted.

The danger of this kind of immunity from criticism is that it removes the ability to attack or to defend a view. If nothing can count against a view, then nothing can be said in its favour. If there is nothing falsifiable in Christianity, it is not clear that it is offering anything positive at all. Immunity from criticism can be bought at too dear a price. Christianity needs to be honest about what counts against its claims. Some have argued that unmitigated, endless suffering counts against the existence of an all-loving God. Paul, the apostle, was quite clear that Christianity is wrong and misleading if there is no resurrection of Jesus from the dead. Both these attitudes stress the importance of evidence and the fact that evidence is double-edged. It may count against as well as in favour of a view.

Faith thus walks the tightrope between no proof and some proof. Obviously, faith is a means of interpretation, but not only that. It is an interpretative framework, which may be more or less justified. It must guard against false standards of proof and also against unreasonable and inappropriate demands for justification. It must also refuse to flee into the realms of irrationality by abandoning all evidence and attempts at justification.

PROOF

David Hume distinguished between deductive and inductive proof. Deductive proof is circular and simply functions on the basis of assumed premises. You get nothing in the conclusion which is not already contained in the starting-point. This is not to say that there is no point in deduction. Logical proof and mathematical reasoning – clear examples of the deductive approach – do help us grasp relations of ideas. But when we are asked to justify the procedure of deduction as a whole, we have to admit that this process requires agreed definitions and proceeds from these to argument.

Inductive proof, on the other hand, is the method of empirical science and scientific discovery. It tells us about the real world. It is open to doubt, but provides us with matters of fact. We are told that it is good for us to include bran in our diet, because generally we lack fibre and this leads to disease. It may be that, in time, medical science will show some hitherto unknown disease or a link with an already existing disease, which is caused by bran. In the end, by a process of induction and experience, we may discover that bran for breakfast may not be quite so healthy a food as we presently believe.

When Christians are faced with the demand for proof, they must beware of holding too high a view of proof in other realms. It is often as if Christianity is some poor relation in terms of proof, while other beliefs may be proved very easily. Hume has clearly shown the limits of deductive proof. Inductive proof has limits, too. It depends on the repeatability of tests and the predictive power such results give. One exception, however, undermines the general law. If I believe that aeroplanes are the safest form of transport and I resolve to fly to the States rather than sail, I may be more than a little disappointed if my aeroplane crashes. The general law may still hold at the statistical level, but this is of no comfort to me. There also comes a moment when there is little point in adding instances to the level of proof. If proof is reached by the accumulation of evidence, then one thousand supporting cases seem as strong as one thousand and one. Hume tells of an Indian prince who refused to believe in snow, for he had no experience of snow. On the basis of induction, he was correct. He carefully measured his belief on his experience to date. This allowed for no new experience. We know that he was wrong.

Induction is limited to what we know up to the present time. This creates difficulties for moments of insight, intuition and creative jumps of thought which often characterize new discoveries. These may be true, and even known to be true, before convincing, inductive proof can be produced. Induction is always open to doubt. It shows only that some new thing is beyond our present experience or else that something is highly improbable. Induction does not and cannot show that something is impossible.

The most common expression of proof is the *principle of verifiability*. We shall look in chapter 12 at some of the problems with the principle, its various forms and expressions, and its application. The whole discussion will show that 'proof' is often a loaded term, presupposing a particular philosophy and its view of reality. The empiricist philosophy is embodied in the principle of verifiability. It is proper to ask whether we should accept these presuppositions before seeking to try to satisfy their demands for proof. Both the proof and the presuppositions may be alien to Christianity.

There are certainly different kinds of proof ranging from the mathematical and logical to the scientific and practical. There are also realms where proof seems notoriously difficult to find. Morality and aesthetics are two such realms. This does not mean that there are no explanations, justifications or evidence for and within these areas of knowledge. The same is true of religion. There is little to fear from modern science which has rediscovered the limits of 'proof'. Modern science claims predictive power for its 'proofs' rather than any hard and final absoluteness. This should make us less afraid of the demands for justification and proof. So often the proof that is demanded or required is only a function of the terms of the *demand* for proof, and the *context* which gives evidence its significance.

FRAMEWORK OF INTERPRETATION

Proof and justification make sense within particular contexts. There are different criteria of proof which are appropriate for different areas of study and reflection. We may also view the same object from different perspectives and form criteria appropriate to those perspectives. There is a splendid example of this in the duck-rabbit figure. When they look at it, some folk see quite clearly that it is a duck. Others are adamant that it is a rabbit. If you suggest the alternative view and turn the drawing to facilitate that interpretation there follows an 'ah-ha' experience when the penny drops and the person sees the alternative animal. The really careful say that they see a squiggle of lines.

The duck-rabbit example is helpful, for it reminds us that differences in views can be exaggerated. There remains a minimum element and description which is neutral. But if we go beyond that minimum and offer an interpretation, we must ask why we interpret things in the ways that we do. To do this is to ask for some account of the adequacy of the models and pictures we use and the accounts we give. This adequacy must relate to the actual disclosure of reality and the accuracy of the picture and of the account. One writer tells a story of the Greek poet, Homer, looking out at a stormy sea and suggesting that Poseidon was angry. In contrast we interpret the wild sea as signs of high tides and bad weather. There are here two competing accounts given of the same sight and we believe that one alternative is better than the other. It is a more correct reflection of reality. The kindly might try to save Homer's account by suggesting that there is a metaphorical point and sense in saying that Poseidon is angry. This interpretation certainly would not satisfy Homer. So often similar reductions of Christianity fail to satisfy Christians and seem to expel both baby and bath water. If the Christians are to reject such reductions, they must be able to show that their framework of belief is a viable and preferable alternative.

This is far from easy, for the notion of *final* proof for anything is extremely doubtful. Moreover, such alternative frameworks are the expressions of the very basic presuppositions people hold. Some have suggested that fundamental assumptions are arbitrary, for we can offer nothing to support them. Others reply that fundamental assumptions are the most necessary of all and are what make knowledge, science and faith possible. We cannot get behind these presuppositions, but this does not mean that every viewpoint is equally valid. Rather there is at this point even more need for a careful presentation of ideas and weighing up of them. The purpose in such a procedure is that reasonable people change their views, beliefs and presuppositions on the basis of evidence.

To give some account of our basic presuppositions and their

preferability over alternatives is to describe the heart and content of faith, the evidence that supports it, the consequences, which flow from it, and the internal and external 'fit' that faith offers. Such an account begins with revelation for the Christian.

REVELATION

Revelation, in the Christian context, is the imparting to humankind of divine truth. It implies a revealing of what is hidden. In Christianity, it refers to God's unveiling of himself and his purposes. Inevitably questions are raised as to how revelation happens, how it relates to other forms of knowledge and belief, and how any revelation may be verified. As we have seen in Barth's emphasis on fideism, revelation is crucial and central. Without revelation, there is no knowledge of God. There are those who prefer to talk of revelation as response and obedience. Others seek to reduce revelation to some pattern of living. Some others argue that religion tells stories in order to encourage people to behave in particular ways and follow a certain way of life.

There are two sets of distinctions which are made in the area of revelation. These are distinctions between (1) special and general revelation and (2) propositional and non-propositional revelation.

General revelation is the view that God reveals himself in everything in general. God has put his mark and stamp on everything. The world, history and the nature of humanity are all facets of God's revelation. Special revelation makes a fundamental distinction between general revelation (which, according to the special revelation view, gives no *specific* knowledge of God) and particular revelation, for example, in Christ, in the Scriptures or in some special meeting with God.

The second distinction describes propositional revelation as consistency in a body of truths expressed in statement form. These truths are revealed to humankind. Faith is the intellectual and personal assent to these truths. Faith is the reception of revelation. Non-propositional revelation is not so much to do with statements about God, as the reality of God's revelation in saving history. Theology is a human attempt to understand the significance and meaning of that saving history. Faith is a trusting obedience in response to the revelation of God.

Neither view is immune from criticism. The propositional view is attacked for its intellectual character. Rationalist and empiricist standards are applied and the propositions of Christianity do not seem to conform to these tests. Hence it is concluded that the propositions of Christianity are meaningless or simply expressions of feeling. The growth of biblical criticism has reinforced this flight from propositional faith. The criticism of the non-propositional view is that it reduces God to the purely immanent, the 'this worldly', and seems to make him dependent on our subjective feelings. This looks like shifting sand; it seems to make truth variable. In fact, it is doubtful whether we can separate the two forms of revelation. Experience of God implies some statements and assertions about him. To give meaningful content to our experience of God, we must make some statements. These must be appropriate and checkable. At the same time, faith obviously goes beyond words and reflects a personal response of obedience and trust. We need to hold fast to both insights.

We shall examine the content of revelation more fully in the sections on the proofs of God and religious experience. There we shall see that we cannot escape from some form of verification and testing. The Christian community provides the proper setting for the judgment of claims to experience God. The criteria used are the standards of Scripture, doctrine, tradition and the understanding of the nature of God in Christ. No human philosophy can show the *actual impossibility* of revelation from God. Nevertheless, the onus rests on Christianity to produce adequate grounds for the belief in and acceptance of a revelation of God.

THE COHERENCE OF FAITH AND REASON

When reason is brought to bear on faith, it deals with the expression of faith rather than with faith itself. There are two ways it may then proceed. It may seek to offer an internal or external testing and clarification. There are those who hold that philosophy leaves everything exactly as it was before the philosophical questions were asked. On this view, reason's task is to describe and offer conceptual clarification. This rests on the idea of 'language games'. To understand reality, we need to look at how language is used and the contexts in which language operates. Theology is seen as a 'language game' which religious people play. Each game has its own rules and inner logic. The philosopher, like the sociologist, can describe the game, its rules, the way the rules function and the way the game is played. Sense and nonsense are purely internal to the game. The tests of what is appropriate, inappropriate, true or false are part and parcel of the nature and content of the game.

Many find the notion of 'game' misleading. It is certainly inadequate for Christianity in its claim to be an objective account of the world and not merely a way of looking at reality. To make such universal and absolute claims is to move into the setting of external verification, in the sense that there may be competing standards of verification and justification. The Christian will have to come to terms with these. The challenge of science in particular has posed a serious test for Christian truth. As we shall see, however, there is no reason for over-defensiveness on the part of Christians.

There are three main tests of truth. Consistency and coherence, correspondence with reality, and some form of pragmatic test provide these standards. Consistency and coherence are necessary for a view to make sense on its own terms. They are necessary if a view is literally to make sense and is not self-contradictory. The second stage of testing is to see how far a view and its claims correspond with reality. The view must fit the facts and match up to the way things are. This is complicated, of course, by the way most views offer their own definitions of 'reality' and 'fact'. Yet it is still crucial that the descriptions given do have some correspondence with reality. The third test is some form of pragmatic one. This is a varied kind of test stretching from the crude and direct form of 'If it works, it must be right' to a popular expression in the philosophy of science which uses the standard of fertility in producing new insights and other theories.

Christianity has tried to satisfy all three, but only in appropriate ways, given the nature of God and of Christian truth. These tests are applied in the context of the tradition and history of Christianity and in the company of the people of God. Consistency means that the view makes sense on its own terms and holds together. It is not self-contradictory. Christian truth must also correspond with the reality of God and be in keeping with his character, plan and revelation. Christian faith must work in the sense of transforming human life and society. Thus the believer is required to talk sense rather than nonsense, to point to the reality of God in ways that are appropriate, and to show the difference God makes to life. Then, indeed, Christianity may be taken more seriously by the unbeliever.

FAITH AND REASON: SOME CONCLUSIONS

Often philosophical problems arise from false dichotomies and the reduction of a complex reality to one aspect of that reality. It is so with knowledge and belief, and faith and reason. They go together. The Christian needs to come to terms with reason and faith and to try to express the Christian faith in reasonable ways. This is not to suggest that people will be won to faith by argument, though argument may help to clear the ground. Neither is it a reduction of faith. It is a call to communicate that faith to a needy world.

The history of the people of God is one of communication: a telling of stories and parables, the preaching of the written Word of God, and the witness of individuals to others. Such communication presupposes that Christianity makes sense. It is the Christian's task to keep on showing that this is true. However, it does not imply that everything in Christianity can be totally understood or will be acceptable to all. God is bigger than our concepts and our understanding of him. We shall inevitably reach the limits of our reason, insight, understanding and language. When we do, we should not be afraid to say so. There is also a proper place for the recognition of fallibility and the possibility of error. We have said too little about sin. Sin, in Christian terms, affects the whole human being and that includes the understanding. People's minds are not perfect. This does not simply mean that we sometimes get things wrong. It also implies that reason is properly used only in relationship with and obedience to God. Our fallen understanding is not a final one. Now we know only in part. Our task then is to seek to conform ourselves and our expressions of truth more and more to the reality of that truth. Christ is the way and the life, because he is the truth. Truth leads into the proper way of living and brings real life. Christians need not fear such truth.

Key words
knowledge. Justified true belief; what we accept as certain.
belief. Trust, confidence, accepting as true.
rationality. Our ability to think and reason.
objectivity. An approach which rests on what is really the case regardless of personal interpretation.
subjectivity. (a) a person knowing something as a person; (b) a purely personal approach based on one's own opinions or attitudes.
context of interpretation. The

setting in which, and by which, we seek to look at and understand things.

presupposition. What we assume or take for granted.

faith. The personal commitment and belief in the reality of God.

evidence. Signs, indications or facts available as proof.

proof. The process of ascertaining the truth or facts.

testing. The process of checking out to see if some thing, quality or person is true or not.

induction. The production of facts to prove general laws in science.

deduction. The process of reasoning proceeding from the general to the specific.

special revelation. The unveiling of truths by God by special and particular means, *e.g.* through the person of Christ, or through Scripture, or some specific event in the life of individuals or groups.

general revelation. The unveiling of truths by God through the ordinary processes of nature or history which are open for all to see.

Reading

C. Stephen Evans, *Existentialism: the philosophy of despair and the quest for hope* (Paternoster Press, 1984).

Arthur F. Holmes, *Contours of a World View* (IVP, 1983).

B. G. Mitchell, *The Justification of Religious Belief* (OUP, 1981).

R. Swinburne, *The Coherence of Theism* (OUP, 1977).

Daniel L. Wolfe, *Epistemology: the justification of belief* (IVP, 1983).

2 Religion: a good mystery?

Mysticism in religion – Some problems of the mysterious – Definitions of the mysterious – God and mystery – Verification and mystery – Practical differences – Quo vadis?

People are fascinated by the unusual and the mysterious. From the work of Edgar Allan Poe to the interest in UFOs, people cannot resist a good mystery. Mysteries baffle us. We do not know how to proceed with them. We lack the necessary knowledge to give a solution. Deep down we feel that even if we have all the facts, there might still be no solution at all. This love of the mysterious finds expression in the fairy stories, myths and magic of many tribes and peoples. It is also expressed in music, art and drama. The aesthetic realm often brings us in contact with a world of mystery which defies any cold, rationalistic explanation.

MYSTICISM IN RELIGION

Religions too have some element of the mysterious. This almost seems to be part of their very definition. In the Christian religion, the theme of the transcendent God, who is totally other, is at the heart of the mystery. Given the differences, stated in doctrinal formulations, between God and man, how is it possible for us to characterize or know the divine? The Christian mystic finds no problem here, for he or she denies that mystery creates a question to be answered. By definition, it is argued, no answer is possible. The mystery is irreducible. All that is required is contemplation and humble investigation of the mystery.

Within the tradition of Christianity, particularly in monastic settings, there has been a history of individuals like Julian of

Norwich, Teresa of Avila, John of the Cross, and their disciples, who have stressed the role of contemplation, ecstatic experience and silence. For these people, Christianity is not so much a matter of dogma, teaching, or even a life lived, but rather of an encounter with God. This direct encounter exposes what we are and what God is in ways that cannot easily, if at all, be expressed in words.

The mystic claims an immediate, direct contact with the transcendent God. This experience is often described as timeless and is a complex business. We need to be careful, in approaching such experiences, to separate out the experiences from the systems of contemplation which lead to such experiences, and those in turn need to be distinguished from the dogma which arises from such experience.

There is a real danger though with any mysterious experience which is claimed to be beyond words. It is of 'declaring the mystery too soon'. In the last analysis, there may well be things which cannot be explained, but that does not mean that *we can say nothing* to describe, defend and elucidate their reality. The appeal to the mysterious may simply be an evasion of the empiricist attack on mysticism which is itself seeking to give some meaning, content and, most of all, verification to the idea of the mysterious. The empiricist appeals to testable experience as the sure guide to truth in every matter.

SOME PROBLEMS OF THE MYSTERIOUS

Not all puzzles or problems fall neatly into the category of the mysterious, as far as religion is concerned. The definitions of mystery will show why this is the case. But even given some understanding of definitions, certain basic problems remain. Thomas McPherson puts it nicely thus: 'What to the Jew was a stumbling-block and to the Greeks foolishness, is to the logical positivists nonsense.' Christianity is full of mystery. It proclaims a transcendent, all-powerful, all-loving creator God, an incarnate Son of that God, who enters time and space, a Spirit who lives in the hearts of men and women today; yet these are not three gods, but one, called the Trinity. In the practices and worship of Christianity, too, the element of mystery is integral. The heart of the Eucharist, or Communion, is the presence of God in the midst of a supper of bread and wine. But how is he present? Where?

The problems of the mysterious in relation to the philosophical questions facing Christianity appear to be as follows.

In examining all the religions, and indeed all the cultural practices, of the world, we find that the mysterious is part and parcel of them all. Mystery seems a universal category of experience. If this is so, how then is the Christian claim for a unique mystery to be judged over and against other such claims? Is there any basis for the claim to uniqueness?

The second area of difficulty likewise holds against all claims of mystic experience. What is the relationship of our knowledge and experience in general to the realm of the mysterious? Is this another form and aspect of human knowing, for example, open only to the highly sensitive? Is it rather to be understood as a kind of experience similar to, yet different from, aesthetic experiences? But in what ways? These questions are attempts on the part of the questioner to uncover the rational content of the mysterious. The retort may well come that such knowledge or experience of the mysterious is, in fact, non-rational, but then the questioner does not know what, if anything, is being said. He or she argues that if there is no link with our normal knowledge and experience, then it cannot be knowing or experiencing which is under discussion. The discussion may then move to the realm of verification, where the questioner is concerned to know the conditions under which a mysterious encounter may be verified or falsified as a true mysterious encounter. How does the participant guard against deception, especially against self-deception?

Two further areas of discussion are found in the realm of mystery. The first is to enquire what practical difference such 'mystery' makes in relation to the Christian faith, if it is an experience which is beyond knowing, checking and even adequate language for expression. Such a pragmatic push often goes hand in hand with an alternative account of mystery. This is usually in a reductionist form, which reduces the mystery from all that it is claimed to be, to a simpler, understandable aspect of life and experience. For example, some might suggest that Christian mystics, and indeed all those claiming mystical experiences, are in fact schizophrenics, who live in two distinct worlds. One they share with the rest of us and that is what we all call the real world. The other world is the product of diseased or over-imaginative minds creating a realm of experience which is a mystery to the rest of us. In this way, 'mystery' is reduced to psychological abnormality.

DEFINITIONS OF THE MYSTERIOUS

The heart of a mystery is something which is hidden or obscure. This is usually held to be inexplicable by the normal procedures and criteria of rationality. What is mysterious cannot be totally hidden, or there could be no knowing at all. Rather there is held to be a realm of what is grasped, which then follows a line into realms of the more obscure. When one begins to grasp a mystery, it seems to result both in an appreciation of the mystery itself and an awareness of one's inadequacy to grasp it. In Christianity, mystery is bound up with revelation, particularly the revelation of God. Before such a mystery, language and intellect fall short of being able both to understand and to express the truth of the religious mystery. Many Christians will testify that the more they discover about the nature of God, the more there seems to be to know. For Paul on the Damascus road, there was an experience which at that moment he did not fully understand. In the years to come, he could describe this as being 'owned by Christ'. What this experience meant for his life was a growing knowledge of Christ, though Paul writes to the Philippians that he had not yet attained perfect knowledge of Christ, but followed after to 'make it my own, because Christ Jesus has made me his own' (Philippians 3:12).

In some ways this explanation of mystery is very similar to the way in which science explains the mysteries of the universe. The mysterious account that scientists give in terms of models and constructed pictures of reality are like religious mysteries because they are able to elucidate other realms of experience and understanding, even though themselves remaining opaque. Often the awareness of mystery is more akin to an emotional experience than to an intellectual exercise.

GOD AND MYSTERY

Karl Barth, following Søren Kierkegaard, suggested that between God and man there was an 'infinite qualitative distinction'. The God of Christianity is hidden from our view and grasp. He is unique. The trouble with uniqueness though is that, by definition, it offers no possibility of comparison with anything else. The gap between the human and divine, the transcendent and immanent, the finite and the infinite, the creature and the Creator, is such that man cannot grasp the mystery of what God is in himself. Any understanding of the mystery is then dependent on some revelation from the divine to the human. This was exactly the pattern followed by Barth in his analysis of the nature of God. God not only revealed to man who he is, but, at the same time, gave man the capacity to receive that revelation.

There are, however, two distinct aspects to the mystery of God. There is the *ontological* mystery, that he is at all. There is also the *conceptual* mystery of what he is and how that is known. The first is the same kind of point hinted at by Wittgenstein when he said, 'Not how the world is, is the mystical, but that it is.' This sense of ontological wonderment at God and the world's existence is held in abeyance as far as the sceptic is concerned, for he wishes to know what God's existence is like before being assured that he exists. This is a point of direct clash with any mystical account of God. It is the 'thatness' of his existence which is at the heart of the mystical experience. The mystic denies that it is possible to define the content of that mystery, but does not shy away from 'pointing' in the direction of the mystery. As the leading example for discussion we shall draw on the work of Rudolf Otto and his book, *The Idea of the Holy*.

Otto suggests that there are five main characteristics in any discussion of the mystery of the Christian God. God is transcendent, revealing, holy, awe-ful and mystical. Each of these themes and descriptions form the nexus for a web of characterizations of his mysterious nature. God's transcendence sets him apart from this world and all that is in it. God is wholly other. He cannot be grasped by, or reduced to, any set of terms which are purely immanent. (We shall return to these points in chapter 4.) Such is the importance of the otherness of God that it has caused people like Don Cupitt to deny the reality of the incarnation, as an attempt to 'reduce' God to human terms. There was a fashionable school of thought in theology called the 'God is dead' school. Theologians who belonged to it argued that God is so transcendent, we can not only know nothing of him at all, but that he is, as far as we are concerned, dead. They summed up the rejection of knowing God by concentrating on Jesus in the phrase, 'God is dead and Jesus is his Son.' The distant, transcendent God of traditional Christianity is unknowable. Declared redundant, he is replaced by Jesus, who was interpreted totally in terms of this world and our shared humanity.

For the mystic (and by mystic we mean someone who has mystical experiences) God is not only a transcendent God, he is also a God who reveals himself. These revelatory experiences are irreducible to set formulae or patterns, but the sense of immediacy and of God's presence cannot be mistaken. In other words, these revelatory experiences are essentially *self-authenticating*. This is not to say that there is no more description to be given. The essential marks of these revelations of God are that they convey feelings of holiness, awe and dependence. For the mystic there is a fundamental difference between a simple or complex aesthetic experience and a religious one. No matter how overwhelming they both may be, the heart of the *religious* mystery is the holiness of God. There is a moral element of goodness and right, and in contrast to that revelation of goodness, purity and righteousness, a sense on the part of the recipient of his or her own sinfulness, impurity and impiety.

The Old Testament examples of God's confrontation of the prophets and leaders – like Moses, Gideon, Isaiah and Ezekiel – all have this element of holiness explicit in the recorded accounts. The proper place for a person receiving the revelation of God is on one's knees or flat on one's face. The person who meets God expects to die. This sense of awe is not only a sense of holiness, but is also itself a category of mystery. Otto uses the terms *mysterium tremendum* and *fascinans* to gather the themes of awe together. He describes the object experienced as the *numen* – something outside us – and our experience of it as *numinous*. C. S. Lewis and J. R. R. Tolkien have popularized the concept in their writings.

There are two aspects to this numinous experience. There is the sense of the nature of what is being experienced and the feelings and reactions elicited by that object in the experience. The marks of the thing being experienced are of its overpoweringness, its awe-fulness, its sense of energy and urgency. The marks of our response to that kind of object are dread, fear, reverence, humility and fascination. The total experience of the numinous is a blend of all of these and more.

An example may help. When we drive near a road accident, where flashing blue lights, ambulances, people and cars are everywhere, we are drawn almost compulsively to look. We know it will be horrible and leave a terrible memory, but we cannot not look. We are fascinated. The sight of tangled wreckage and mangled bodies, and of the grief and strain of the onlookers fills us with a sense of the futility of life, the stupidity of cars and driving, and a sense of our own mortality and weariness. Our speed is suddenly reduced. The conversation falls still. The mystery makes us all tremble. If we may add the essence of these feelings to the sense of holiness, we are beginning to approach Otto's account of the mystery of God.

The main aspect still missing is that of the sense of the majesty and divinity of God and the parallel evocation of feelings of absolute dependence, finitude and creatureliness in response. This overwhelming experience is not so overwhelming that we forget our rightful place in the order of things. It is the Creator and we are his creatures. This is precisely what Job experienced, when at last he met God face to face. Job came with so many questions and doubts on his lips, but in the light of the reality of God, he accepted that he could not understand. It was enough for Job to know God and to have met him face to face. This gave him a perspective for all that had happened to him, though it did not explain it.

There is a mystery in God and his revelation towards us. As well as revelation and an unveiling of God, there is a continuing hiddenness. The same pattern is seen in the incarnation, where 'the Word became flesh . . . we have beheld his glory' (John 1:14), yet it was only those who had eyes to see who grasped the presence of Christ, the Son of God. Further, the God who reveals himself, and yet remains hidden, is a God who also reveals himself as a God to be worshipped. The awe and its appropriate response of humility leads naturally into worship. It is the correct response to the mystery of God. This same mystical experience is not to be interpreted in terms of the experience alone. Once we have had some religious experience the focus of attention ought not to be the experience itself, but rather the object of the experience. If we concentrate on the experience alone we shall be misled. The object delineates both the nature of the experience and therefore the appropriate modes of response to it. The Christian belief is that the God who reveals his mystery is not simply an object, but rather he is a personal God. His nature is such that we may apprehend something of him, but can never comprehend all that there is to know. We truly catch something of God, without encompassing the whole of his nature and being. We know something of God, but do not know everything.

VERIFICATION AND MYSTERY

Contemplation is often the natural setting for the Christian mystic. Here apophaticism rules OK. The rule here is often one of silence. The mystery is beyond speech. If, however, there is nothing to be said, then this certainly guarantees that nothing may be said *against* mysticism. Equally, nothing may also be said *for* it. Thus not only does verification of mystical experience become impossible, but its very meaningfulness must also be in question. The empiricist approaches the mystical, as he does all else, demanding that it conform to his criterion of sense experience. But this seems too narrow an understanding of experience, for, as we shall see, it rules out all moral and aesthetic as well as religious claims to truth. The mystic has responded to the empiricist challenge with two emphases.

Primarily, the mystic claims that mystical experience is self-authenticating. It is *sui generis* – of its own nature – so that it cannot be reduced to anything else, for nothing else is comparable. It is utterly unique. Mystical experience carries within it such an intrinsic quality that the only solution to questions and doubts is to have a mystical experience for oneself. This is a parallel move to the 'intuitionist' line in perception, knowing and morality. If someone asks why a thing is wrong, we may respond that it is obviously wrong. If the person persists with the question, we are driven back to a position like 'Well I just know it is wrong. Intuition tells me'. Some things are known by intuition. Nothing can be behind an intuition. It is the end of the matter.

Obviously, for those who have such direct experiences, it may well seem to be the last word, but this is of little help to those who do not have such intuitions. This is where the fear of 'declaring the mystery too soon' is crucial. The mystic must point the way to the non-mystic so that the possibility of such an unique experience may begin to be understood and even become a reality. He might well do so along the lines of Otto in the previous section of this chapter. This brings the non-mystic to the crunch of his problem. If he has followed all the instructions about how to have an experience properly and has done all that is required, yet fails to have a mystical experience, how may he be sure that there is such a thing?

Before suggesting some response, it is important to examine the mystic's second emphasis when confronted by the sceptic. The mystic describes the mysterious experience as non-rational. This is not a claim that it is supra-rational and even less that it is irrational. Rather it is the claim that intellectual and rational criteria may be inappropriate here. You cannot see microbes through binoculars, even if you reverse the binoculars. The mystical realm cannot be reduced to some logical formulation or interpreted in the categories of other areas of thought. It is ineffable and inexpressible. As Wittgenstein put it, 'There is the inexpressible. This *shows* itself; it is the mystical' (my emphasis).

PRACTICAL DIFFERENCES

If ordinary tools of thinking and knowing are inappropriate in judging the validity of the mystical, and personal attempts to do likewise are unsuccessful, there might still be some kind of support offered along lines previously suggested. Here we ask what difference such experiences actually make. It would be odd if some overwhelming, awe-ful experience of the transcendent left no mark. Moses left his father-in-law's flocks and led the people of Israel out of Egypt. Gideon freed the land from the Midianites. Isaiah and Ezekiel became prophets.

Certainly the biblical view of mystical experience is that it radically affects people. The same is true in the traditions of the church where mystical experience is expected and encouraged. Such experience may affect both the mystic and others. The mystical experiences of a young girl at Lourdes led to the radical transformation not only of a small village community, but also of millions of pilgrims world-wide. Not a few have been healed in some way through their pilgrimage there. This does not mean we have to accept the validity of the experience, but it shows that practical consequences are claimed and expected to follow from mystical experience. It is not possible to argue backwards here. Difference afterwards *does not prove* the reality of an experience. Nevertheless, in the absence of other appropriate evidence, it appears to offer the best hope of some kind of check on the meaning and validity of claims of mystical experience.

It is certainly noteworthy that the religious community of believers who most often administer such checks on authenticity would be looking for some signs of radical transformation as a result of the mystical encounter. Absence of practical effect would cast doubt on the reality of the experience. Thus it should be no surprise that Christians look for signs of spiritual growth and maturity from those who claim to have had some special experience of God. When someone claims that they have been 'filled with the Spirit', one simple test is to contrast the quality of life lived since the experience with the life lived previously.

QUO VADIS?

The mystic is confronted by a double set of demands. His Scylla and Charybdis are the rationalist and the empiricist. The rationalist requires the mystic to conform to normal conceptual and logical standards of rationality. The empiricist demands conformity to a particular definition of experience in terms of the senses. Both need to be avoided if the mystic is to be true to his or her own understanding of his experience. The mystic, nevertheless, should testify, ever aware of his or her own frailty and the possibility that he or she may be wrong. The mystic must, in principle, be open to falsification.

Mystics are important for Christianity, for they remind us that we cannot sew up the whole of God in a neat package. Our knowledge as human beings is fallible and incomplete. Part of true wisdom is the recognition of the limits of our knowing. The mystic also shows us that what there is to know is complex. God, if he is God, cannot be fully expressed in a simple theological aphorism or set out in a slide for a microscope. This double theme of the limitations of our human capacity to know and the realization that there is far more to be known than time and ability permit, may be tellingly illustrated by a story from Nikos Kazantzakis. Four friends bring a dispute about the nature of God before the Pope.

'Understand God, Yannakos?' said the Pope, horrified. 'But Man is a blind earthworm at God's feet; what could he understand of an incommensurable greatness? I too, when I was young, used to protest and question like you. I didn't understand. One day my Superior, on Mount Athos, told me a parable. He often expressed himself in parables, God keep his soul!

' "Once upon a time," he said, "there was a little village, lost in the desert. All its inhabitants were blind. A great King passed by, followed by his army. He was riding an enormous elephant. The blind people heard of it. They had heard a great deal about elephants and were moved by a great desire to touch this fabulous animal, to get an idea of what it was. About ten of them, let's say the notables, set out. They begged the King for permission to touch the elephant. 'I give you permission, touch it!' said the King. One of them touched its trunk, another its foot, another its flank, one was raised up so that he might feel its ear, another was seated on its back and given a ride. The blind men went back enchanted to their village. All the other blind people crowded round them, asking them greedily what sort of thing this fantastic beast, the elephant, was. The first said: 'It is a big pipe that raises itself mightily, curls, and woe to you if it catches you!' Another said: 'It is a hairy pillar.' Another: 'It is a wall, like a fortress, and it too is hairy.' Another, the one who had felt the ear: 'It's not a wall at all; it's a carpet of thick wool coarsely worked, which moves when you touch it.' And the last cried: 'What's that nonsense you're talking? It's an enormous walking mountain'." '

The four friends burst out laughing.

'We are the blind ones,' said Yannakos, 'you're right, Father. Forgive me. We explore his little toe-nail and we say: "God is hard, like stone". Why? Because we haven't gone further.'

If we apply this story to our knowledge of God, it is clear that we lack the ability to know God fully *and* that he is far beyond all human knowing. It tells us something about us and something about God. The category of the mysterious will be part of human knowledge and experience of God, where we cannot comprehend all that God is and fail to encapsulate God. Mystery, in the Christian context, reminds us how great and different God is and how human and frail our knowledge is. Of course, this may also be true of all our knowing and understanding, but within Christianity we are not only recognizing human limitations. We are also affirming the divinity and otherness of God.

This same God is, in Christianity, a God of order who is rational. He is the source of all rationality, and the one who gives and sustains rationality in all things. There is the hint in the New Testament that the time of knowing in part and seeing through a glass darkly will come to an end. What is now a mystery to us will become part of the ordinary in eternal life. Then, perhaps for us as for Job, all the questions and doubts will fall into place and perspective in the full knowledge and experience of the living God, seen face to face.

Key words

the mysterious. The obscure and fascinating which goes beyond known comprehension.

encounter. A direct meeting for oneself.

mysticism. An approach to God which stresses direct communion with God, often through awe-inspiring experiences.

awe. Reverential fear.

numinous. The felt presence of the divine. The feelings of the worshipper in the presence of God.

authentic. Proved or accepted as true and genuine.

intuition. A clear and distinct perception by the mind. A direct act of knowing that something is true, *e.g.* when 'the penny drops'.

limitations of knowing. What there is may go beyond our ability to know what there is.

Our human ability to comprehend may not be perfect.

Reading

C. S. Lewis, *The Problem of Pain* (Fontana, 1957).

R. Otto, *The Idea of the Holy* (OUP, 1968).

A. W. Tozer, *The Knowledge of the Holy* (Kingsway, 1984).

R. C. Zaehner, *Mysticism Sacred and Profane* (OUP, 1969).

3   Is faith just a paradox?

Logical paradox – The paradox of mystery – Poetic paradox – Religious paradox – Responses to paradox – The limits of language – Living with paradoxes

One main area where mystery seems to have been expressed, and yet these expressions have been much criticized, is the realm of paradox. This also relates to theological language, which is often attacked on the grounds that it is paradoxical. It makes statements which appear to be nonsensical, while claiming that these statements have genuine meaning. The statement 'God became man' makes the empiricist complain about the nonsense of the transcendent becoming immanent, the divine becoming human, the other assuming identity with something normal. It is not only individual statements that cause problems, but also the juxtaposition of sentences such as 'God loves sinners' and 'God hates sinners'. The theologian argues that both are true descriptions, but they appear to contradict each other. How are we then to proceed?

When confronted with a theological statement which we describe as a paradox, we should immediately put this description in its whole context. This means that we should place such a particular paradox in relation to what we understand by paradox in general and compare it with other known examples of paradox. We should also place it against the backdrop of all religious language and other forms of religious paradox. This will be the structure we shall follow, adding two main lines of thought. The first is how we might set about trying to eliminate or come to terms with a paradox. The second is to examine the relation of paradox to truth and meaning, as well as the limits of our language and understanding.

'Paradox' seems to have two basic meanings. The first is

that of a self-contradictory, or an essentially absurd or false, statement. But this is in fact derived from the notion of a statement contrary to received opinion. This second sense is sometimes expressed in talking of someone's behaviour as paradoxical. Very roughly, this division in meaning may be characterized as being, on the one hand, logical paradox and, on the other, paradox in the sense of mysterious or inexplicable. When we use this latter sense to describe people and their behaviour we are suggesting that there is no obvious rational explanation for their behaviour, or that they have two apparently contradictory notions or beliefs and yet manage to live with them both. We shall return to this theme of living with paradox. It seems, however, that there are two main senses of 'paradox' – the logical and the mysterious.

LOGICAL PARADOX

If we take the first notion of logical paradox, we find that philosophers have puzzled over such paradoxes for years. Perhaps one of the first was Zeno in about 300 BC. His classic example is of a race between a tortoise and Achilles, where the tortoise has a handicap, but Achilles covers half the distance between them with every bound. As Achilles leaps to half the distance behind the tortoise, the tortoise creeps on a little further. Achilles then covers half the distance now separating them, only to find that the tortoise has yet again crawled on. The net result is that, somehow or other, Achilles never quite catches the tortoise up.

Another example of such a paradox is that of a cake which is never finished. At a tea party, everyone is invited to cut a slice of cake. The only condition is that a piece must always be left on the plate. It looks as if the cake will never be totally eaten, for each cut leaves a slice to be sliced yet again. Of course, the cheat in all this is the assumption that it is possible to cut cake in ever finer slices, thus leaving slices to be sliced. Logically, this seems a possibility. Practically, our hopes and our cakes will soon crumble.

In modern logic there are other similar paradoxes, for example, that of the null class. The null class is the class of all those who are not in a class. Thus a class is formed of those who are not members of a class. If there are indeed members of no class, then they are members of the class of not-being-members-of-a-class. If, however, they are not members of the class of not being class-members, then they are members of another class. Thus the paradox is of a class of things which are not members of any class, yet are members of the class of not-being-members-of-a-class.

Each of these paradoxes is a clear example of how, by a process of logical thinking, one arrives at a position which is contradictory. We are left with more than a slight uneasiness about how to proceed, or even quite where we stand in relation to logical paradoxes. We do not want to admit or accept them, but we are not quite sure how to dissolve them.

THE PARADOX OF MYSTERY

There are also the paradoxes of the mysterious or surprising. In a very real sense, the woman who retains her love for the man who has burdened her with a child out of wedlock, mistreated both her and the child physically and mentally, and done all that he could to harm her, is and must be something of a paradox. This is a mystery and indeed surprising, for our reason and common sense call out for a sensible and safe rejection of the man. Yet the woman's love encompasses the unlovable man who may even despise her affection. So too with the martyr – perhaps a man who has given up all wealth and security to go to a dangerous foreign land to aid those in underdeveloped areas. He falls into the hands of some evil communists, who try to make him renounce his beliefs and to denounce his village friends, in return for safety and immunity from harm. He prefers to be shot keeping faith with his friends and ideals.

Both these cases – the woman and the martyr – may be described as paradoxes of the mysterious. We cannot easily explain such behaviour. But we could have used the example of Galileo and his notion of the earth's motion. It appeared obvious that the sun moved, and that the earth was flat and stationary. This was the prevalent opinion and common sense. Galileo suggested that the earth moved and not the sun, and that it was round and not flat. Here indeed were prime examples of paradoxical statements contrary to perceived common sense, though not to logic.

POETIC PARADOX

To be comprehensive, we ought to look at the paradoxes of literature and poetry. John Keats said, 'Beauty is truth, truth beauty.' Here we are not confronted with total identification of beauty with truth but rather with a hyperbolic statement of something the poet wished to express. He stated it thus for effect, to be noticed, to be startling and different, and simply to make his point. This statement is certainly paradoxical in the sense of surprising. There are examples of paradox in our human lives, as social animals, in our description of the world and in the way we communicate with each other. In all linguistic spheres we can use paradoxical statements for effect.

RELIGIOUS PARADOX

Having tried to draw a distinction between different kinds of paradox in order to draw a division between our reaction to them and the way we dissolve or accept them, we turn to paradox in religion. It is far from clear whether paradox in religion is to be taken in a logical, a mysterious or a poetic sense. This is not helped by the approach to paradox of philosophers and theologians. Most often paradoxes are stated and then the statement is analysed, often to the point of absurdity, even though a paradox may not be the only way of expressing the idea in question.

Philosophical writing tends to fasten on the notion of God and attempts to say that it is in itself a paradoxical concept. That is to say it seems self-contradictory. God and his relation to the world are often treated in the same way. If God is to be seen in the world, how can he be kept distinct from his world and the created order of things? If he is kept distinct enough to be God, then how can he be seen in the world? The result is religious paradox. Another example is the incarnation. How could God become man and yet still be God? In addition religious people often express themselves in paradoxical ways. For example, 'Make me a captive, Lord, and then I shall be free.'

The problem of the religious paradox is what sense or meaning we can attach to each example. Are we to allow that they say anything at all? Are they just nonsense? If they are nonsense, is it useful nonsense? What could or would count as evidence for us to be able to accept these paradoxes? There are two basic questions about paradoxes: first, how do they claim to truth and meaning? and second, are they genuinely useful or not? It may be that we are not really clear what the problem of paradox is, but just that we feel uneasy about it. It is this uneasiness and the ways to cure it that need our attention. Thus we must clarify both the problem and the solution.

RESPONSES TO PARADOX

It is only apparent
One of the main responses to the problem of paradox is to try
to deny that there is a paradox. One tries to minimize the
apparent paradox by dissolving the apparent contradiction. This
is done either by removing one or other of the terms, or else
by clarifying the full meaning of one or both of the terms so
that the distinction is made clearer. When the believer says
'Make me a captive, Lord', he or she is asking to live a life of
full and total obedience to the will of God. When the phrase
'and then I shall be free' is added it is thus not working against
a concept of captivity in the negative sense we normally expect,
but is drawing attention to the way in which those in relation
to God are freed from sin and able to live lives of genuine
freedom. In knowing God, we discover our true selves.

This kind of move amounts to a denial that there is a paradox
at all. The appearance of paradox is not essential to the cognitive
content of the statement. In this way, an attempt is made to
dissolve the paradox by stressing its poetic and thus rhetorical
power. Such a move is required in religious language where an
almost studied delight is taken in paradox, with the intention,
one sometimes feels, of confusing rather than enlightening.
However, one still wants to say that the problem of paradox is
much more basic and serious for this solution of clarifying the
meaning of the terms to be applicable every time. Rhetorical
paradox may be forceful in making a point, but it rests for its
effect on the fact that the point made is itself simple and sensible. If it were a genuine paradox, a second level of analysis
would be necessary to make clear the function of paradox.

It must conform to logic
Often the paradox just seems plainly self-contradictory. This is
the position taken by many philosophers of religion towards
much of 'God-talk'. There are different levels of possible
response to this. The initial one must be drawn from Wittgenstein and his description of paradox being accompanied by
'a slight giddiness – which occurs when we are performing a
logical sleight of hand' (*Philosophical Investigations,* p.412). In
reality the philosopher may be saying no more than that logic
creates problems for theological statements. The theologian may
reply that logic has its own problems when applied to the wrong
sort of thing in the wrong sort of way. May it not be the case
that the religious paradox is a paradox only because of the

paradoxical situations to which the relentless application of logic pushes us? There is no necessary reason that theological paradoxes should behave in the same way as logical ones, nor be treated by rules of logic from other spheres of life. Of course, the theologian still cannot, if he wishes to retain a rational standard and basis for his faith, refuse to be consistent. He must not be self-contradictory. Nevertheless, when a purely logical analysis of religious statements is made, one is left with the giddiness to which Wittgenstein refers and a feeling that logic may not be the best tool to use. Different areas of life and thought have different logics. We need to explore why particular logical systems are appropriate to some areas and not to others. We need to look at the presuppositions behind the logician and the theologian as they debate the nature of paradox. It is crucial to expose these assumptions on the part of the critic of religious paradox, for they may be questionable. Logic is a tool and not a master. It should serve us rather than rule us. We must examine its use with care.

It is expressing the inexpressible
Even if this attack on logic by the theologian fails, there is still the other form of paradox to be discussed, that of surprise and mystery. One can try to make out a case that theological paradoxes are the same in nature as those mentioned earlier to do with love, the nature of the earth and poetry. To do this one must elucidate the points of similarity and try to measure whether they are sufficient to make a genuinely viable analogy. On the other hand, one could claim that these paradoxes are the distinctive marks of a true, and indeed *the* true, theology. Such paradoxical theological language is proper, for such language is *sui generis.*

Both lines of escape have problems. If we opt for the similar analogy approach, one must show that beyond human terms and expression there is a genuine divine content. If God is involved in and with the world, is he still sufficiently different to be God? If one moves to the other horn of the dilemma and argues for the uniqueness of theological language, then its relation to human standards of truth, meaning and understanding becomes a problem. What appears to be offered is a suprarational (or is it a sub-rational?) leap or step into an unknown where what appears to be false is true and what is true, false.

Yet behind both approaches there is a common thread which is of great significance in examining paradox. Both kinds of argument are saying that paradox arises from trying to express what in a sense is inexpressible and incomprehensible. Love and theology are ultimately inexpressible in the sense that everything about them cannot be put into words with nothing left over or out. Both are incomprehensible on any but their own terms and require a way of approaching them which is true to their nature and sensitive to their own standards and functions.

Herein lies a tension. It is the tension of the possible and the impossible. If Christianity is true, then there must be some elements of incomprehensibility about it. This is what faith and belief are about, and why they are so important. But the greater the claim to be incomprehensible, the less clear it is what it means to say that Christianity is true. There is again a problem here of meaning and truth. Paradoxes are claimed as expressing truth, but their form seems to remove hope of clear meaning. The believer must make clear what standards of meaning and truth are applicable in religious language in general and in terms of religious paradox in particular. This will help put in context the problem of saying the unsayable and stating the unstatable.

THE LIMITS OF LANGUAGE

If Christianity and what it says about reality is true, then we are surely talking about the very limits of our language and our understanding. How can our reason hope to be able to understand what is absolutely different from itself? Our reasoning cannot negate itself completely, so if we are to conceive of things superior to reason, it would have to be by means of reason itself and its capacity to conceive. As Kierkegaard put it, 'The supreme paradox of all thought is the attempt to discover something that thought cannot think' (*Philosophical Fragments*, p.46). There are a few levels of analysis possible here. The giddiness of the logical paradoxes soon returns when we try to think the unthinkable and say the unsayable. When we try to express the paradoxes of love and martyrdom in terms of factual statement, making language with no room for the experiential aspects of being in all their fullness, then paradoxes result. There is quite a similarity between the issues of paradox in general and those of religious paradox. This should make the philosopher more reasonable as he approaches the religious paradox.

In the last analysis it is the notion of the ultimate that we must stress. For it is here that our language and our comprehension break down. It is just as impossible to state in statements how statements are related to existence, as it is impossible to picture in a picture how a picture pictures what it pictures. Our language breaks down at the ultimate and so too do our criteria of truth and meaning. It may thus be that we cannot adequately judge by our usual standards what is to be said about the ultimate.

LIVING WITH PARADOXES

We have not established the validity of religious paradoxes in themselves. We have tried to create a background which is more sympathetic to the possibility of these paradoxes being meaningful and significant. We have argued that there is little difference between religious paradox and paradox in other areas of life. The real test, however, is whether or not we are prepared to live with paradox or are so disturbed by the presence of paradox that we dissolve it at all costs. Theology may claim that there is a proper use of paradox and must therefore establish that necessity at each and every point of its claim. The difference made by such paradoxes and the context in which they are claimed and expressed become crucial guides in responding to paradox. We do judge by fruits.

It is also the case that paradox seems likely to occur at the frontiers of human knowing, and because of the limits of human rationality. Scientists seeking to describe the nature of light present it as both acting in wave and in particle form. Both descriptions are necessary, yet seem to create a paradox. In the end, the scientists can only state what the situation is and work on expressing why that is the case as fully as possible. It is at the point of limit and of the ultimate that our minds begin to boggle. The danger is that instead of recognizing our own limits, and living with an appropriate untidiness, we seek to force our usual standards of meaning and truth in judging what breaks through and beyond those standards.

We have tried to make a case for taking paradox seriously on its own terms, for religious paradox bears many similarities to other paradoxes in human experience. In the next chapter, we shall focus on one paradox in particular and see what sense can be made of it.

Key words

paradox. An apparent contradiction.

nonsense. Literally having no sense, no meaning and unable to be understood.

religious language. The words

and symbols used by the community of believers.

limits. The boundaries that cannot be passed.

self-contradiction. A statement or set of statements made by an individual which nullifies or destroys itself.

the mysterious. The obscure and fascinating which goes beyond human comprehension.

logical paradox. An apparent contradiction based on the rules and structure of logic alone.

poetic paradox. An apparent contradiction expressed in literary and poetic ways.

religious paradox. An apparent contradiction which arises within a religious setting.

apparent paradox. What seems to be a contradiction but is not.

the inexpressible. What cannot be put into words properly.

paradoxes of human life. Experiences and expressions we encounter as people which do not easily make sense but are still real.

Reading

R. Hepburn, *Christianity and Paradox* (Watts, 1966).

J. Passmore, *Philosophical Reasoning* (Duckworth, 1961).

4 God: up there and down here?

*A split infinity? – The sceptic's case – The intuitionist's case –
Reducing God to the transcendent – Bringing God down to size –
Is the gap really necessary? – Grounds for belief in transcendence
and immanence*

We have examined the nature of paradox in general, but the real
problems arise when one is confronted by particular paradoxes.
How is it to be interpreted? What meaning can be given to it?
We shall look at the issue of transcendence and immanence.

A SPLIT INFINITY?

The God of Christianity is a transcendent God. There is an
'infinite qualitative distinction' between God and humankind,
and between God and the world. Yet the biblical picture of God
is of a God who is intimately involved with the world. There
are two aspects to God and his activity. These are the aspects
of *transcendence* and *immanence*. The transcendent God is
different in being from other beings. All other beings are created
things, but God is pictured as the Creator, himself uncreated.
God is also different from other levels of reality, for these levels
are finite, corruptible and less than perfect. The Christian God
is infinite, incorruptible, perfect and holy.

At the same time and in the same breath, the Christian affirms
that God is not only the Creator of the world, but is also its
sustainer. There is no hint here of a maker who simply gets the
process in order and leaves it to its own devices, as Deism
argues. Rather God is seen as intimately involved in every level
of the world and its sustenance. Without him, nothing would
be. This is not simply an interplay of God with nature. It is God
creating and controlling nature and history. It is an expression

of the sovereignty of God, in which God rules nature and is involved in the realm of the history of human affairs. History is seen as the arena of God's activity and as a process which lies under the ultimate control of God. Thus God interacts with and relates to humanity and all its doings.

This God of transcendence and immanence is also held by Christians to enter into time and space while still retaining his essential transcendent features. 'The Word became flesh' means that the transcendent God, retaining his uniqueness and essence, became immanent. The infinite became finite. The incorruptible put on the corruptible, yet retained its incorruptibility. At this point, the philosopher has had enough. The unkind cry, 'Nonsense!' The more gentle ask for some careful account of how transcendence and immanence may be expressed. Renford Bamborough has suggested that there are basically three approaches to transcendence and immanence. These are the views of the sceptic, the intuitionist and the reductionist.

THE SCEPTIC'S CASE

The sceptic's case is quite straightforward. The gap between transcendence and immanence is so great that it cannot be bridged. The sceptic examines the language of Christianity and its talk of God: 'Our Father who art in heaven . . .'. For the sceptic, the problems begin with what is meant by 'Father' and 'in heaven'. When the Christian replies that by saying 'Father' he is not referring to 'father' in a physical sense, nor in the sense of one who begets children, the sceptic responds with two objections. Antony Flew calls this first objection 'the death of a thousand qualifications'. He argues that the Christian takes a word which is familiar to us all. It makes sense in the immanent realm. The Christian then qualifies his use of the term, by suggesting that it is not quite the same as in normal usage. He then qualifies and qualifies again. Flew argues that, in the end, the concept dies the death of a thousand qualifications, for it is emptied of all genuine content and meaning. There is nothing left at the end of the process. The gap is too great to be bridged by the qualification of concepts.

The second attack from the sceptic relates to the idea of 'stretching concepts'. The sceptic argues that the Christian proceeds by taking a concept from the immanent realm and then stretches it to apply to the transcendent realm. The sceptic argues that there is such a world of difference between the immanent and the transcendent that our human, immanent concepts snap. They are stretched beyond breaking-point, and literally no sense is left at all. 'Love' is a meaningful term when applied to parents and children, husband and wife, friends, lovers, pets and owners, and a host of this-worldly relationships with which we are all familiar. To talk of a transcendent, infinite, all-mighty, all-perfect God 'loving' means nothing that is recognizable or intelligible to humankind. The sceptic argues that the gap between transcendence and immanence is so great that we must accept only what we actually know. That, of course, is all within the immanent realm alone.

THE INTUITIONIST'S CASE

In contrast, the intuitionist accepts that there is a gap between transcendence and immanence, but is more optimistic about bridging the gap. The man of faith knows that the transcendent and immanent come together in the reality of God revealed in Christ. The man of faith knows in a moment of insight or intuition in which the 'impossible' becomes possible. The intuitionist is not always able to say very much about the intuition, its basis, its form, or the means of testing it. He argues that you will know when and if you intuit for yourself. The intuitionist accepts that there is a gap but denies that rational reflection will be of much help. Personal experience of the intuition provides the key.

The problem, however, is that it is not clear what kind of key is being provided. Such a retreat to intuition seems very attractive until we inquire what is meant by 'intuition'. Then the problems begin, for it may be so deeply personal that it escapes general description. The conditions under which the intuition happens cannot always be specified with great accuracy. Indeed, even when the conditions are expressed and someone fulfils these conditions, the problem may be that they still do not have the necessary intuition. The intuitionist replies that they obviously did not do the experiment properly. The difficulty with this response is that nothing will count as having done the experiment properly, except success and having the intuition. Yet it is the reality of just such an intuition which is supposed to be tested. One is left with the feeling that it would be lovely if the intuitionist were correct, but that there is not sufficient detail to clarify what is being said, far less to convince the genuine seeker after God.

These problems with the intuitionist's approach should not

drive us back into the arms of the sceptic, for his view has difficulties. The sceptic makes certain assumptions about knowing and reality, which he does not always make explicit when he attacks. These are often narrow empiricist assumptions about language and reality. Words are supposed to picture reality and, unless I can see the result of the picture, the word is thrown away as rubbish. But this picture theory rests on the idea that reality can be experienced only through the five senses. There is, in this view, nothing beyond sense experience.

The problem is that when the sceptic approaches the relation of transcendence to immanence he comes with a ruler to judge all else. The ruler may not be relevant or useful. Likewise, his acceptance of the picture theory of language is an attempt to put all language in a single strait-jacket. The truth of the matter is that language has a depth and variety of relationships with reality, as poets and writers are continually revealing. The sceptic's case has many problems.

REDUCING GOD TO THE TRANSCENDENT

The reductionist believes that both the sceptic and intuitionist are wrong. Their error, it is suggested, lies in accepting the gap between transcendence and immanence. The reductionist believes it is possible to bridge the gap by reducing one to the other. Such a reduction may happen in either direction – of transcendence to immanence or of immanence to transcendence.

If one tries to reduce the immanence of God entirely to the transcendence of God, one is left with a completely transcendent being. God is the totally other, separate from the world. The ground of this otherness may be ontological or qualitative, both in God's being and in his nature. God's being is infinite. Such being cannot be talked of as 'being' in the same sense as finite being. God is holy and perfect. Such holiness and perfection cannot bear to look on sin and corruption, far less have contact with the imperfect and sinful. If God is transcendent, then it is clear that there is no way from the world to God. There are no features or aspects of the world which would help man to know or understand God. The categories of transcendence are foreign to immanence. There is a more serious problem of knowing for man. How can man – the corrupt, finite, imperfect sinner – think of or know the infinite, holy, incorruptible God? If God is transcendent, there can be no place for intimate communion between God and man. If God is distinct from the world, then it is in no way clear what kind of contact God could have with the world.

An emphasis on transcendence, in an extreme form, and every reduction of immanence to transcendence, must inevitably put God so far from the world that he can have no concern with it. If his being is so different in kind from ours, it is not clear what kind of relationship he could have with the world or man, for how could he show himself? If he is so holy, then he cannot bear to look upon sin and could not approach us. Moreover, such talk of 'approach', 'looking' and 'being' is highly metaphorical and, on the basis of a totally transcendent view of God, would seem to be illegitimate.

A retreat to analogy is not really helpful, for an analogy to work requires that we know both terms to ensure a proper fit in the analogy. The comparison between two terms is the base of analogy, but if there is knowledge of only one term, analogy is just hopeful gesturing. If there is only transcendence, analogy will not work. If God is reduced to the totally transcendent, he is placed not only beyond our being, but also beyond our knowing. We have no means of reaching, understanding, or even catching the faintest glimpse of him. In short, the transcendent God becomes so unknowable, other and separate that we can neither have dealings with him nor he with us.

In a strange way this is almost the aim of those who reduce God to the totally transcendent. Certainly they believe that there is no way for man to reach up to or understand God. They thus stress the initiative and grace of God, who approaches mankind. The problem is that, having put God beyond all human comprehension, it is hard to see what human concepts may be used to talk of this 'approach' and used to grasp the grace of God. Some theologians so stress God's priority in salvation that human beings seem nothing more than helpless objects in a divine game.

Those who stress this transcendent reduction, like Rudolf Otto and even Don Cupitt today, seem to believe that there is still a way for man to note the presence of the divine. Otto talks of the fear and dread which come in experience of the numinous. This is an anxiety which marks an encounter with the holy and living God. A similar emphasis lies in the experience of wonder and amazement at there being a world at all and at the nature of the world. This wonder and amazement are supposed to be intimations of the reality of the God of otherness. The difficulty with both lines of suggestion is that they can offer no reason why the experiences of fear, dread, wonder and awe should not be ends in themselves with any number of different causes. It is not clear how a truly transcendent God could 'cause' anything in this world. The transcendent God, once placed at that infinite distance from man, is unable to bring any form of help or succour to mankind in their predicament. God is too heavenly to be of any earthly use.

BRINGING GOD DOWN TO SIZE

If the transcendent horn of the dilemma is too painful to allow lingering ease, there remains the other reductionist attempt. This is by far the more popular resting-place in the modern age. The transcendent God is reduced to the immanent. God is reduced to the world, to the processes of nature within the world, to the 'ground of our being' which underlies all reality, to man, to some aspect of personality, or to whatever the latest theological fashion decrees. This literally means that God is reduced to man, being, or to the world. The immediate question must be why this reduced reality should be called God. It is to make God in our own or chosen image. There seems a genuine difference between the worship of God and the worship of man, being or the world as God. Effectively, if God is reduced to something else, then there is no God. Certainly, such a God is indistinguishable from us and our world. He is too near us and our predicament to be of help and succour. He simply becomes part of the problem. He provides no avenue of escape, far less an opportunity and reason for worship.

It is difficult to see how one might be thoroughgoing in this reduction to immanence because of the multiplicity of things and the problem of evil. The world, being, mankind are all full of such diversity that it is hard to see that God might be one set of such. The existence of evil, corruption and imperfection seems a rank denial of the traditional account of God as sinless, incorruptible and perfect. If God is reduced to the immanent, then his moral nature must undergo radical transformation. If the God of transcendence is so far removed that he was of no earthly use, then the God of immanence is so near to mankind that we cannot properly identify, recognize, relate to and know him. God, for his part, could do nothing to help us.

No matter the direction that reductionism moves along, the end result is meaninglessness and nonsense. Reductionism offers no viable alternative to the gap between transcendence and immanence. What is crucial is the standard we have used to reject both moves from the reductionist. That standard has been the traditional concept of God as both transcendent and immanent. The use of this standard is no mere attempt to retain historical continuity within the Christian faith. It is used in the firm hope that none of the sceptics, intuitionists or reductionists have said the last word on possible attitudes to understanding transcendence and immanence.

IS THE GAP REALLY NECESSARY?

A third alternative to the two different reductions would be to accept both horns of the dilemma, not in the form of a gap between the transcendent and the immanent, but as interpreting these as equally viable, acceptable, intelligible and non-contradictory ways of describing God. It is certainly true that the biblical writers find no problem in shifting from talk of God as transcendent to talk of him as immanent.

The problem is that of beginning with a gap. But can the gap be prevented? A parallel case may show us a fruitful way forward. Traditionally man was divided into two parts – the mind and the body. This became the central area of debate between the rationalist and the empiricist. The rationalist held that knowledge of the world of sense was dependent on the mind and understanding. Reality was mental and known with certainty only by the mind. In a way, the rationalist reduced the body to the mind, at least in epistemological ways. The empiricist reduced in the opposite direction. He held that reality was entirely in the realm of sense experience or of the body. Thus the mental life was reduced to the body and the mind to sense experience. The criticism of both views was that they failed to do justice to the complexity and variety of mind and body.

Recent philosophers, especially P. F. Strawson, have suggested that the basic error is to begin with a gap or division between mind and body. As an alternative, he argues that the basic reality is that of a *person*. A person may be regarded, described and understood from two different angles or perspectives – mental attributes and physical attributes. Thus the person is the basic unity, and 'mind' and 'body' are rather ways of looking at that unity and aspects of it. There is no gap. Thus the problem is not so much solved as *dissolved*. But are there any grounds for suggesting that this line of dissolution may be justified in the problem of transcendence and immanence?

When we talk of the transcendent or of the immanent, these are used relative to something else. To be transcendent is to be transcendent to the created world. To be immanent is to be immanent in the created world. Both descriptions are relative to the concept of a created world. The key term here is 'created'. If one believes that the world is created, then there is implicit in that doctrine of creation, notions of transcendence and immanence. The power that created is over and above the world we know. Nevertheless by its creative act it is somehow involved in and with the world. If the Christian or believer in the created world lays too great a stress either on the characteristic of transcendence or of immanence to the exclusion of the other it leads to distortion. To talk meaningfully of transcendence and immanence presupposes that the world is created. It is part of the framework that presupposes the doctrine of creation and the doctrine of the Creator God, who acts in transcendent and immanent ways. Both expressions are part of his activity, as both mental and physical expressions are part of a person's activity.

In contrast, if one does not believe in a created world, any talk of transcendence and immanence literally does not make sense. There may be some metaphorical sense, but no literal one. We now see that there are two different presuppositional frameworks in conflict. It is essential therefore to clarify what it is to accept that the world is created and what it is to reject the world as created, and the grounds for both positions. Any justification of the doctrine of a created world would not be based on transcendence and immanence, but on some other grounds such as religious experience or rational proof. Nevertheless such a belief would entail a belief in the transcendent and immanent as ways of describing the activity of the one God. If such a belief is plausible, there is a possibility of a new approach to the question of transcendence and immanence.

GROUNDS FOR BELIEF IN TRANSCENDENCE
AND IMMANENCE

If someone were to attempt to hold the two aspects together, on what grounds might such a position be adopted? Some might argue that the immanent seems to point to something beyond itself because of the order, variety, morality or whatever else it happened to display. It might be proposed that the world points to something beyond itself, by the fact *that it is* regardless of *what* it is. In other words, the world itself demands some notion of purpose and meaning beyond itself. The problem is why we should look beyond the world for something more, when it may be that this world is all that there is.

What might suggest that there is something beyond the world? Some philosophers like H. H. Price and Colin Wilson have suggested that the reality of the paraphysical and paranormal point beyond the immanent. Spirits, ghosts, psychokinesis and telepathy are sufficient grounds for the postulation of something beyond the world as experienced through the five senses. Others have emphasized our experience of forces and powers greater than ourselves. In light of the force of the tide, or of gravity, man is filled with an awareness of power, and of something greater than themselves. This is a sense of the transcendent and one is conscious of both the desire to grasp, harness, control and understand it, as well as being grasped and controlled by it. It is doubtful if we know enough of the paranormal, or have sufficient reason for confidence in what we know, to hope for some genuine knowledge of the transcendent from that source. As for the awareness of power, this may be a person's psychological make-up addressing itself, to creating and fulfilling its own need. Alternatively, that power may well be there and have a totally immanent explanation for its existence.

Rudolf Otto has formalized something of the attempt to show the transcendent in his description of the numinous, and the sense of fearful awe and wonder we experience at certain moments of our lives. He attempts to argue from this experience to the reality of something greater than ourselves. Yet this 'proof' rests on the self-authentication of the experience itself, and we are back to the position of the intuitionist.

The Christian believes in revelation. This revelation is based on the grace of God. In that sense man cannot know God, unless and until God reveals himself to mankind. The God of Christianity is a God who chooses to reveal himself and his nature to man. The Bible is a record and expression of that revelation which is also expressed in nature and morality, but finds its full and final form in the revelation of Jesus Christ. He is God in terms we can all understand. Once a person is able to accept the notion of the grace of God, there is no inherent unintelligibility in the concept of revelation.

The sticking-point for the non-Christian confronted by Christian claims is the acceptance of revelation. What is crucial here is what content is claimed for revelation as objective. The Christian claims that God is Creator and that he became incarnate. These claims are based on divine revelation. Both these doctrines of creation and incarnation hold together in unity the angles or aspects of transcendence and immanence. The transcendent God not only creates, but sustains and rules the immanent realm of the world and of humanity. The transcendent God became immanent in human flesh, in space, time and history; yet he retained his transcendence. God 'showed' himself to us in a form that we could understand, that is in our own terms; but, it is claimed, he still retains his full godliness.

There is thus a possible solution to the problem of transcendence and immanence in the doctrine of creation, and in the person of Christ. The crux, is, then, how one regards Christ and the Christ-event. If one begins on the side and viewpoint of transcendence, then one must come to grief. Likewise, if one begins from the side of immanence, what remains is no 'good news'. The Christian demands that one begins with Christ in all he said, did and was in himself. This goes beyond the mere academic exercise of an intellect or the 'intimations of immortality' or the numinous. It comes to an affirmation of Lordship and divinity, as it did for Thomas: 'My Lord and my God!'

In John's Gospel, chapter 14, Philip says to Christ, 'Show us the Father, and we shall be satisfied.' He was a good empiricist and a good reductionist. It is claimed that everyone would be satisfied if God were reduced to a test-tube, a scientific formula, or an essence. In one sense this is true, for the ghost of God would be laid for ever. In another sense, however, this would bring no satisfaction, for the Creator, almighty, eternal God would have disappeared. Plato, in his *Republic,* struggles with transcendence and immanence in relation to his concept of the Form of the Good, or the Form of Forms. The question the reader wants answered is how we may grasp this and know it for ourselves. Plato's response is to turn our attention away from the mere shadows flickering on the cave walls, and even the shadows of the objects in the daylight sun, to the sun itself. Facing the sun in a final coalescence of knowing and being one experiences the transcendent and immanent.

There is a painting of a labourer toiling in a field. His head is bent low by his work. His gaze is fixed on the furrow and field. Yet hovering above his head is the glory of paradise. He does not see it, for he is not looking in the right place. 'There is none so blind as those that will not see.'

Key words
transcendence. Referring to God standing over, against, independent of, and above the world.

immanence. A way of understanding reality purely in terms of complete involvement with the world of physical and historical reality. The rejection of any explanation for reality outside of the world.

scepticism. The view that we cannot arrive at any certainty at all, especially by using our reason.

intuitionism. The view that knowledge or morality stems from clear and distinct perceptions by the mind.

reductionism. An approach to issues and problems which tries to make the complicated seem simple by reducing it to the key themes or points.

infinite being. Usually the being of God, understood in terms of having no limits of time or space.

created world. The world around us seen and interpreted as originating in the action of God bringing it into being.

analogy. An agreement or likeness between things which helps us understand the one thing by reference to the other.

logical gap. An unbridgeable interval between ideas or concepts because of the nature and content of their definitions.

presuppositional sense. Clarifying the meaning of what we assume or take for granted.

revelation. The unveiling of truths which cannot be reached by reason alone. It is used to refer to God's unveiling of himself and his will through nature, history, the prophets, the Decalogue, Christ and the Scriptures.

Reading

H. Bavinck, *The Doctrine of God* (Banner of Truth, 1977).

E. L. Mascall, *He Who Is* (Darton, Longman and Todd, 1960).

R. Swinburne, *The Coherence of Theism* (OUP, 1977).

K. Ward, *The Concept of God* (Collins, 1977).

5 So you think you've got problems!

Four kinds of evil – Traditional approaches: monism – Traditional approaches: dualism – The Augustinian theodicy – Evil is privation – The aesthetic conception of evil – Two objections – The Irenaean theodicy – Difficulties – A proper context for the understanding of evil – Some philosophical notes – The Christian view of suffering – The positive value of suffering

As I write this chapter, the television set announces yet more deaths in Iran, Southern Africa and Belfast. Most of us feel that death is bad and evil. Death is the very opposite of life. It is literally meaningless. It causes suffering often to those who are dying and to those left behind. Before the reality of death we seem powerless and helpless. But if we reflected a little more we might see things differently. Death might be seen as part of the natural order, simply part of what it means to be mortal and human. It is all too easy to label things as evil without really asking what that means. So what is evil and, if it is a problem, how are we to deal with it?

FOUR KINDS OF EVIL

Most of us are familiar with one basic sense of evil. That is *physical evil*. This meant originally the actual physical sensation of pain and discomfort. Gradually this sense was extended to the notion of mental anguish in relation to suffering, both in the sense of the pain we might feel being away from home for a long time and also the pain felt when we watch others suffer and feel sympathetic towards them. Both physical and mental pain obviously vary greatly according to the individual. Some seem almost oblivious to pain, while others seem to be over-sensitive.

A second kind of evil is *natural evil*. This refers to what we call evil in the natural realm. Disease, earthquakes and natural disasters would all come under this category. There is evil in nature itself.

A third kind of evil is *moral evil*. By this is meant evil originated by human beings. We can see examples of this at many levels. Man's inhumanity to man, to the world and to themselves is clearly seen as coming from mankind themselves and they bear responsibility for that. This is what is traditionally included under the idea of sin.

The final category is that of *metaphysical evil*. This is the most difficult to understand, but is related to the very nature of finitude, contingency and being imperfect in an imperfect world.

TRADITIONAL APPROACHES: MONISM

The monist holds that, in fact, everything is good. To be more precise, monism argues that everything is of one nature. It would be possible for everything to be evil, but traditionally monism, in relation to the problem of evil, has suggested that everything is good. There is no evil. Evil is an illusion. This kind of view is held by Christian Scientists and also by Hindus.

The view has led to humorous attempts to outline its position. The following limerick is one such attempt.

> There was a faith-healer of Deal,
> Who said, 'Although pain isn't real,
> If I sit on a pin
> And it punctures my skin,
> I dislike what I fancy I feel.'

The monist view seems obviously unsatisfactory, for it appears to be pure escapism, in the sense of pretending what is real is not real. This cannot be successful. Monism simply refuses to recognize the problem, and rather redescribes it. This is no way to deal with the reality of suffering and pain. Neither does this approach offer any reason why, if pain is only an illusion, so many suffer from such a comprehensive illusion.

TRADITIONAL APPROACHES: DUALISM

Monism holds the basic and absolute unity of everything at all costs, even that of taking the reality of evil seriously. Dualism, it may be said, goes to the opposite extreme. Dualism, as its name implies, divides the world and reality into two. This is the pattern in Plato (though not all commentators accept that) and Zoroastrianism. There are both good and evil deities, which are engaged in a battle with each other. The mixture of good and evil in the world, and of pleasure and pain, simply proves that there are both sorts of powers – that of good and evil. Dualism does not necessarily offer any analysis of the eventual outcome, but as is usual, the goodies are supposed to win, and the baddies to lose, in the end.

The two philosophical approaches of monism and dualism have passed into Christianity and religion. Both Christianity and other religions have tended to hold some uneasy compromise between the two approaches, trying to hold them in balance. Two main positions have characterized theology and philosophy of religion throughout Western history. These are the approaches of Augustine and Irenaeus.

THE AUGUSTINIAN THEODICY

The term 'theodicy' means a justification or defence of God. The need for theodicy stems from the claim that God is both good and all-powerful. If God is good, then why does he allow evil to happen? The answer might be that he cannot help it. That would then deny that God was really all-powerful. If he is all-powerful and evil still occurs, it seems as if he does not use his power to rid the world of evil. Thus he is not good. But, by definition, as far as the Christian is concerned, God is all-powerful, so the Christian wants to uphold that God is both good and all-powerful. This means that the Christian tries to defend God by giving some kind of solution to the problem of evil and suffering.

The Augustinian view has two key notions. The first is that evil is a privation, and the other is what is called the aesthetic conception of evil. These stem from Augustine's Manichaean past: dualism and the struggle between good and evil were very much part of the beliefs of Manichaeism. In rejecting this, Augustine stressed a monist type of view.

EVIL IS PRIVATION

Evil in itself, Augustine argued, is not anything real. It is simply a corruption of good. It is falling short of goodness rather than an independent reality. Evil is thus always parasitic on good.

It is an absence of good, and so is a movement towards non-existence. Augustine believed that goodness is the most real thing. All falling short of goodness is a move away from reality. Augustine supports his theory by describing the genesis of evil in terms of the free-will choices of angels and men. Again, he is careful to emphasize that this does not make evil a positive thing, but rather it is a turning away from a higher good, particularly from God. This is the classic description of sin. Sin is falling short of God's standards. It is failing to do and to be what God intended. Accordingly, since God is good, he must punish sin. Thus we have the real reason why there is suffering in terms of disease and disaster. These are the natural consequences of the fall of man. Man falls from God's standards and so must inevitably be punished, or else the fact of God's goodness would have no relevance to God.

We must not fail to see the complexity of Augustine's view. He is giving a double definition of evil. It is first of all sin in the sense of falling short, and that is the true basis and cause of all sin. The second sense of evil is the *fruit* that sin inevitably brings – the penalty and punishment of sin. In essence, however, for Augustine, evil is negation and deficiency.

THE AESTHETIC CONCEPTION OF EVIL

Closely allied with this idea of evil as privation is the notion of evil interpreted from another perspective. If we look at a tapestry, we see that there is an intermingling of threads and patterns. To highlight particular threads and patterns, dark threads are set against light ones. The light colours are seen in all their glory by the contrast with the dark colours. The overall effect, when seen from above or as a whole, is pleasing and aesthetically beautiful. If each thread were examined individually, it would seem uninteresting and displeasing. Augustine builds on this kind of analogy. What appears to be evil is only what is seen in isolation. We are in fact viewing things from too limited a context. In this way, distortion occurs. What we call evil is a necessary part of the universe. If we were able to view the universe only as a whole, we would then clearly see that the totality is good. When we call things evil, it is because we never see the whole. It is God alone who sees the whole and, in fact, he is the great designer. Thus we can have confidence in him and in his judgment. Some people have described what lies behind Augustine's view as the principle of plenitude. The universe is a better place, having a wider variety of things

and experience, than it would be if everything were monochrome.

TWO OBJECTIONS

There are two main objections to the Augustinian view of evil.
The first is to question why God did not make us differently.
If we are made such that, when faced with the choice of doing
good, we choose to fall short of that standard, then it seems
obvious that God could have done a better job. He could have
made us so that we always, without exception, chose the good.
In this way, both evil, in the sense of sin, and evil, in the sense
of the penalty for sin, would have been avoided.

The debate on this has centred on a defence of free will. In
response to the question whether God could have made us so
that we always chose the good, the reply comes that such a
'biasing' on the part of God would have robbed us of free will.
In making men and women, God created them with the capacity
to choose goodness or to refuse to choose goodness and thus
fall short of his standards. If he had made people so that they
'had to' choose the good and could do nothing else, then they
would not have had freedom. Indeed, it is argued that they
would not really be people at all. Instead they would be like
programmed robots, acting on the basis of orders and unable
to disobey. The critics have responded with the suggestion that
God could have made people so that they freely chose goodness
all the time. The problem is, how we would know whether they
were truly free to do differently, if they never chose anything
but goodness. It is also debatable whether it makes sense to
create people who are free to do only one thing. Is this genuine
freedom, or is it another, more sophisticated level of control by
God?

This leads quickly to the second point, which has bedevilled
philosophy of religion. If God allows evil, he is either lacking
in love or in power. If he really loved us, he would never allow
us to suffer in any way. If he does really love us and yet we
still suffer, then he is lacking in the power to control us and
evil. Either way, the traditional picture of God is called in question. His love or his power must be redefined because of the
problem of evil.

Such pleas for a redefinition would require a very careful look
at what it means to say that God is all-powerful and all-loving.
To be all-loving does not necessarily mean letting people do
whatever they like or removing all consequences of actions and

behaviour. To be all-powerful does not mean an ability to do the logically impossible or the nonsensical. God cannot make square circles, but that says nothing about his power. As part of its defence, the Augustinian view would try to see the likely effect on man's relationship with God of some change in the pattern of God's activity, if we are assuming that a truly all-loving or all-powerful God would act differently.

There is even more at stake here than man's relationship with God. There is also God's relationship with the world. What kind of world would result from such interference and control on God's part? If God were to step in to prevent evil and its consequences, what would our world be like? Imagine a drunk person leaping from the top of the Empire State building in New York. As he falls, he thinks, 'So far, so good.' At the very moment he is about to be splattered on the sidewalk (pavement) of New York, somehow or other he floats to a gentle landing. God has intervened. The speeding car suddenly slows down and avoids a crash. Mrs Jones, in the kitchen slicing onions, discovers that her knife suddenly turns to jelly as she is about to chop off her little finger. Chaos would result if God were to intervene in the world in these kinds of ways in order to prevent or restrain evil. The regularity and order of the world would disappear. With the disappearance of that regularity and order our ability to understand, relate to and act upon the basis of regularity and order of the world would come to an end.

Any retreat to the next world to put things right does not seem a proper escape for Augustine. Given that at that point we may see the whole and so realize that evil was not really evil, we would also be faced with a presumably unaesthetic and displeasing existence. All that we experienced would be good and pleasurable rather than their opposites. Heaven must therefore lack the variety that evil appears to provide. Of course, Augustine might respond that in heaven not only has sin been dealt with finally and absolutely but also that our nature has been transformed. If we no longer fell short of the standards of goodness of God, by God's grace, then the privation of evil would disappear. With its disappearance, the aesthetic conception of evil also disappears, for it makes sense only when evil occurs and when the falling short happens. In that sense, the heavenly situation of all goodness would make both notices of evil, as privation and as aesthetically useful, redundant.

Augustine's own view is in a state of tension and contradiction. The stronger the view that evil is a privation resulting from sin, the less it is possible to hold to an aesthetic view of evil. Like the monist, Augustine is in danger of failing to do justice to the reality of evil, pain and suffering. The same kind of criticism will reappear in connection with the Irenaean view of evil.

THE IRENAEAN THEODICY

This defence of God's goodness in the light of evil was popular in the early church through the writings of Irenaeus. It regained importance in the nineteenth century mostly due to the influence of Friedrich Schleiermacher. In contemporary philosophy of religion John Hick has been a powerful proponent of this view, particularly through his work *Evil and the God of Love*. The general tenor of these three writers can be simply described.

Before the fall, Adam was a child. He was *not* a mature, responsible adult. Rather he stood at the beginning of a long process of development. Adam was created in the image of God. He was yet to be made in the likeness of God. He had the *form* of God, but lacked the *content* of God. We can see the same sort of situation if we look at someone who has the makings of a good football player, but lacks the particular skills. He has a general idea but has not grasped the individual particulars which will transform him from potentiality to actuality. This distinction between image and likeness and form and content stems from a particular interpretation of Genesis and the account of creation there. The account of the Garden of Eden is an idyllic interpretation of the childlike Adam in his immaturity.

The process of development truly begins with the fall. The fall of man was an absolute necessity. It was a growing up experience. It was learning the hard way. Humanity had to experience some degree of freedom and autonomy, otherwise they could not become adult. In the setting up of one forbidden tree, humanity is confronted with the freedom to choose. The freedom to choose is a choice of obedience or disobedience. One can either go God's way or one's own way. In choosing the one or the other, a person is beginning to grow up as a mature adult. Teenagers reach a point where they can question the values of their parents. They become adults when they decide for themselves to adopt the values of society or parents or else to create another set of values. It is only if one is truly free that one can enter into a fully adult relationship of love and trust. The parallel is exact with humankind according to the Irenaean account. It is only when people are truly free both to accept and reject God that they have adult maturity. Given such freedom, people can enter into an adult relationship of love and trust with God. Anything prior to that expression of freely chosen love and trust is simply childish dependence.

The presence of evil in the world is explained as a necessity. The necessity is to help people grow and develop. The aim of evil is to mature people. Naturally, it is humanity learning the hard way. The presence of evil ensures that people can learn. Evil and suffering open up the possibility of choice, without guaranteeing or biasing the direction to be chosen.

The world is then seen as a vale of soul-making. At the present time, we lack truly developed, perfect souls and the process of evil will correct that imbalance. Hopefully by the end of this life, we shall have achieved adult maturity, and a proper relationship with God. Obviously, there are situations where life is cut short prior to the completion of that process. In this sense, the Irenaean theodicy readily accepts a notion of purgatory. Purgatory is the culmination of the process of soul-making. It is the final stage of purification before people are truly and properly related with God.

In the Irenaean view, God is ultimately in total, sovereign control. He is working his purpose out. He sends evil and suffering, not to punish people but rather to help them. People are truly helped to be what God intended, when they are developed and grow in maturity. Freedom is necessary to develop and to mature people, but the price of such freedom is suffering. If a person is to be responsible, he or she must learn to take responsibility for his or her actions. That is, he or she must be able and willing to accept the consequences of what he or she does. Whatever a man sows, that he will also reap. Evil is the natural result of certain choices which people make. God allows such evil to reinforce people in their freedom and responsibility. A person who has suffered arrives at development, growth and maturity.

DIFFICULTIES

The criticisms of the Irenaean view are similar to those of the Augustinian view. The critic emphasizes the problem in relation to God. Either God is all-good – if so he lacks the power to overcome evil – or else God is all-powerful, but lacks the goodness to eradicate evil. Why does God choose to allow evil to bring about maturity and growth? Is there not some easier way? Why did God not make us perfect in the first place? Why did he not create us so that we were already mature adults and fully grown and developed? To fail to make us perfect suggests that God is not really all-powerful or that he lacks either the good will or the power to make perfect creatures. Thus we return to a tension between the goodness and the power of God. Certainly, the critic asks why God makes the road to maturity and perfection such a difficult one.

The Irenaean view is ultimately monistic. It seems that evil is not truly evil at all. Always there is a point behind evil and that point is towards good. Evil is a helpful growing thing. It provides us with lessons that cannot be learnt in any other way, just as a parent might spank a child for its own good. But does pain do this? Does it really bring maturity and growth? In some cases has not God overdone his work? The amount of pain and suffering which some people experience seems totally out of proportion to any lessons they might learn. In fact, sometimes the experience of pain and suffering makes people bitter and extremely anti-God and anti-human. For every example of people coming through to greater maturity in response to suffering, there are as many (if not more) examples of people who have been destroyed by the experience of pain.

A further difficulty with the denial of evil as truly evil is that it makes the traditional doctrines of redemption and of the cross unnecessary. Certainly the Old and New Testaments take evil and sin very seriously and reveal a God who acts decisively in Christ to redeem men and women from the power and reality of sin and the consequences of evil. Redemption and the cross create some theological problems for the Irenaean view.

In the end, behind the Irenaean view is the idea that evil can be explained. Evil has a point and a direction, if we can but understand it. This sounds suspiciously like the Augustinian, aesthetic concept of good and evil forming·a privation of good. We might question whether or not such a view makes the unreasonable, reasonable. In other words, evil seems to us to be totally incomprehensible and irrational. It is nonsensical. So will any explanation be possible?

There is, too, an optimism in the Irenaean view which suggests that everything works out fine in the end. But what assurance do we have that in the end all will be well? John Hick replies to this critique with his parable of the road. Two men are walking along a road. The one believes it leads to the celestial city. The other believes it leads nowhere. Hick's point is that, in the end, one of them is right and the other wrong. The test is not strictly speaking a fair one. For the unbeliever, there is never a point at which his view is proved true or false.

For the believer, there is no point at which his view can be proved false to him. Presumably, when he reaches the end of the road, if there is no celestial city, he has no knowledge of the lack of such a city. The picture of verification offered is inadequate.

A PROPER CONTEXT FOR THE UNDERSTANDING OF EVIL

There are, it seems to me, three basic positions, which it is important to separate in coming to grips with the problems of suffering. The first is the position of the Christian. That view can be stated as, 'There is a God, but why is there evil?' The atheist has a different position. It states, 'There is no God, but why is there evil?' The agnostic offers a third alternative, which asks, 'If there is a God, why is there evil?' If we take each one in turn, we discover that no amount of evil will make the Christian change his or her mind. The Christian's statement is a statement of faith. He or she believes that there is a God and that belief is based on past experience, present reality and future hope. Belief in God is the ultimate presupposition of the Christian. It provides the framework of life and thought by which to interpret all else. The Christian recognizes that there is a problem of evil, but his or her interpretation of the problem is always in the context of God. Given a belief in the reality of God and his goodness and sovereignty, how then is the Christian to cope with the problem of evil? The Christian confesses its reality, but the existence of evil will not and cannot threaten the existence of God. That is already presupposed and the basis for interpretation of any possible understanding of the reality of evil.

The atheist holds the opposite view. He or she denies the reality of God. There is nothing, as far as he or she is concerned, which counts for God's existence. There is nothing which can prove God's existence. The atheist has his or her mind made up. However, he or she recognizes that this still leaves him or her with the problem of pain and suffering. Suffering is real, but how is it to be explained? The atheist's difficulty is that pain and suffering are irrational and seem to serve no purpose. Pain, evil and suffering defy explanation. They cannot be reduced to any logical system of thought. As far as the atheist is concerned, evil does not count for or against the existence of God, There is no God. The atheist is much more concerned to respond to the genuine problem of suffering.

This problem of evil for the atheist has led some Christians to ask why evil matters if there is no God. Indeed, they go further and ask why anything at all matters. Often the alternative to Christianity in the light of evil is pessimism, which excludes meaning and significance in every tragic situation.

The question for the agnostic may be expressed as, 'If there is a God, who is all-powerful and all-loving, why then is there evil?' For the agnostic, the problem is really a question of 'God' – who and what is God? It is a conceptual problem, relating to a proper understanding of the nature of God. It is not really a problem of evil. Evil and suffering are relevant only in so much as they relate to God. Agnostics are concerned with the consistency and meaning of Christianity and especially the consistency and meaning of 'God'. They are not truly concerned with evil in and of itself. They are concerned only with the reality of evil in as much as it seems to conflict with the picture and concept of God, traditionally given. Ultimately, we must try to give them some kind of answer.

SOME PHILOSOPHICAL NOTES

One of the dangers in theology's response to philosophy is that it is so terrified by the realm of the philosophical, that it ignores the help philosophy can give. There are, for example, many philosophical comments about the nature and concept of evil which would help put evil and suffering in a context which might be more favourable to the Christian position.

If someone seeks to deny the reality of evil, then, in a real sense, they also deny the reality of good. Like hot and cold, you cannot have the one without the other. Evil and good seem to be like two sides of the same coin. There is evil and evil is a reality. It is not simply an appearance. It cannot be reduced to part of the whole pattern of good. If there is an attempt at such a reduction, then not only is evil reduced, but so also is good. Evil's reality depends upon the reality of good and presumably vice versa.

When we ask a question about evil and suffering, we run into a particular danger. The danger is a desire to impute to the universe, or to God, a purpose like our own. Inevitably, we judge everything from our own point of view. But in so doing we are in danger of imagining that God is just like us. The demand for justification for the problem of evil may be an attempt to push God into a human mould, demanding that God answer in human terms. It may be a projection of God in our image and an attempt to limit our understanding of him by ourselves. What lies behind this particular philosophical thought is the fear of man becoming the measure of God's creation. Man can seek to 'reduce' God by asking for explanations to fit in with human understanding. If there is a gap between man and God, then that gap may mean that there are some things which man cannot understand. God's ways may not be man's ways.

There is a lot of nonsense talked about the problem of evil. Some people suggest that the problem of evil is just like a mathematical sum. We add together all the pains and evils in the world to create the problem of evil. There is something extremely odd about such a calculation. We cannot add together my physical pain and my mental pain. It makes no sense to try to make a grand total of my sore head and my sadness at leaving home. This is rather complicated, especially when I try to add together my pain in the neck and your pain in the neck as well as your grief when your favourite football team is beaten. Nor can I add to the grand calculation all the pain which individual animals feel. It is also impossible to make the addition of natural disasters to this motley collection of pain and suffering. In other words, there is *not* a problem of evil, which is the *sum of all* the pains and evil in the world. This is not to deny the reality of each individual pain and suffering, but rather to emphasize that, if there is to be any hope of an explanation, it must deal with these pains and sufferings individually rather than with some great conglomerate. There is no one thing which feels all the different kinds and different degrees of pain.

In Rudolf Otto's book, *The Idea of the Holy*, he gives some interesting examples of dysteleology. Dysteleology is the negation of all purpose. It is the opposite of teleology. He gives an example of the ostrich, who goes to all the trouble of laying eggs, and then forgets where they were laid. In its forgetfulness, the ostrich tramples the eggs in its own nest. There is no meaning and purpose in such an action. In the same kind of way, pain and evil seem to lack meaning and purpose. They are literally nonsensical. They cannot be reduced to sense or any rational system. They are irrational and, in the end, perhaps we can simply say that this is the way things are. We cannot reduce this state to any other level of explanation.

It often seems that questions about pain and suffering are not really asked at the universal level. Rather they are asked at the individual level, and that is right and proper. The real question is perhaps not, 'Why is there pain and evil?' but rather, 'How can I cope with my pain and suffering?' In other words, the real question as far as many philosophers are concerned is a psychological one. 'How can I cope with pain and suffering? How can I give or find some meaning and purpose in these experiences which seem irrational and meaningless?' These are questions about our psychological ability to cope with the world as it is.

THE CHRISTIAN VIEW OF SUFFERING

Earlier, we suggested that there needs to be some Christian response to the agnostic. The Christian does not make a response by describing the beginning of the world. He or she describes an original creation which was good and perfect. This picture of the beginning is a picture of a reality where pain and suffering were not present. Likewise, the Christian points to the end of the world and to situations where evil, pain and suffering will be banished. The pictures in Isaiah 11 and Revelation 21 offer a description of a perfect world where evil has no place.

The Christian must also face the world as we actually know and experience it. In one sense, he or she recognizes that there can be no total and ultimate answer to evil in the here and now. If such an answer were possible and we understood it perfectly, then evil might well cease to be evil and a problem.

The Christian too confesses that his or her intellect is limited. There are some things which he or she cannot know. For the person of faith, there may come a time when he or she is content to trust that God knows, and that God knows best. In classical terms, this is to recognize that people may be confronted by mystery, as we saw earlier. There are some things which are too great for us to understand. The danger, of course, is that we may declare the mystery too soon and fail to push our understanding and intellect to its proper limits. However, the Christian need not retreat into mysticism without pointing to some meaning in the nature of evil and suffering. He or she can make some suggestions which may encourage others.

Ultimately, Christians look for the source of evil in two different directions. Firstly, they point to another level of reality and to the influence of the devil. The devil is the source of much evil in the world, argue the Christians. There is some kind of cosmic conflict between good and evil which is being waged in 'heavenly places'. Christians are caught up, as is the whole of the world and creation, in that cosmic struggle. Evil then can be partially explained by reference to that struggle and to the power of evil and the devil. The second source of evil is in ourselves. Human sin in the fall is figured as a refusal to accept God or to obey him and as a desire to break his law. We try to be God and to lead our own lives. In the end, we reap the consequences of this action. The consequences, for the Christian are a loss of relationship. This is total and absolute. It is firstly a loss of relationship with God. Humanity is alienated from their Creator and they are no longer what they were created to be. Men and women are rebels who are out of joint with their true source and origin.

This loss of relation, secondly, affects individuals' relationships with themselves. Many point to the alienation which is present in modern-day life, as a mark of our inability to relate properly to ourselves. We suffer from fear, dread and from a lack of will. The good that we want to do we cannot, and the evil we want to avoid, we fail to avoid. Humanity is lost, anxious and troubled. We have lost our innocence and now know the difference between good and evil, but are unable to do the one and avoid the other.

The third aspect of this loss of relation is a loss of relation with our fellow men and woman. This is evidenced by wars and by many criminal actions. It is shown in the apathy and indifference which allow people to die of poverty and malnutrition. The great statesman, Edmund Burke, expressed the problem here in a different context: 'The only thing necessary for the triumph of evil is for good men to do nothing.' At root this is the shelving of responsibility. People refuse to take responsibility for themselves and their fellow human beings. Rather they seek to blame their circumstances or other people. It is an interesting thought that in the Garden of Eden, when Adam was confronted by God with his sin, his initial reaction was to blame the woman. 'It was not me, it was the woman.' Then he blames God. 'It was the woman *you* gave me, so it is all your fault, God.' Man, out of relationship with his fellow, seeks to blame others.

Finally, mankind is out of relationship with the world. Many interpreters of the Genesis story stress the close relationship of mankind to the world. As humanity falls, so, too, the world is affected. You see this not only in Genesis, but also in Jeremiah 1 and in Romans 8. Mankind is no longer in a proper relationship with the animal kingdom or with nature as a whole. Man's cruelty to animals and the dreadful effects of man-made pollution reinforce this picture of the breakdown in relationship with nature. A lack of care, the overuse and abuse of the world are signs of mankind's lack of responsibility for the natural realm.

There is, however, a tendency towards anthropocentricity. Humanity becomes the centre of all things. Are the mosquito and the snake evil? Or are they evil only as far as man is concerned? In other words, is it fair to describe things as evil in themselves, which are simply evil with reference to man? Earthquakes are a result of the earth maintaining a certain temperature throughout the planet. If the temperature becomes too great, then there is an eruption, which we call an earthquake. This is called evil only when it affects human existence. A tidal wave in the Antarctic, where no-one lives, is not considered evil. A tidal wave in Brighton, which wipes out a thousand people, would be called evil. The only difference is the presence of people. The tidal wave remains the same. Is then the tidal wave evil or is it evil only for us? Some go so far as to suggest that people themselves are to blame for building their houses where tidal waves and earthquakes are likely to come.

Anthropocentrism may be equally evident in relation to our understanding of animals and talking of their pain and pleasure. We may be guilty of the pathetic fallacy. This assumes that animals feel as we do and that their experiences are the same as ours. Do animals truly feel pain and pleasure in the same kind of way as we do? The danger is, again, of judging everything by the standard of our own reactions, rather than by seeing things in themselves and as they actually are.

THE POSITIVE VALUE OF SUFFERING

The Christian wishes to affirm that there are positive values in suffering. He or she recognizes that the same conditions, which make it possible to suffer in the physical, emotional and mental state of man, also make it possible for us to have a sense of enjoyment, happiness and contentment. The human sensitivity to pain is likewise a sensitivity to pleasure. We cannot experience the one without at the same time being open to the experience of the alternative. Grief and pain at the loss of a loved one arise because of the relationship of love and interdependency that has gone before. The very situation and condition of life which allows us love, joy and shared happiness in a relationship carry within them the implicit threat of loss, suffering, pain and grief. Of course, we can prevent ourselves feeling the loss and pain of bereavement, by having no close human or family relationships, but that, in itself, seems sub-human.

Pain may also be seen as a warning. Often, when people suffer heart attacks, the first attack is very slight. The doctor describes this as a warning. The patient must take things more easily in future. A child, who accidentally touches a red hot fire, will know to be more careful in future, when confronted by any kind of blaze. Pain and suffering may, then, be interpreted in God's providence (his good care) as warnings to beware of danger. Leprosy provides an example of the value of pain. It destroys the ability to feel anything at all. Victims may suffer severe burns because they cannot feel the heat of fires and so do not know to avoid them.

Pain can bring about positive good. This is when it serves a purpose and is willingly endured. We are not here thinking of sadists or masochists, but of the pain endured to save others. In recent times, Argentinian and British servicemen suffered and died for a cause they believed to be just in the Falklands 'war'. A motto on many war memorials reads, 'Their sacrifice shall not be in vain.'

Many people have interpreted suffering as a positive opportunity. It is an opportunity *to do good*. This means it creates the possibility of serving and helping others. It gives opportunities to show the love of Christ. It is also an opportunity *to be good*. It offers an opportunity for the heroic, which enables us to suffer and yet, in the midst of suffering, to encourage others. Often clergy, who visit those who are suffering extreme pain, come away talking of a sense of peace and glory there. They feel that the sufferer has been more help to them than they have been to the sufferer. It is also an opportunity for God to be with us in our suffering. An opportunity presents itself to come nearer to God and to participate with God in suffering.

This idea of participating in suffering with God also relates to Christian responsibility. Christians have a responsibility to be Christ to the world. It is to bring his love and his healing to those who suffer, whether in physical, mental or spiritual ways. Pain and suffering in the animal kingdom and in the pollution of the world remind man of the need for a right relationship with both. Our responsibility is to care, preserve and shape nature and the natural realm. Pain and suffering which result from our sin remind us of our sinfulness. This means that we are reminded of the need for salvation. Every example of evil is an example which reminds us of Christ's forgiving and dying love. The traditional view of an evangelist is of someone proclaiming that he or she has been bitten by a dog, but in

Christ there is a cure for the disease.

Some Christians argue, too, that suffering does, as Irenaeus suggested, offer an opportunity for growth. In 1 Peter and Romans 5, we have various pictures of the development which follows from the experiences of suffering. Suffering teaches us endurance. Endurance brings us proof that we have stood the test and that proof is the ground of our hope. There are some things that we can learn only the hard way. Suffering will teach us the necessary lessons. The common picture is that of a chrysalis. A little grub spins itself into a cocoon. In the fullness of time, the grub begins to struggle. As it struggles, it changes, developing into a butterfly. As part of the struggle, it must burst out of the cocoon. The struggling develops its wings. Eventually there comes a point, when it is strong enough to break through the cocoon. At that point, it is able to fly. In a mistaken fit of kindness, some person may try to cut away the cocoon. If he does so, he will destroy the possibility of that grub becoming a beautiful butterfly.

Suffering, too, can be seen as punishment. Often in the Old Testament the suffering of the children of Israel is seen as a result of their sin. God is pictured as allowing defeat in battle, famine and disaster because of the wickedness of Israel. The danger is that we may interpret *all* our suffering as punishment for sin. Christ himself was confronted by the scribes and Pharisees, who wished to know whether a man, blind from birth, was so because of his own sin or the sins of his parents. Christ's response was to see in that suffering an opportunity for God's grace and power to be shown. It was not a chance to blame, either the man, his parents, or God. Suffering, then, may be seen as coming from God in two senses – either as a punishment or, as earlier suggested, as an opportunity for the glorification of God. But neither of these senses means that all suffering comes from God. Man's sin and the reality of the devil suggest the very opposite.

One of the most honest things that Scripture has to say about the problem of suffering comes in the book of Job. Job is a man who suffers, not because of anything he has done, but as part of a test. His test is to see whether or not he will love God for God's own sake, rather than for anything that God does for him. Thus, when evil comes to Job, his immediate response is one of praise and thanksgiving to God for everything. 'The Lord gave, and the Lord has taken away; blessed be the name of the Lord.' The rest of the book of Job is given over to a debate, which centres round the theme of suffering and its relationship with sin. It is obvious that Job is not suffering because of sin. He is not being punished for any evil that he has done. However, the explanations of his comforters for evil and suffering are all inadequate. What then is an adequate explanation and response to the problem of suffering?

The book of Job affirms that it is when man meets the living God face to face that suffering is seen in its proper context. It is interesting that, in the meeting between God and Job, there is no solution offered in terms of an explanation of suffering. Nevertheless, in the light of his experience, Job no longer looks for an explanation of suffering and evil. It is enough to experience God.

If that is true in the Old Testament, how much more true in the light of the New Testament revelation of Christ. The ultimate affirmation of faith on the part of the Christian is that nothing can separate him or her from the love of Christ. There is no experience of evil, suffering or even of death itself, which can disturb the relationship between the Christian and God. In the light of that relationship, then all things can be endured and faced. The last word from the Christian is a word of triumph. It is the triumph of the overcoming of evil by the life, death, resurrection and glorification of Christ.

The Christian response to the problem of pain and suffering is to recognize its reality and the Christian responsibility to work for the eradication of pain and evil. At the same time we must set the problem of pain and evil in a context. This context has, to some extent, cut down the size of the problem by showing that it has different facets. It also helps create a way of coping with the psychological problems of pain and suffering. Thus the emphasis on the relationship with the living Christ is a means of coping with pain and suffering on an individual level. The problem of pain and suffering is not only a Christian problem. Are the alternative solutions any better?

Key words

evil. Wickedness, the opposite of good, that which causes displeasure and pain.

monism. The view that everything that exists is part of a united whole and there is no fundamental separation between good and evil.

dualism. In relation to the problem of evil, the view that the world has a fundamental division between the reality of good and the reality of evil, and that they are in ultimate conflict.

Manichaeism. The religion of Mani which stressed a framework of world conflict and redemption in terms of the struggle between good and evil. This view influenced and affected Augustine, who wrote attacking it after his conversion.

theodicy. Name given to any attempt to justify the goodness, justice and power of God in the light of the reality of evil in the world.

goodness. The source or ground of positive value; what is morally desirable.

all-powerful. The quality of God of omnipotence; the ability to do anything which is not logically impossible.

privation. The view that evil is a lack or falling short of the good rather than a positive thing in itself.

aesthetic view. An interpretation of the problem of evil which tries to view the experiences of human beings as a whole, and which sees that whole, with its mixture of good and evil, black and white, as better than a world of experience which is simply monochrome.

fall of man. An account of the failure of men and women to obey God's commands, as pictured in the Garden of Eden, and the results of that failure.

free will. The view that individuals can choose to act or believe without force, or necessity; the notion that people are responsible for their own decisions and actions and are not predetermined by God.

suffering. The experience and enduring of pain.

purpose. Aim, direction or design towards a particular end.

relationships. The connections or feelings that prevail between people or with things.

anthropocentrism. An approach to understanding the world or humanity, or a way of life, which puts human beings at the centre rather than God.

triumph. The Christian notion of victory over evil, suffering and death.

Reading

Stephen T. Davis (ed.), *Encountering Evil: live options in theodicy* (T. and T. Clark, 1982).

B. Hebblethwaite, *Evil, Suffering and Religion* (Sheldon Press, 1976).

John Hick, *Evil and the God of Love* (Fontana, 1968).

C. S. Lewis, *A Grief Observed* (Faber, 1966).

C. S. Lewis, *The Problem of Pain* (Fontana, 1957).

Alvin Plantinga, *God, Freedom and Evil* (Eerdmans, 1974).

6 Is there life after death?

Denying mind and soul – Three problems – Starting with the person – Definitions of immortality – The arguments for and against immortality – The biblical view of immortality – The philosophical problems of immortality – A note on hell

Traditionally, a person has been held to consist of two parts – the soul and the body. The soul has been identified with the mental life and the body with the physical. According to this view, in dreaming and in death the soul is freed from the body and able to roam, where it wills. This two-aspect view of man is called dualism. In the debate between the rationalists and the empiricists, dualism was called in question. For Descartes, a person had both soul and body, but the important thing was the soul. The mental life was the real self, and the body a kind of shell inhabited by the essential person. Although the mind and the body did connect and interact through the pineal gland, it was the mind that was the important thing. In contrast, David Hume denied the reality of the soul and of the self. The self for him was simply a bundle of impressions or sensations. There was no 'thing' which was the self. It was a useful figment of the imagination used to hold together the impressions people received.

The debate continues today. Some, convinced of the reality of the soul, argue for its existence on the basis of our direct experience of consciousness, memory and the mental life as a whole. They argue this view in the following way. If I intend to do something, the intention is real and actually happens. If, for some reason, I am unable to fulfil the intention, because of some unforeseen circumstances, the action never occurs. There is no outward manifestation of that intention, but I know that it was real. The essence of the argument is that there is a direct awareness of the self, which cannot be denied. This experience is irreducible and fundamental. Usually, it is claimed that the nature of this self cannot be totally explained. It is a mystery, but nevertheless a reality. Indeed, it is held to be the basic reality by which we experience and interpret the world. The essence of this reality is freedom. I am free to think and choose whatever I will. Other forces may seek to control the expressions of my thoughts, desires and will, but I am what I think, feel and will. The rest of the world may have a certain view of who and what I am, but only I know the real 'me'. It is hidden inside my head. It is my personality and my true self. It is thus a small step from this account of the true self, to the notion that I do not depend on my body, and may survive bodily death and dissolution. The soul is immortal. By following this line, the rationalist is reductionist. He reduces the person to the soul or mind and the mental realm of spirit.

DENYING MIND AND SOUL

In sharp contrast, the rise of modern science has led to the philosophies of behaviourism and materialism. Desmond Morris typifies the behaviourist view of man. A person is essentially his or her behaviour. I consist of what I have done, am doing and am about to do. The so-called mental life is simply the disposition to behave. All is explained in terms of behaviour and behaviour states. The materialist takes this line of analysis a stage further. He suggests that what is called the mental life may be explained without remainder in physical and physiological terms. Sensations, feelings, indeed the whole of the 'inner life', are all brain states. 'Man is simply a physical, material reality. There is no soul or mind.' The person is reduced to certain chemical and physical states.

Both sets of explanation seek clarity by reducing the problem of the gap between the mind and the body. It is suggested that one is simply the expression of the other. There are, however, problems both with the rationalist and the behaviourist/materialist accounts. The reduction to the mental alone seems to be parasitic on some physical grasp of reality. Will, feeling, intention and memory are not purely mental happenings, for they are caused by, or directed to, happenings in the physical world. When I recall a past memory with fondness, it is set in a particular time and place, with recognizable physical features. There is also the problem of the dependence of the mental on the physical. What I eat, and the condition of my body, affect the way I think and feel. Drugs, alcohol and other physical inputs may radically affect the content and quality of my mental life. Thus the relationship of mind to body is more complex than the reduction to the mental alone suggests. As for the possibility of post-mortem, after-life existence and survival, that requires more evidence than that of the pre-mortem mental life.

THREE PROBLEMS

The behaviourist/materialist reduction fares little better. The variety and intensity of mental life is in no way captured by talk of behaviour and physical states. There seems to be no possibility of a one-to-one reduction. When the physicalist account has been given, it seems that there is still more to be said. The responses to the behaviourist and materialist views tend to follow two main lines. The first is the denial of the ability to express the view as true. If man is simply a collection of physical attributes, what makes a collection a collection? What holds a collection together? Further, even if there is such a collection, how does such a collection form a theory, test its adequacy, and accept its truth and validity? If everything is just a piece of physical matter, then the thought life is a purely physical function. In that case, the materialist thought, 'Everything is reducible to matter', is itself reducible to physical matter. Likewise, the non-materialist thought that 'Everything is *not* reducible to physical matter' is reducible to physical reality, if the materialist view is correct. We are thus confronted with a choice between two sets of physical reality. The problem is not only how on earth to choose between them, but how we might think, reflect, choose and affirm the truth or otherwise, if the view were correct. The materialist cheats by standing on the rationalist ground to proclaim his or her thesis of the rejection of rationalism. Such a stance is illegitimate. This line of argument in no way proves the falsity of the materialist case. Rather it reveals the difficulty in the expression and propounding of that thesis as true.

The second line of criticism of the behaviourist/materialist reduction is that of common sense. Common sense argues that, even if behaviourism/materialism were true, it would make no difference at all. People would still go on feeling, thinking, intending and acting as they do at present, believing in the reality of the mental life. The society and legal system, which presuppose the freedom of man and his non-determined nature, would continue to treat people as if they were free, and not simply the victims of chemical, physical or psychological forces. The argument is essentially that behaviourism and materialism cannot be true, for they make no difference to life, even if we accept them.

A third line of attack criticizes the materialist claim of identity between things which cannot be measured. 'Feelings are brain-states,' argues the materialist. I may not wish to deny that statement, but rather to deny that this is *all* that feelings are. When I feel sad, this does not simply happen to coincide with a brain-state. The brain-state is a necessary, but not a *sufficient* explanation of my feeling of sadness. The facts of the situation and my response to that as a person are intimately bound up with my feeling of sadness. There is far more to my feelings than the description of a 'brain-state'.

STARTING WITH THE PERSON

Recent philosophers, such as Peter Strawson, have revised our approach to the dualistic understanding of human nature. If you start with a gap between mind and body, then that gap will inevitably remain. Why, then, start with a gap? Instead, it is suggested that the basic category of understanding is that of a 'person'. A person may be viewed from at least two angles or directions. These are predicates which describe the mental life and the physical characteristics. Both are aspects of the one unity, which is the person. In this way, there is no gap between the different aspects of man's personality.

A similar line is taken by some scientists, such as Donald MacKay. They suggest that there are a number of different, possible descriptions of reality. Chemistry, physics, cybernetics, psychology and sociology all offer descriptions of man and his nature. These are not 'true' descriptions in any absolute or exclusive sense. They are rather aspects or angles of under-standing and ways of looking at reality. Thus, there is no conflict between the different pictures, be they mental or physical. For there is no ontological or absolute claim made with the description. Ways of looking at reality are not to be confused with reality in itself.

DEFINITIONS OF IMMORTALITY

Ancient people believed that the world was not an end in itself, but was here for a purpose. The world was going somewhere and people had some part in that goal. Man was interpreted as having life beyond the here and now and some significance other than in the present.

It is interesting that the final goal is often seen in moral terms. There will be some correction of the balance between good and evil; good will be rewarded and evil punished. As in Kant's thought, there seems to be in ancient thought a clear connection between the point of doing good and resisting evil in the here and now and the theme of reward, punishment and fulfilment of the moral nature of the world. Times do not change very much. The evolutionist, the Marxist and the Christian still believe in a final goal and purpose for the world in which mankind has an essential part. The evolutionist believes in the continual improvement of life and the 'intensification of consciousness'. Man has a special role to play in the development of that consciousness. The Marxist believes that humanity is in the midst of a great economic struggle in history, which will lead to a classless, struggle-free society. The Christian's view of the goal of creation is defined by an understanding of God. The difference between the Marxist and the Christian is not necessarily in the moral and community references, which are part of the final goal, but rather in the role played by God.

Given the variety of pictures of the end, and of the significance of man's efforts in that end, it is important to recognize that science and philosophy cannot provide a final test for the truth or falsity of accounts. As with talk of the beginning, talk of the end is talk of an absolute state, which is different in kind from our experience of proximate beginnings and endings.

We may know much about how things come into and pass out of existence, but we have no experience of everything coming into and passing out of being. There is thus no scientific evidence as such to act as a final arbiter for the pictures we may be offered. Philosophy may not prove or disprove the validity of the picture of the end, but that does not mean that philosophy has no role. It offers a means of testing the sense and nonsense of what is said, in the light of the internal coherence of the view, and of its match with our understanding of man's nature as we now know it. Such knowledge, however, is not final. Christians need not be hesitant in proclaiming their account of the goal of man and history, recognizing that other accounts are in no better or worse a situation than theirs. Other philosophies are faced with similar difficulties of evidence, validity and proof. This, of course, is no invitation for sloppy thinking, but an opportunity to show the challenge of the Christian view.

When you start doing philosophy, you are always told to define your terms. You soon learn that there are different ways of arriving at a definition. One of the most fruitful is by a negative process of saying what you do *not* mean in order to arrive at what you *do* mean. When the Christian talks of immortality, he is not referring to the realm of wishful thinking and fear of death. Obviously, people may make up an idea of immortality to help them cope with the fear of death by offering some hope of life beyond the grave. There is a world of difference between those who are driven by fear to fabricate an account of eternal life, and those who are convinced that they have eternal life here and now. When the Christian defines immortality he does not mean the idea of living on in our children and our grandchildren. Immortality is not some faint family resemblance visited upon the third and fourth generations. Nor is immortality the memory of what we were. To live on in the memory of friends or relatives, in the pages of a book, or in a sound or video-tape is not the same as some personal existence beyond the grave. Immortality is not our influence living on after us. Nor is immortality our absorption in the whole of reality or some other level of being. When the Christian talks about immortality, he or she is not dealing with the conceptual problem of trying to picture the world without us, or the difficulty in accepting that life continues in our absence.

When Christians talk of immortality, they are not talking of the immortality of the soul in the way that Plato did, although many people think they are. For Platonists, the soul *is* the real, essential person. It is different from my body, which is part of a passing, transient world. My body will die, but, it is argued, my soul will go marching on. In contrast, Christians are talking of the eternal existence of a *whole* person with spiritual and physical attributes. This definition is always expressed in relationship to and with the God who made men and women.

THE ARGUMENTS FOR AND AGAINST IMMORTALITY

The arguments against immortality have both a simple and a complex form. The simple argument is that there is insufficient evidence to prove the reality of immortality. This may be countered by realizing that there are many things which we accept without having sufficient evidence. But, more seriously, it all depends on how we define 'evidence'. Too often the critic of immortality has accepted empiricist presuppositions. He then brings his standard of evidence, that is sense experience, to the notion of 'immortality' and announces that it has failed the test. There is no way it could ever pass that test. The test itself assumes the falsity of what it then seeks to prove is false. There needs to be some other ground for the examination than empiricist presuppositions.

The simple line of argument holds not only that there is insufficient evidence, but that immortality is purely a self-centred desire of human beings to reinforce their own importance. Of course, this may be true. There are people who are self-centred and desire some significance beyond the here and now for themselves. The fact that there are such people does not necessarily mean that immortality is false. There may be good grounds for the view as well as bad ones. That a poor argument is used by someone does not automatically mean that their position is false. It means only that those particular grounds are inadequate.

The more sophisticated argument against immortality draws heavily on the materialist view. Life consists purely of the physical, and every aspect of life can be explained in physiological and psychological terms without remainder. There is no such thing as soul or mind and, accordingly, no prospect of any post-mortem existence. We are our bodies and, when our bodies die, so do we. The response to this kind of argument follows the criticism we examined in the first part of this chapter. It is to suggest that, even if this view happened to be true, it is impossible in fact to accept the argument as valid. The second line of response is to argue that the materialist account is inadequate to the facts and facets of personality and our experience of reality. The depth and variety of human experience, personal and social, and the expression of this variety in legal, social and community life demand a more satisfying account of humanity and human nature than the materialist is able to offer.

Unfortunately, the arguments in favour of immortality fare little better. They start with the almost universal desire for an expression of a belief in immortality. Simply because many people desire something, and even believe in that thing, does not make it real or true. The majority view has no monopoly on truth and reality. The pro-immortality argument is often based on the moral nature of the universe. Good is to be rewarded and evil is to be punished. Our experience of the here and now suggests that correction of the moral balance and dispensation of just rewards and punishment does not always happen in the present life. Accordingly, the balance will be restored in the after-life. Regardless of the many difficulties in the notion of a moral universe and its proof, problems remain. Even if we accept the moral nature of reality, there is no necessity to look beyond the moral nature of reality in itself. There may be nothing beyond or behind that reality. That may simply be the way things are.

The main line of argument on the part of Christianity takes its root in Scripture and the nature of God.

THE BIBLICAL VIEW OF IMMORTALITY

For the Christian, there is no belief in a ghost in the machine, or a shadow man hiding in the body, waiting a painful release. The biblical writers are unafraid and unashamed in their use of pictures and symbols. The biblical position begins with God and his creation of mankind in his own image. Man is not like the rest of creation, for he and she are created for fellowship with God. This creation of men and women free to respond to God implies also the freedom to reject God. Sin entered the garden in rejection of God and his ways, and with sin came broken relationships, separation from God, and death. Death is seen as an interloper and an enemy to be fought and overcome.

The Old Testament is cautious and shadowy in what it reveals about life beyond the grave, with one or two notable exceptions. The full expression of the Christian view of the after-life comes in the account of Christ's life, death and resurrection as the New Testament writers reflect on the historical events of Jesus' life. There are four key elements to this account – resurrection, judgment, new creation and the presence of God.

There is no immortality of the soul for Christians. Rather they believe in the resurrection of the body. It is the whole person who enjoys eternal life, rather than just one aspect of the person. The proof of this resurrection rests on the resurrection of Christ. Paul does not shrink from the issue. If Christ is not raised from the dead, then the dead are utterly gone, we are still in our sins, our gospel is nonsense, and we are to be pitied most of all (1 Corinthians 15). The resurrection appearances of Christ, and the promises he made concerning resurrection, are the grounds for Christian hope of life after death. This is the restoration of the relationship with God and the fulfilment of God's intention in creation. In Christ, men and women are to be what they were created to be eternally. The biblical writers are clear that all are to be resurrected, both the just and the unjust, and that the resurrection is a prelude to judgment.

The picture of judgment centres on the role of Christ the Judge. Judgment is presented in relation to our motives and behaviour towards others, as well as our relationship with God. The Bible does not flinch from pictures of reward and punishment. Heaven is the setting for eternal enjoyment of the blessing of God. It is free from all pain and suffering. The chief mark of heaven is the presence of God and the worship man gives to God. Hell is pictured vividly in painful terms. It is the destination of the wicked, and is eternal separation from God.

The Christian view of eternal life has been criticized as 'pie in the sky when you die'. This is a misrepresentation of the biblical account. Eternal life is presented as a quality of life which begins in the here and now. Eternal life comes as part of the new creation of Christ. Those who know, love and serve Christ are pictured as being new creatures, transformed by the power of Christ. That process of transformation is completed in the new creation of everything at the end of time. Humanity and the world are both transformed. The perishable puts on the imperishable and the mortal immortality.

The essence of eternal life is living in the presence of God. It is to be with God. Here the biblical language and pictures begin to falter in light of the reality. Glory is the mark of the presence of God and the believer is to partake more and more of that glory. In the light of the presence of God, there is knowledge, understanding, unity and worship.

THE PHILOSOPHICAL PROBLEMS OF IMMORTALITY

Regardless of whether the post-mortem existence is held to be that of an immortal soul or a resurrected body, the essential philosophical problem is what kind of existence this will be. Accounts of the immortality of the soul do not seem to offer any basis for existence except as a pale reflection of the earlier embodied existence. Such a parallel is illegitimate, for its success depends on concepts and experiences which are dependent on the body and close interaction and relationship of soul and body. The post-mortem life, if it consists of the soul alone, cannot be like the pre-mortem existence. Thus the notion of an immortal soul and its continued existence is rejected along the lines of the incomprehensibility of the account and the impossibility of proof and testing.

The problem with the notion of resurrection is still that of identity. What is the *continuity* and *discontinuity* of post-mortem and pre-mortem existence? Two candidates are presented for consideration. These are body recognition and mind recognition with some reference to permanence through time.

The body recognition requires that there be some relationship between the body before death and the body after death. It is interesting that Dives is pictured as recognizing Lazarus after death, which is all the more noteworthy considering that he ignored him during life. The body of the person must be sufficiently similar for it to be considered the same person. This is not a watertight concept. We all change and develop. Our physical appearance, shape and size change radically in the span of our human life. The seven ages of man are clearly recounted in Shakespeare's *As You Like It,* with the different appearances of the same person at different moments of his life. But is it the *same* person? Is the worldly-wise man of business the same person as the helpless tot who cried every night many years before? The answer is both 'Yes' and 'No'. There is continuity in time, but there is discontinuity in appearance, shape and experience. This criterion of bodily recognition is made all the more complex by the cases where a person suffers serious illness, brain damage or some shattering experience. The physical appearance may remain the same, but people may still say, 'He's not himself just now.' He may never be 'himself' again in that sense, but if he is not himself, then who is he? The continuity is even harder to maintain when it comes to the link between the body before death and the resurrected body. The physical body decays and disintegrates, but the resurrected body is pictured as incorruptible and immortal. How may these two be connected?

There are similar sets of problems with the other criterion of mind recognition. What mental continuity should there be between the pre- and post-mortem states? Memory is held to be the key to continuity. My memories are unique to me, so it must be possible for me after death to remember what happened to me before death, or else 'I' am not the same person. This test is difficult to envisage, for the intervening experience of death seems to be traumatic and to put an end to all experience. Moreover, my memory is often faulty, changes when jogged by others and cannot be tested by myself. If I try to check on a memory, I may simply misremember again, a state of affairs Maurice Chevalier immortalized in his rendition of 'Yes, I remember it well'. Unfortunately, he did not remember, and only the presence of another corrected his memory. But how may we be confident that another's memory is any more reliable than our own, and even if it were, how might we prove it?

There can be no return to compare the memory with the original. Perhaps two memories are worse than one.

The understanding of life after death depends on some notion of continuity, and that means both mind and body recognition. The first flaw is in trying to separate these two aspects into separate ontological realities. They are rather aspects of the whole person. This is of little help in the testing of the continuity and discontinuity of the person. Obviously, no-one expects life after death to be the same as life before death. This discontinuity is allowed for, but how may the balance between continuity and discontinuity be affirmed and tested?

For Thomas, the disciple of Christ, the problem was the same. Dead people just do not rise from the dead. The Jesus who had appeared to others seemed the same Jesus; yet his body seemed different in what it was able to do. For Thomas the solution of the problem came not in reflection on the possibility, but by encounter with the reality of the resurrected Jesus. In this area most of all, Christians need not be so hesitant about their faith. The evolutionist and the Marxist have faith too, but in very different philosophies. The limits of science and philosophy are very real in dealing with immortality. This does not mean that anything goes. We are still bound to be consistent, coherent and to present a case which matches reality in so far as that may be understood. This makes the essential issue our understanding of God and especially of God in Christ. It is how we respond and react to the evidence of the creation of reality by God, and the resurrection of Christ, which will form our presuppositions concerning immortality.

If John Hick is to be believed, then the end of all things will offer a kind of eschatological verification. When we die, or get to the end of the road, it will be seen whether or not there is eternal life. Sadly, such verification would work only positively. If there is no eternal life, then we shall never know it for certain.

A NOTE ON HELL

Some philosophers, notably including Ian Ramsey, have been uneasy about the concept of hell. This unease is not the general unease about escapism from the present world into some future state, nor of the danger of fear or greed motivating our behaviour in the here and now. Rather it is an unease about hell based on moral repugnance. Hell for them is morally repugnant, for it conflicts with and contradicts the notion of a God of love and mercy. Such a God would not allow any to perish and suffer eternally. God's love and mercy must not fail and hell is seen as such a failure. The logic of this view ends in universalism, which means that eternal life with God is for all.

Despite the obvious attractions of such a view, it is a rejection of the plain sense and meaning of Scripture and conflicts with the biblical concept of God. God is, of course, presented as a God of love and mercy, but that love and mercy are defined with righteousness, holiness and judgment. No ultimate conflict is seen by the biblical writers in the affirmation of God's love and of his justice. As with immortality, the debate centres on our concept and picture of God, whence we derive that picture, and how we express and support the presentation of its reality.

Key words

soul. The spiritual, rational and immortal aspect of human beings.

body. The physical and material nature of human beings.

mind. The mental faculties of human beings.

immortality. Infinitely prolonged existence of the self or soul.

rationalism. The view that certain knowledge is to be found through the use of reason.

behaviourism. The view that a person consists of nothing more than one's behaviour or states of behaviour. The denial of an 'inner' life in human beings.

materialism. The view that reality and humanity can be totally explained without remainder in terms of physical reality.

reductionism. An approach to issues and problems which tries to make the complicated seem simple by reducing to the key themes or points.

memory. Faculty by which things are recalled.

common sense. Accepted by ordinary people as true.

the whole person. The refusal to divide a human being into elements by holding a total view of every aspect of human being.

ways of seeing. Means of interpreting or looking at things.

purpose. Aim, direction or design towards a particular end.

bodily resurrection. The raising from the dead of the physical body of a person.

judgment. The pronouncing of sentence according to what a person deserves. In theology, God's passing of sentence on men and women.

continuity. Connected in time or space in an unbroken way.

body recognition. To know again, and identify as the same, because of the physical similarities.

mind recognition. To know again, and identify as the same, because of the mental similarities and connections, usually of memory.

hell. The abode of the damned; a place or state of endless misery.

Reading

William Hasker, *Metaphysics: constructing a world view* (IVP, 1983).

D. Gareth Jones, *Our Fragile Brains: a Christian perspective on brain research* (IVP, 1981).

T. Penelhum, *Survival and Disembodied Existence* (Routledge, 1980).

D. Z. Phillips, *Death and Immortality* (Macmillan, 1971).

7 The problem of prayer

*Presuppositions rule OK? – What is prayer? – Prayer changes God
– Prayer changes things – Prayer changes people – Prayer as
dependence – Prayer as performance – Prayer as living – Prayer as
contemplation – Prayer as relationship*

What is prayer? The demand for a description creates a quandary. Is the question a request for a religious account, or for a philosophical or psychological account of prayer?

The questions people ask limit the answers that may be given. The barrister is expert at asking questions in such a way that only the evidence which is favourable to his case is presented. The very asking of the question often excludes other vital information. Likewise, the assumptions behind a question limit the appropriateness of the response. The problem in any approach to prayer is that different levels of account may exclude each other. The philosopher, in his approach to the subject of prayer, is looking for criteria for the validity of the notion and practice of prayer. The difficulty is what will count as adequate criteria. Within the religious realm, there are criteria for proper and improper praying. There are ways of telling when prayer is happening and of judging its propriety. From the external observer's viewpoint, it is perfectly possible to give a psychological and a sociological account of praying, but the adequacy of those accounts may be questioned.

PRESUPPOSITIONS RULE OK?

There are two main philosophical approaches to prayer. The first falls into the empiricist camp. It asks whether the language of prayer and the mode of prayer, *e.g.* a believer talking to God, literally make sense. (By making sense is meant a correspondence with reality.) The empiricist examines the word 'God' and cannot understand what in reality corresponds to the description offered by the believer. If there is no such object, any notion of communication and intercourse with a non-existent being is nonsensical. Accordingly, while prayer may well have some genuine psychological purpose, getting the believer in a proper frame of mind to cope with the world, it cannot be understood as a communication with a transcendent reality called God, who responds in action.

The second philosophical approach stems from the functionalist approach, which seeks to analyse how language is used, as we see with the phrase, 'Don't ask for the meaning. Ask for the use.' This line of thinking interprets religion in a descriptive way. Prayer is seen as a facet of the religious life. The meaning and nature of prayer is understood only in the context of religious praying and the purposes and roles such prayer fulfils in the religious community. Prayer is then seen as a kind of 'language game' which has its own internal coherence. The task of the philosopher is to uncover the depth grammar of prayer in light of the religious tradition and understanding in which it takes place. It is a *depth* grammar because even the believer may not fully understand what he is saying and doing. It is only by careful attention to what is said and how that functions in the religious community that such grammar can be uncovered.

What is noteworthy is the different presuppositions involved by the two approaches. The empiricist is demanding, 'Come up to my standard.' The linguistic analyst is saying, 'I simply describe. I leave everything as it is.' The former has a clear set of criteria in terms of meaning and truth to which prayer must conform if it is to fulfil the claims it makes and the descriptions offered for it. The latter is concerned to penetrate to the internal criteria which the community of believers hold in relation to the practice of prayer. It is through this probing that the linguistic philosopher hopes to uncover the true meaning of prayer.

Obviously, the different presuppositions create different questions. But care needs to be exercised in responding to the empiricist's questions. He or she is seeking to shift the focus of the debate from prayer itself to the prior issue of God's existence and the nature of his being. That is not an illegitimate approach, but it is not the sole content of an adequate analysis of prayer. The believer assumes God's existence, and prayer is the expression of a relationship with that God, not a means of establishing his existence. The 'if there is a God, show yourself to me' kind of prayer is not typical of what believers take the essence of prayer to be.

WHAT IS PRAYER?

For most of us prayer is most obviously a physical attitude. 'Hands together; eyes closed' sums up the way we do it. But what do we do? We address God. Prayer is speaking to God. This suggests, however, a one-way form of communication. Prayer is rather an interactive communication with God. But what do we communicate with God about and what is to be the result of such communication? The standard religious society talk on the subject of prayer breaks prayer into four distinct parts expressed by the initials ACTS. Prayer, is *adoration, confession, thanksgiving* and *supplication* (also called petition). When people are involved in prayer, they may be engaged in any or all of these activities.

They may be 'adoring' God. This kind of praying stresses the worship of God. God is worthy of praise and adoration, and there are suitable prayers and emphases within prayers, which attempt to give God recognition of his nature and the right response of humanity and the world to his majesty. It is interesting that the phenomenon of *glossolalia* (speaking in tongues) is most often described in the context of adoration and praise praying. It is seen almost as a shifting into a 'higher' gear of praising God, when ordinary language breaks down and cannot express the inexpressible. It is then that the 'tongues of angels' take over or are taken over as an even more suitable means of expressing adoration.

The second form of praying is confession. This is the confessing of sin to God and the seeking of forgiveness, cleansing and the power to make a new start. Confession does not tell God anything he does not know already, but expresses to him our sorrow and contrition for what we have done. At the same time, it is an accepting of responsibility for our shortcomings. An essential part of this confession seems to be the desire to do better next time and a request for help in that struggle.

The third form of prayer is thanksgiving to God for all he is and does. As 'thank you' is the appropriate response to the giving of gifts, the prayer of thanksgiving expresses our gratitude to God. This may also act as a reminder and as a corrective to pessimism and complaint. The chorus advises us to

> Count your blessings, name them one by one,
> Count your blessings, see what God has done.

The net effect of such a procedure is 'and it will surprise you what the Lord has done'. Prayers of thanksgiving express gratitude to God, but also act as an encouragement to interpret life in the light of the goodness of God.

The fourth form of prayer is supplication. Petitionary prayer has been most subjected to philosophical critique, as it involves the notion of asking God to act in the world in particular ways. These requests are obviously not purely the expression of selfish desires, though it is all too easy to characterize prayer as trying to make God do what we want. The Christian view of petition is that it is right and proper to bring all our wants and requests to God. This is not simply to have them satisfied, but is also a means of checking that our will is in conformity with God's will. Also involved is the view of prayer as a means of ministering to the needs of others in the world. Intercession is praying to God on behalf of those in some kind of need. In every aspect of petitionary prayer, there is the clear assumption that God is both willing and able to act in ways which can be seen to be answers or responses to our prayers.

These different kinds of prayers may happen both in formal, highly liturgical community settings or in the private simplicity of a believer alone with God. No matter what the setting, the attitude of the one praying would be seen to be that of a worshipper, who comes to God, not in a brash, demanding way, but as a suppliant recognizing his absolute dependence on God. These keynotes of worship and dependence seem to be at the heart of true prayer.

This description of prayer will still leave the philosopher unsatisfied. Some more direct description of the problems posed by philosophy, and the responses believers can make, is still required. There are two sets of themes here. Prayer *changes* things and prayer *intrepreted as* something else.

PRAYER CHANGES GOD

Is the intention of prayer – particularly petitionary prayer – to change God? The first problem arises with discussion of whether God is changed by the addition of knowledge. In other words, in prayer, do we tell God something he does not know already? If God is omniscient, then we cannot tell him anything he does not know. The philosopher thus argues that if we cannot tell God anything there is no point in praying. God already knows what we want and need. But there are many occasions when we say things to people who already know these things. They may know the details, or they may know us so well that they have pieced the information together without our telling them. In neither case does this obviate the importance of telling. When we say 'I love you' to those we love, they know this and have heard it a thousand times before. That does not make the telling any less worth while. Likewise, when a child tells the teacher of some new, exciting discovery she has made, the teacher knows all about it, but that does not make the teacher less eager to hear the news.

The second problem fastens on the immutability of God, instead of focusing upon his omniscience. God does not change. But if he does not change, what is the point in praying for God to do something? His mind is made up already. If it is not, then he is a God who fails to see the need, and who does not love sufficiently to do something unasked. Or is he plain fickle and persuaded by the last person who talked to him? These alternatives seem to suggest a weakness in love or a weakness in ability.

There are at least two lines of response to this difficulty of God's immutability. The first is to see the mechanical nature of prayer being offered here. It is a coin-in-the-slot picture. Pop in a prayer and out pops God's answer. The philosopher's picture of prayer seems very man-centred. It sounds as if prayer begins to depend on the one who is praying. Prayer depends on us; and how often, how well and how many of us are praying. If the conditions are right, then God has to respond properly. This mechanical picture of prayer is not adequate. Prayer is a relationship in which there is interaction. God is affected by our prayers, but being affected does not necessarily mean that his essential being and nature change, nor that he is simply the victim of the last feeling or last prayer. God has his own integrity.

The second response is to the philosopher's challenge over prayer changing God's mind. It is to look at some examples. Jesus rebuked those who had a picture of God as one who had to be cajoled to make any impression or to be persuaded to listen at all. God loves to give gifts to his children. In the pages of the Old Testament we have several classic cases of prayer apparently changing God's mind. The first is when God is planning to punish Sodom, and Abraham intercedes for the city to be spared if ten righteous men can be found. There are also many examples of Moses pleading to God to spare the children of Israel in the wilderness, when, yet again, they have been disobedient and have complained against God. It is interesting to see how both appeal to the mercy of God and remind him of his true nature. Moses also usually appeals to the past promises of God, as well as to God's reputation among the nations. What we learn from these accounts is the same as in the teaching of Jesus. There is a God whose heart and good will are turned towards man, but also a God who recognizes the seriousness of sin.

In all this, we have talked of God as a person, but this is the very heart of the difficulty for some philosophers. How can the immanent talk to the transcendent? How can a human being talk to God? Has God ears to hear? Is he a listening object? Where and how does he listen? These questions drive us back to the presupposition of God's existence and his nature. These problems about prayer arise from problems about knowing that there is a God and what that God is like. They must be dealt with on their own terms, rather than in the context of a discussion of prayer. This will be done in chapter 11.

We have to use anthropomorphic language, for we are human. The God of the Psalmist was contrasted strongly with the gods of wood and stone, who had ears but did not hear, eyes that did not see and mouths that did not speak. Because the Psalmist believed in a personal God, he prayed in anger or in joy, expressing his relationship with that God. We shall return to this theme when we describe prayer as relationship.

In the end, the person who prays to God in order to change God's mind does not seem to have grasped fully what God is like. The Christian doctrine of God is of a God who is omniscient, all-loving and sovereign. We may pray to this God and communicate directly with him in prayer, but it is always as his creatures. Our requests are to be seen in the light of his will being done on earth as it is in heaven.

PRAYER CHANGES THINGS

The same presuppositional problem is obvious in the philosopher's question of how prayer changes things. By this is meant not so much the question of how human prayers might cause a divine being to act or react, but rather how the divine being, in the transcendent realm, can act in the immanent realm. There is a subsidiary problem here. If God acts in the natural realm in response to prayer, then what becomes of the natural order of things? Can God interrupt the laws of nature at the request of the believer? This theme is dealt with in our discussion of miracles in the next chapter. The root of the problem, and of any proffered solution, depends on whether God and the world are two independent realms or whether God is intimately bound up with his world. The Christian has no doubt that God can act in the natural realm and indeed the prayer of faith looks expectantly for things to happen. Elijah, on the hill of Carmel, prayed and expected results. He got them. Is our hesitation to prove the efficacy of prayer in a similar fashion a question of doubt of God and of his ability to act? Rather, it seems a proper hesitation concerning ourselves and our ability to discern what we ought to pray for in the world. 'Nevertheless . . . thy will be done' is not an easy get-out clause tacked on at the end of a prayer to save face. It is rather an honest awareness that we do not know what is best and how to pray aright. It may be that Christians have to learn how dangerous a weapon prayer is, and that if we do pray, then things will happen. This is no 'interruption' of a 'natural' world, but another aspect of God's interaction with the whole of creation, the secrets of which we have still to learn.

PRAYER CHANGES PEOPLE

One main line of retreat from the difficulties of prayer and its effects on God and on things is to deny that these are really of the essence of prayer. Prayer is about changing the *pray-er*. When we pray, we are, in fact, coming to terms with what we are praying about. We are clarifying our own minds. We are trying to steel our wills to act in particular ways. We are conforming ourselves to the will of God. These descriptions of the heart of prayer seem to rely heavily on a psychological view of what prayer is. Christians would acknowledge that there is a crucial psychological element in prayer, but this is very different from reducing prayer simply to a psychological tool or trick to keep ourselves going. Of course, there is an aspect of praying in which we are expecting to be affected by our prayers, but that is not the sole purpose and nature of prayer. There are easier and more direct ways of telling myself something and of clarifying issues.

Yet prayer does change people. The saintly life of prayer proves that. We must not over-react to the psychological account. There is a real sense in which the pray-er is changed by communion with God, but that is more akin to the way people change as their relationship and communication grow and develop with others. It is not simply a matter of psychological adjustment. It is rather a personal relationship.

PRAYER AS DEPENDENCE

This tendency to fasten on one aspect of prayer and one way of looking at a complex whole is likewise propounded by those who describe praying as the expression of our dependence on God. There is some biblical support for this view. Job prayed that he might have the opportunity to present his case to God face-to-face. When God appeared to him, all the questions disappeared. It was enough to see God in all his glory and to realize that he, Job, was as nothing before God. He was absolutely dependent on God for everything. While accepting the insight that prayer is an expression of dependence, it is not only that. The believer holds that prayer is also a communication and a building up of the relationship between the believer and God.

PRAYER AS PERFORMANCE

J.L. Austin stressed the use of language to perform something. The naming of a ship or the pronouncing of a man and woman as husband and wife fall into this category. Some have tried to interpret prayer in similar ways. The liturgy may encourage this in parts. The confession and absolution in most liturgies seem to act in a performative manner. The priest saying the words of absolution makes them effective. He 'performs' the action. While again offering some insight into some parts of prayer, this will not serve as a basis for a single, total interpretation of prayer.

PRAYER AS LIVING

The old Latin tag suggested that *laborare est orare* (to work is to pray). Not only work, but the whole of life, it has been suggested, is essentially prayer. This kind of defence against the philosopher's attack removes prayer as an activity from scrutiny, by making it synonymous with the religious way of life. This is not only to evacuate the concept of prayer, but radically to alter the description and practice of the believer, who sees prayer as vital in, but not as equivalent to, the Christian life. Those who hold such an equation may be termed contemplatives.

PRAYER AS CONTEMPLATION

There is a mystical tradition of prayer, which moves away from the strong linguistic emphasis in prayer to a focusing on silence and an interpretation of prayer as a kind of mystical vision. Prayer is still a form of communication, but of an inexpressible, apophatic kind. The trouble with the inexpressible, as we have seen, is that we can say nothing *against* it. In that sense, it is secure from all attack. It is also the case that we can say nothing *for* it, in the sense of propounding its reality and anything of its content. Expressing the inexpressible is 'catch 22' all the way. The reality of the mystical tradition of prayer will not serve as an adequate base for an understanding, critique, or defence of the variety of terms and forms that prayer encompasses.

PRAYER AS RELATIONSHIP

We began by stressing the importance of the starting-point for any approach to the nature of prayer. For the believer, that starting-point is a relationship with a personal God. This is not some individualistic thing, but it makes sense only in the context of a tradition and a living community of people who share that kind of relationship. The tradition and the community thus, in practice, act as a check for the validity of prayer in all its forms. Religious language, in the context of prayer, may be meaningless, misused, or plainly wrong. The community, in its present life and tradition, forms a means of checking that prayer is genuine.

While the community may act both as a check and as a focal point for the expression of prayer, through, for example, a liturgy, there is a strong emphasis on the individual practice of prayer. Whether formal or informal, such prayer is expressed in the context of the relationship of the believer to God. If God is personal, he may be addressed and petitioned. Requests and responses make sense only if the God to whom they are directed, and from whom they are expected, is genuinely personal. If he is personal, there are still fundamental inequalities in the relationship of the believer with him. The believer comes in worship and with a sense of dependence as a creature to the divine, omniscient, all-loving, sovereign God. The believer comes because God invites this and sustains the communication. If prayer was meaningless and pointless, believers would soon give it up as a worthless activity. Rather, they claim to find that prayer not only makes sense, but also brings an increasing openness to the activity of God in the believer's life and in the world.

Key words

prayer. Communication with God which may consist of praise, worship, asking, thanksgiving, confession.

questions and criteria. Things we ask in order to understand, and the standards by which we judge the answers.

meaning. The sense and import of words and sentences. What is intended to be conveyed, understood or signified, usually by actions or language.

function. The way something (*i.e.* language) operates, and the role words, sentences and grammatical forms play in communication.

presuppositions. What we assume or take for granted.

petition. Request or supplication in prayer to God.

omniscience. The quality of knowing everything.

immutability. The quality of being unchangeable or invariable.

change. Becoming or making different or other.

contemplation. Meditation or fixing or focusing of one's mind on something.

relationship. A connection or feeling that prevails between people.

Reading

John Calvin, *Institutes of the Christian Religion,* Book 3, chapter 20, 'Of Prayer' (Westminster Press, 1980).

P. T. Geach, *God and the Soul* (Routledge, 1969).

C. S. Lewis, *Letters to Malcolm: chiefly on prayer* (Fontana, 1966).

D. Z. Phillips, *The Concept of Prayer* (Blackwell, 1981).

Carroll E. Simcox, *Does God Answer?* (IVP, 1985).

8 Do miracles happen?

An object of wonder – Contrary to our knowledge of nature – Seeing as – An extraordinary event caused by supernatural agency – Justification: how or why? – Standards of justification – Hume and experience – Rules and their exceptions – Scientific method and miracles – Miracles and causes – Foundation of a religious system – The naturalist and the supernaturalist

In the popular mind, science has disproved the idea that miracles can happen. This is not merely bad science, but also shows a failure to understand that each scientist, and every science, presupposes certain things which may or may not be the case. Whenever people make sweeping claims – as some are making for science – it is important to ground these in actual fact. So what are the problems which the believer faces in approaching the question of the possibility of miracles? First of all, we must define what is meant by 'miracle'.

AN OBJECT OF WONDER

The basic linguistic sense of miracle suggests that it is something which produces wonder and amazement. A miracle causes those present to be astonished. It may also produce fear. In this connection, there is also involved the notion that we cannot explain what has happened by usual means. If we were to explain it, then that would remove the sense of wonder. If it is genuinely inexplicable, then there is no room for the scientist to do any work, for he specializes in the explicable.

There is, however, a serious weakness in this definition of miracle. If we accept it at face value, everything and anything which causes wonder must be miraculous. The Grand Canyon, a Picasso, and the way that Scotland plays football would all be miracles. This is true particularly if the event or object is inexplicable. Again this part of the definition creates its own difficulties. The behaviour of some people I know may well be totally beyond my comprehension, but that does not make it miraculous. Of course, my knowing and someone else's may not be the same. They may be much more intelligent and better informed than I am. If that is the case, then what is a miracle for one person may not be miraculous at all to someone else. The kinds of achievements which science has produced for us today would be truly miraculous to a person from the Middle Ages, even though every child today accepts them as commonplace. After all, the scientist can explain what is happening and cause it to happen regularly; so the wonder of the whole thing disappears. This definition of miracle is scarcely adequate.

CONTRARY TO OUR KNOWLEDGE OF NATURE

Augustine argued that miracles were contrary to our knowledge of nature, but not to nature itself. In other words, miracles were inexplicable to us at present, but given new discoveries, it would be possible to understand the true order of nature which 'broke through' in the miracle. If we hold that God is in charge of the whole of nature and creation, then a miracle creates a problem for us. It goes against that order. Traditionally, theologians have argued that a miracle goes against only our understanding of the ordering of nature, but not ultimately against the true order of nature itself.

The relationship between order and exception is a key one and we shall return to it. But as this view stands, it is no better off than the previous definition. A miracle is simply inexplicable so far. This means that yesterday's miracle is tomorrow's commonplace. All miracles are then vulnerable to scientific explanation. There are natural causes behind every miraculous event. What room does this leave for the agency of the supernatural? It can mean only that the supernatural is what causes the whole of the natural. Any apparent breaking in of the supernatural is really the natural in its reality showing itself. The problem then is that the natural and the supernatural become the same thing. Somehow God – or his equivalent – lies behind the process of nature, but a miracle is nature showing itself as it really is and showing too that our view of nature and how it behaves is inadequate. In this definition miracles are really natural, if we but knew enough. It is hard, therefore, to see what purpose talk of God or the supernatural has in explaining the miraculous. This has led some to reinterpret miracles as follows.

SEEING AS

John Hick and Friedrich Schleiermacher have argued that what we call miracles can all be explained in other ways. There are various ways of looking at the world among which is the scientific, but it is not the only way. A miracle, then, is any and every event, when looked at from a religious point of view. A miracle is something that we experience as having religious significance for us and our lives. A sunset is basically light refracted through particles of matter in motion, but that in no way captures the aesthetic beauty of a fiery sky at dusk. Seeing the miraculous is like wearing a particular pair of spectacles. You see things in a different light and context. If we look at the feeding of the five thousand this way, then it appears obvious that all those who had packed lunches shared them with those who did not have any food. The miracle that happened was that Jesus, by his words, persuaded those who had something to share with those who had nothing.

This kind of definition will, not surprisingly, leave many Christians dissatisfied that the true essence of miracle has been captured. It is all too naturalistic, but it has also other philosophical problems. On this basis, a miracle is evident only to the eyes of faith. No unbeliever can appreciate the miraculous, far less recognize it. He has the wrong spectacles. It means also that any and everything can be said to be a miracle. A cornflake at breakfast, a human pulse, a straight bat in a cricket test match and an ant carrying a grain of wheat would all fulfil the terms of this definition. But this is to evacuate the sense and meaning of the word 'miracle', so that there is no point at all in using the word. If everything is a miracle, then miracle has no meaning which differentiates it from other descriptions. If I call everyone 'dear', then the term is devalued and there is no one person, or very few, who are especially dear to me. If I mean what I say, then everyone is dear to me. I would then have to develop another system of giving worth to people, or else settle for having the same attitude to everyone, and no special relations with anyone.

Not only is the word 'miracle' made redundant, but events are reduced to the same level of significance. If a miracle is *seeing as*, then I either see it as or I do not. That means that there is no room for degrees of seeing as. On this basis, the growth of an oak tree from an acorn, or a falling star, has the same value and significance as the resurrection of Jesus Christ. Both the unbeliever and believer must find this equivalence difficult to accept. The Christian claim concerning the reality of the resurrection seems to demand a different standing from tree development. This view of miracles certainly makes itself immune from criticism by scientific attack, but the immunity is bought at the price of vacuity.

AN EXTRAORDINARY EVENT CAUSED BY SUPERNATURAL AGENCY

There is a sense in which a miracle is an extraordinary event and therefore must cause wonder and amazement, but the extraordinariness stems from the fact that the particular event shatters the very fabric of our understanding of nature and its processes so far that we are compelled to attribute its cause to a supernatural power. The apparent laws of nature are broken, not in any meaningless or irrational way, but rather in the context of God's plan and purpose. Miracles, according to this classic statement of the position, do not merely *happen*, but are *intended* for a particular purpose. They are a sign or token that the divine is present in an exceptional way. When John the Baptist enquired, through his disciples, whether Jesus was indeed the Messiah, the message sent back recounted the miracles done. Among the signs that the Messiah had indeed come were the blind receiving sight, the deaf hearing, the lame walking and the good news being preached to the poor (see Luke 7:19–22).

This view is subject to a number of attacks. It presupposes the existence of God. What sense of 'event' and 'cause' is there which can be applied to divine agency? How can the transcendent God intervene in the world without destroying that transcendence and becoming merely another part of creation itself? How can we be sure what the sign is meant to signify? It may and does often mean different things to different people. We would require some independent verification and identification that the sign was genuine. These questions are all concerned with the same kind of problem. How is it possible to justify a claim that a miracle has occurred?

JUSTIFICATION: HOW OR WHY?

As mentioned before, the questions we ask limit the answers

106

we may receive. If I ask a man whether he has stopped beating his wife, then I am assuming two things. I assume that he has a wife and that he was or is a wife-beater, neither of which may be applicable. So we need to be cautious when people demand justification in these ways. Firstly, are they entitled to ask and be given justification at all, or is the demand itself illegitimate? Secondly, what, if anything, will satisfy them as justifying the miraculous? The danger is that when philosophers say, 'Justify it,' there is nothing at all which will prevent them saying, 'But that does not satisfy me and my standards.' What is crucial is the actual standards that are being applied. An inch ruler is an inappropriate instrument for measuring the movement of an electron. Not all standards are appropriate or relevant.

This is the problem with the question 'How?'. If I want to know how a miracle has occurred, and by that I mean, what caused it to happen, then I am confronted with the kinds of problems created by exceptions to the laws of nature and inexplicable events. If it is an exception, and if it is inexplicable, the demand for causal explanation is pointless. The problem with a miracle, if there really are such things, is that, by definition, no-one will be able to tell you how it is done. If they can, it ranks the same as other explicable events. To say that God did it, is not to reveal *how* the event happened, but to point to the fact that there was some divine purpose and agency behind it. Neither of these can be exhaustively described without making man God or reducing the divine to the human. Accordingly, there can be no naturalistic description or explanation of how a miracle has happened, and that by definition. If there could be, it would no longer be a miracle. That leaves open the possibility of a supernatural explanation. But that again, by definition, must be of a very different kind from the normal human explanations.

If I suggest that God did the miracle, and someone asks the 'how?' question, all I can do is to describe the nature of the God who is able to do such things. I have and (unless God tells me the answer) can have no idea how he works. But that does not mean that I am left with no questions at all. One primary question, given the definition of miracle suggested in the classic view, must be, 'Why has it happened?' This question tries to discover the point of the miracle, what it signifies and, in that sense, what God is trying to say through it. If there were no such point or relation, then the event would be totally irrational and unrelated to all else. It would be a nonsense to everyone. Nonsenses are not miracles.

STANDARDS OF JUSTIFICATION

The fact that the demand for justification must be carefully analysed for legitimacy and presupposition does not imply that there are no proper demands for justification. There are two main bases for justification not just for miracles, but for all the things we claim to know and believe. These are *reason* and *experience*. The problem with trying to use the standards of reason in connection with miracles is that reason, both inductive and deductive, has produced a standard of its own, which we call the laws of nature. It is these laws which are supposed to have been broken. Thus it is the very standard of reason itself which is being called in question. A claim for a miracle suggests that reason will fall short when it tries to measure this event and to reduce it to some pattern. It is not that a miracle is irrational, for then it would be nonsense, but that a miracle is pointing to another level of reason and action – that of the supernatural and divine. Reason then seems to be ruled out as an appropriate instrument to examine the miraculous. That leaves experience.

HUME AND EXPERIENCE

David Hume's attack on miracles in his essay 'On Miracles' is well known and provides a key understanding about the role of experience as a standard for judgment. Hume argued that 'a miracle can never be proved so as to be the foundation of a system of religion'. He accepted the classic definition of a miracle as 'a transgression of a law of nature by a particular volition of the Deity, or by the interposition of some invisible agent'.

Hume raised certain logical problems for the concept of miracle. He was concerned that, when believers tried to convince people of the truth of their faith, they pointed to miracles as proof. The problem was that such an appeal to revelation was being used as a proof for revelation. Thus the believer was 'cheating' by assuming what he wished to prove in the argument designed to prove it. Hume also saw that the essence of a miracle was the overriding of a law of nature. The problem, Hume argued, arises when we try to 'spot' a miracle. We need to use the system of the laws of nature to 'spot' anything and everything. This is basically the way experience works. There is, however, an extreme oddity in using the laws of nature to discover some event which goes contrary to those very laws of nature. Hume argued that there is a logical nonsense about the idea of miracle which depends on using a frame of reference to discover the miraculous, which is then set aside by the miraculous. There are two possibilities. Either there are laws of nature, which are universal and are based on our experience, thus there are no real exceptions to those laws (that is, there are no miracles, for an exception merely proves that the law is faulty), or, in contrast, if there are no laws of nature, then there cannot be exceptions or miracles in relation to these non-existent laws. We shall return to this below.

Hume continued his attack, based on his empiricist philosophy, with four basic arguments. He held that

first there is not to be found, in all history, any miracle attested by a sufficient number of men, of such unquestionable good sense, education and learning as to secure us against all delusion in themselves, of such undoubted integrity, as to place them beyond all suspicion of any design to deceive others, of such credit and reputation in the eyes of mankind, as to have a great deal to lose in case of their being detected in any falsehood, and at the same time attesting facts performed in such a public manner and in so celebrated a part of the world, as to render the detection unavoidable.

This is indeed a powerful test, but Hume then adds as an afterthought, 'All of which circumstances are requisite to give us full assurance in the testimony of men.' If Hume is serious, then he is crying for the moon. It is doubtful if, on Hume's terms, there ever has been, or will be, an event which could measure up to his standard for full assurance. If we applied this strictly, we would never believe anything.

Hume's second argument rests on the basis that

the way in which we commonly conduct ourselves in reasonings, is that the objects, of which we have no experience, resemble those, of which we have.

He moves from this to consider the passions of surprise and wonder, and how these give a sensible tendency towards the belief in these events, from which they are derived. Hume argues that there are people who are psychologically prone to talk about miracles, and to seek to experience and to evoke in others more surprise and wonder. But the fact that there are people who are prone to exaggerate and make false claims tells us nothing about whether or not miracles occur. At most, Hume shows us that we need to be careful in examining such claims. It does not show the impossibility of the miraculous. Indeed it can be argued that to be able to judge false claims, and to know that there are those who counterfeit experiences, presupposes some idea of real experience and genuine claims. Even an insane person may speak the truth.

The third argument is that there is

> a strong presumption against all supernatural and miraculous relations, that they are observed chiefly to abound among ignorant and barbarous nations.

This lacks force. The mere fact that stupid people easily believe what is false does not mean that they never believe anything that is true, or that more sensible people do not believe truly and properly in miracles. Merely because people are barbarous does not mean that they do not believe true things. Perhaps Hume makes too much of the supposed ignorance and barbarity of these nations. In their ignorance, they assume that events will always happen in the same way, and that experience will conform to what has been experienced. This is nothing else than the principle of induction, which, in essence, is the same for all civilized men. Hume thinks so highly of this principle and its basis in experience that he commends an Indian prince, who refused to believe in snow because he had no experience of such a thing. Such a refusal was reasonable. It was also wrong.

The fourth argument is based on the fact

> that there is no testimony for any (miracle) even those which have not been expressly detected, that is not opposed by an infinite number of witnesses, so that not only the miracle destroys the credit to testimony, but the testimony destroys itself.

The cash value of this is that different religions claim different miracles and these must contradict each other. This is not conclusive. The fact of conflict does not prove that neither position is true, only that both cannot be held.

While none of Hume's specific arguments counts against the concept of the miraculous, there is an important theme which underlies Hume's position. It is the issue of rules and their exceptions. Antony Flew has continued Hume's attack.

RULES AND THEIR EXCEPTIONS

When someone claims that a miracle has happened, they are claiming that the natural order of things has been interrupted. To do the work of science and history, we need to assume that things are basically regular, that the past and the future conform to the present. When Christians talk about the miracles of Jesus, they are talking about past events. But such events appear very different from events today. They appear to break the normal ordering of things. Can a genuinely miraculous event be known on the basis of historical evidence? It goes against the natural order of things.

Flew's argument is that the concept of miracle is parasitic on the concept of the natural order. If a miracle is to be a miracle, it is so only in contrast to the order of nature. But they are exceptional to that law of nature and call such laws into question. If there is no natural order, there is no miracle, but if there is a natural order which holds, then we cannot allow miracles.

The oddity is that as soon as a miracle violates a law, it is seen that there was nothing there to violate at all. Rather than a problem unique to the concept of the miraculous, we are dealing with a general difficulty concerning scientific change and discovery. This is the basis of the scientific method of induction. One forms a hypothesis, tests it and, if one finds a contradictory fact, one has to modify accordingly. If there is only one exception to a law, then one is certainly cautious about that law, but it does not mean that the whole law must be disregarded. Bertrand Russell makes the point with a story I have adapted.

The previous principal of my former college used to keep hens. At 8.30 each morning, he would open the henhouse and throw in a handful of grain. The hens would reason as follows. 'For 353 days now it has been the same. 8.30, door opens and then we get a handful of grain.' At 8.29 on the three hundred and fifty fourth day, all the hens would be expecting a feed in one minute's time. But once in a while, instead of grain, one would get its neck wrung.

That shows the problem of induction. All the evidence may point in a particular direction and we may form a law to cover these cases, but that law can never be totally closed. With the world as it is, the possibility of exceptions cannot be ruled out. Now if that is true in the natural realm, it is even more the case in the religious realm, which claims to deal with the divine and its rich and vast possibilities.

111

There is an important point here. Recent emphases in Christian circles have stressed the possibility of healing and the miraculous as the *norm* and not the exceptional. This creates a major problem for the concept of miracle. If miracles are unique events, there seems no sense in which one can expect them. If miracles happen all the time, then is it the miraculous we are talking about? This leads back to Augustine's position in which the argument states that we are simply becoming aware of the true level of reality and of God's action – at that point miracles are regular occurrences. If this is the case, we need to coin a new word to describe 'miracle', for we have changed its meaning and sense and are in danger of misleading and being misled by trading on a traditional view, while using it in a different sense all together.

SCIENTIFIC METHOD AND MIRACLES

Science is concerned with evidence, proof, testing, repeatability and prediction. By the very nature of the concepts at work there can be no scientific testing of the miraculous which will satisfy either the scientist or the believer in the miraculous. The scientist will not rest until the miracle has been explained and, in that sense, 'explained away', so that it can no longer be seen as miraculous, but has some normal explanation. The believer must not and cannot dispute that there needs to be careful examination of each claim that a miracle has happened, but must stress that there cannot be explanation in terms of what has happened previously, for the miraculous is something uniquely different.

Science cannot rule out in advance the possibility of the miraculous. Laws of nature have no power to determine events. They are simply descriptions of the state of scientific knowledge to date. They are open to change and revision in light of new evidence. The occurrence of the miraculous does not necessarily disprove a law of nature, but does remove any idea that natural laws are totally closed. Even if in fact they were closed, the true scientist can never know this, for he is never in a position to have all the evidence and to know that he has it. He is in the same position as the hen waiting for the grain.

We are in danger of accepting Antony Flew and David Hume when they demand a certain type of explanation and justification for a miracle. The trap to be avoided is that of imagining that there is only one sort of explanation. Explanation varies according to the object to be explained and to those to whom the explanation is being given. The strict materialist, the poet, the disinterested observer and the lover may all explain what being in love means, but the type and content of each explanation would reflect the different areas of interest of each person.

When a scientist is confronted by a claim for the miraculous he must regard this as a genuinely open question, or else he is cheating by begging the question in his own favour. That means that the burden of proof must rest on the believer. The scientist cannot rule out the possibility of a miracle. He must examine each case on its own merits. This is all that anyone could ask for or want.

MIRACLES AND CAUSES

Not every event which causes a total break in the normal or natural continuity of events is a miracle. There may be no necessary religious significance in any particular event which would entitle such an event to be termed miraculous. Such care must also be applied when examining the break in the natural process, for such a break must be a genuine one. There must be some difference between the way in which this particular one has happened and normal happenings, or else the idea of the miraculous has changed its meaning altogether.

A miracle cannot be an uncaused event or one which has no reason behind it. There must be the evidence that the specific agency involved is supernatural. We have to show that God did it, rather than someone or something else. This is more the task of theologians than scientists or philosophers. They must outline the standards by which true and false miracles are distinguished. We need safeguards against trickery and gullibility and we need to avoid confusion with the notion of providence. If God is in control of everything, in what way is he more especially in control of a miraculous event?

One important test here must be that of *fitness*. A miracle must fit in with the structure of a religion and make sense within a particular doctrinal stance. This is what was meant when we talked of the need to interpret the sign and its significance correctly. A miracle which has no connection with a particular theological insight, event or position would not really be a miracle at all, for it would have no connection with the whole of a religious position.

FOUNDATION OF A RELIGIOUS SYSTEM

This notion of the meaning of the miraculous event being found in the context of the religious position as a whole is relevant to an important point with which Hume concludes his case. He argues that 'a miracle can never be proved to be the foundation of a system of religion'. The point is that circular reasoning is involved if we try to argue that a miracle is proof for the divine, for one has already assumed a concept of the divine to formulate any talk of the miraculous. Hume is arguing for independent evidence for the certainty of revelation. We cannot use a miracle to prove the divine, but it may still be a sign of the presence and purpose of the divine.

If the theologian unpacks the concept of an all-loving and all-powerful God, he may show that there are certain classes of action which fit in better with God's character than others. Given the reality of God, then these actions are more likely to occur and would make sense given the nature of God. They would be signs of God and his activity, that is miracles.

THE NATURALIST AND THE SUPERNATURALIST

The television breaks down. My friend gives it a kick and it starts up again. Both the naturalist and the supernaturalist accept the explanation – that there was a loose screw. A father sitting in his chair asks his son to fetch the newspaper. The boy sits still, but the paper floats over towards the father. 'How did you do that?' asks the father. 'I don't know,' replies the boy. The naturalist will not rest until he has discovered the mechanism. He believes that, in principle, everything can be understood.

My television set falls to the ground and smashes into a thousand pieces. Suddenly, the pieces all fly together again and normal service is resumed. This last example seems to suggest something totally inexplicable. The supernaturalist holds that there are some events which cannot be fully explained. The naturalist argues that, given enough time and sophistication, all will be explained.

Both disagree over what is explicable. The naturalist holds that all is explicable, but is he entitled to such optimism and faith in rationality? Why should there not be totally inexplicable events – random happenings in the world? Given that possibility and the reality of different levels of explanation, the naturalist cannot rule out the miraculous.

The supernaturalist holds to the miraculous by faith. He argues that science does not and cannot say everything and that there are different ways of experiencing and grasping reality. Not all inexplicable events are miracles, for a miracle must fit in with the character and purpose of God. Miracles do not happen; rather they are planned.

Patrick Nowell-Smith describes this position by saying that there are certain events caused by boojums, but that no-one can tell the principles on which boojums operate or what they will do in the future, because this is the nature of the boojum. How then is it possible to discover whether or not there are boojums? If we are consistent in our talk and action in relation to boojums, if we behave in appropriate ways when they happen, if we provide tests for true as opposed to false ones, then there is a *prima facie* case for taking the concepts seriously. This is the stance the Christian must take over miracles. The crunch is whether the naturalist can offer a more adequate account of alleged miraculous events than the believer. Then and only then can it reasonably be claimed that miracles do not happen.

Key words

miracle. An interruption of the apparently natural order by the will and purpose of God.

sign and wonder. A remarkable event which causes surprise, fear or astonishment, and acts as a pointer to some purpose or reality beyond itself.

explicability. Able to be understood and explained.

nature. The phenomena of the physical and material world.

supernature. An order above the physical and material which controls and directs.

rules and exceptions. Principles of established order, and how we express what is happening when something does not conform to that order.

seeing as. To perceive the world in a particular way, and to interpret things in light of that.

cause. What produces an effect; or the bringing about by agency, power or influence.

justification. The process of giving adequate grounds for something.

Reading

Colin Brown, *Miracles and the Critical Mind* (Paternoster Press, 1984).

Norman L. Geisler, *Miracles and Modern Thought* (Paternoster Press, 1982).

E. and M.-L. Keller, *Miracles in Dispute* (SCM Press, 1972).

C. S. Lewis, *Miracles* (Fontana, 1960).

R. Swinburne, *The Concept of Miracle* (Macmillan, 1971).

9 Has science made faith obsolete?

Creation: some problems – Creation: some responses – Time and eternity – Theological science – Critique – Conclusion

The history of ideas reveals a close relationship and dependence between science and Christianity. The early and medieval churches happily used scientific knowledge and understanding to express the truths of Christianity. Indeed, some claim that much of the rejection of the church by society in later centuries was because the church clung to an outmoded view of science and reality, which had nothing to do with the essence of Christian truth. In modern times, the traditional partnership of religion and science has been dissolved in the face of the debates over evolution and biblical criticism, and the growth of the psychological and sociological sciences. For some years it was commonly supposed that science had disproved religion. Scientists seemed in the forefront of the sceptical attacks on Christianity. This was particularly the case with the development of logical positivism and its close dependence on empiricist philosophy and the physical sciences.

The optimism about science and the belief in the objectivity of scientific accounts of the world have been modified as modern science has matured and as people reflected on the nature of scientific activity. Scientism, and its belief that science will provide the cures for all man's problems, has all but disappeared, except in the hang-over reflected in common fallacies about science in the popular mind and in some philosophical questions put to religion. With the work of Albert Einstein, in particular, there was a less absolutist flavour to scientific claims. The scientist offered *one* way of looking at reality. That way of looking must be consistent and coherent on its own terms. It must correspond with reality as it is experienced under specific conditions. It must also be the best solution available. Thus there are a whole set of criteria bound up in what counts as the best available solution. It might mean the simplest solution, or else what works best, or that this approach will lead to other successful theories.

While few today would regard the content of science as offering the final and absolute picture of any reality, the method of science in terms of hypothesis, testing and experiment, and the development of laws or general theories, is the most basic way of understanding the world in which we live. Rather than talking very generally about issues in religion and science, we shall limit ourselves to the notions of creation, time and eternity, and theological science, before drawing some general conclusions about how we may view the relationship of science and religion.

CREATION: SOME PROBLEMS

When the clash between science and religion was at its height in the last century, the issue at stake was that of creation. The scientist argued that the world could be understood perfectly well in terms of itself, without reference to anything transcendent or divine. The creationist argued that God made the world. The sceptical philosopher then got to work on the account the believer gave of creation. The believer believes in God as the maker of heaven and earth. This act of creation is not by a process of emanation, where some aspects of the divine filter down to the material realm and give it a distinctive flavour and purpose. The doctrine of creation does not present any notion of eternal creation, or of the pre-existence of matter, whether good or bad. The creation account begins with God. 'In the beginning God created. . . .' is the context for all that follows in the Genesis pictures of the start. This God was not compelled into creation either by material to hand, or by some lack in himself. He did not have to create, but rather he chose freely to create as an act of grace and love.

This creation by God is a creation out of nothing (*ex nihilo*). He does not use previously present material. The creation of God is a creative act which brings everything into being. He creates what it is and ensures that it is. In John's Gospel, God's activity through Jesus the Logos is described as all-embracing, 'Without him was not anything made that was made' (John 1:3). God is different from his creation. He is not created. He is not dependent. The created is not independent. It depends for its existence, nature and continuance on God. This creative act is an act of power on the part of God. In acting in power God makes nothing evil. The creation is good.

Such a view of creation is part of an understanding of, and relationship with, a personal God. It does not make sense apart from a framework of religion and morality as a way of life lived in the context of God. The creator God is the Lord and Sovereign of man and the world. Man is made in a particular way and for a particular purpose. His chief end is to glorify God and to enjoy him for ever. The doctrine of creation makes sense only in the context of a relationship between God and man.

There are problems, though, about how much sense the notion of creation makes. The critic begins with beginnings. He asks whether it is possible to talk of an absolute beginning at all. The problem lies in our limited experience. We have lots of experience of proximate beginnings and endings, but no experience of absolute ones. How would we recognize one if we saw one? Moreover, the philosopher suggests that to talk of God creating out of nothing is to imply that 'nothing' is something. It is to use the language of substance, stuff and content, when, in reality, there is no such content or stuff. It is therefore illegitimate to use that context as a jumping-off point for God.

This brings the critic to God and the problems of talking about God existing before creation. Such talk implies time and a setting which God inhabits; but if there is nothing and no time, how can God 'exist' at all, far less 'occupy' a particular setting? To talk of God as creating is to imply that God is an agent, and that creation is an event. The critic argues that we cannot assume that God is an agent because that also assumes both that he is personal, and that he is able to act. Likewise we cannot assume that creation is an 'event', for that term implies part of a sequence and a happening in time. Both these usages are illegitimate, it is suggested. Creation, for the sceptic, can be neither an event nor a happening in time.

The critic also argues that a perfect God could not create, for that would be to add something that was lacking before. The perfect cannot lack anything. Nor could a perfect God create the world we have, for the presence of evil, mutability and corruption in the world deny that the God defined by Christianity could be the author of the world we inhabit.

The critics find that they cannot accept the Christian doctrine of creation because it does not make sense to them. They also claim that scientific explanations of the beginning of the world are more adequate than the biblical and theological account. Science has 'disproved' the biblical account of creation.

CREATION: SOME RESPONSES

Christians recognize that to talk of creation is to talk of an absolute beginning, different in kind from our experience of beginnings in the world. They argue that the evidence for such an absolute beginning cannot therefore rest on the world and its features, for there is no final way from the world to God. This was the problem with so many 'proofs' of God's existence. The grounds for a belief in the doctrine of creation are based on revelation. The question then becomes whether or not such revelation makes sense. It is possible to say something here to give content to the sense of revelation of the fact of creation. When we talk of this making sense, we are talking of whether it fits with what we know of God, and with what we know of the world.

Science depends on an order and intelligibility in the nature of things. It also draws on the notion of end, or purpose, in reality. The doctrine of creation offers a basis and explanation for that order, rationality and intelligibility. It comes from the God who created. This order makes science and knowledge possible. It explains, for some, the objective moral nature of things and humanity. It explains the differences between man and nature. If mankind is made in the image of God, they are in some ways the same as the world – created, coming from dust – and yet they are different – the final created being, the bearer of the image.

What we in fact have is a hypothesis, or picture, which offers an explanation of why things are as they are. The tests must then be the classic scientific tests of coherence and consistency, correspondence with reality as specified, and some pragmatic or disclosure test (discussed in chapter 11). The main challenge to the viability of the creation account depends on the problems with the doctrine of God, and the presence of supposedly better alternatives. Obviously, any talk of God will be anthropomorphic and be set in temporal terms, but that is not to reduce God to the temporal. It is the only way we have of talking at all. To suggest that because we have no experience of absolute beginnings or acts of God's creation, we must therefore say nothing, is to describe a method for the death of all science and knowledge. As for the scientific accounts of the beginnings of everything, it is by no means clear that there is, or can be, any evidence which would favour their acceptance rather than the Christian view. There are many common problems in all attempts to talk of how the world began. Christianity is no worse off than other views in those respects. Science cannot disprove the religious account, nor would it claim so to do. No evidence can be presented one way or the other, for there was no-one there to observe, and what counts as evidence is really an extrapolation backwards from the present. It may not have been like that at all. Different ways of regarding the same reality may well offer compatible accounts. They need not contradict. They must not be reduced to each other, if clarity and truth are to be retained. We shall return to this theme.

TIME AND ETERNITY

Augustine said that, when no-one asked him what time was, he understood it perfectly. We may feel the same. When is the present? The past is no longer. The future is unreal. But at what point is 'now'? Heraclitus complained that we could not step into the same river twice. Time is like the flow of that river. We are not sure that time exists. In dreams or sleep, time stands still. But what is time? It does not happen, but is the context in which happenings occur. Time is a means of measurement and movement. It may be regarded as absolute or relative to the thinker and observer. It appears like a series, but where does the series begin and end? Kant argued that time, like space, is a fundamental category of experience. It is a means by which or through which we experience all that we experience. Time is therefore unanalysable, as far as Kant is concerned. Others have suggested that it is misleading to ask what time is, for to frame the question in that way is to imply substance. Some prefer to see time as a pattern. Music may be interpreted in a variety of ways and, in the same way, time may be seen as offering a variety of interpretations. The very variety of views reveals the general difficulty of understanding and defining time.

In understanding God, there are particular difficulties in relation to time. God is seen as Creator, but what is the relationship between the immutable God and the changing world? God is pictured as active in history, but how may someone outside time affect the sequence of time? God is claimed to have become incarnate in the person of Jesus, who entered time and space, but in what sense can the infinite enter the finite, temporal sequence and retain something of that infinity? Human relationships with the God of Christianty are not interpreted as existing in this life alone. They begin in the here and now, but go on into the there and then. Heaven is the setting, and eternity the frame of reference. This brings us to the most difficult problem for the philosopher, as he approaches the Christian account. God is eternal. Man is created and redeemed to enjoy eternal life. But how is this possible? How may the perfect, immutable, eternal God affect, and be affected by, a contingent, finite, changing and corruptible reality called man? How can there be a purpose in time set by a Creator outside time, and how can there be a fulfilment beyond time for those of us who dwell in time?

A variety of interpretations of eternity are offered. For some it is everlasting existence. It is a realm of eternal similarity, where there is no change or adaptation. This view seems to conflict with any dynamic account of God and to present him as static. It is also possible to ask what kind of life it might be, where no change or movement occurred. A second view is of an existence that is timeless in the same sort of way that mathematical proofs or general laws are timeless. A third view is to suggest that talk of eternity is a poetical exercise emphasizing the stability of certain human facets and truths. A fourth view emphasizes that, from God's perspective, *totum simul stant* – everything stands as at one moment.

It seems obvious that whenever and however we talk of God, there will be some problem. This is especially true in relation to time. Human talk is not designed for divine concepts. We expect our words to fail. Care must be taken not to force our anthropomorphism too fiercely into the divine realm. The biblical writers are happy to use pictures and metaphors to express the difference between man and God's grasp of, and relation to, time. Eternity is about a divine perspective on things. Time is about a human perspective. In that sense, talk of eternal life is more appropriately talk about God from his perspective. Man's perspective cannot reduce the eternal to its own narrow scope.

This need not overwhelm the Christian, for whoever deals with the concept of time runs into similar problems. To talk of it appears to make it substantial. Science, like religion and philosophy, can only seek to offer different perspectives, the values of which must be judged on their respective merits. There is no absolute perspective. For the Christian, then, what is important is whether the idea of an eternal God bringing man into an eternal relationship is coherent, corresponds with reality and makes a significant difference.

THEOLOGICAL SCIENCE

One recent and important attempt to force a new relationship between science and religion is expressed in the work of T. F. Torrance. He offers an account of modern science and then draws parallels between science and theological science.

Science

Modern science is the key to a return to proper theology, and an escape from the quagmire of modern theology. We have undergone an upheaval as a result of Einsteinian physics and quantum mechanics, similar to the great upheavals in thought of earlier centuries. Basic epistemological questions have again come to the fore in such a way that both the sciences and theology are forced to rethink the basic questions of their fields of study. Thomas Torrance claims that, more and more, science is going to dominate our thinking, therefore it is imperative that theology comes to proper terms with it. Fortunately, the work of Albert Einstein and his successors is helpful to theology in that it forces theologians to work in a proper scientific fashion, basing their work on the nature of the objects within their fields of study. Einstein has presented two main themes, which are important for the theologian. The first is the basic respect and sense of awe and humility which stem from appreciating the eternal mystery of the world. This is joined with the second, that there is a direct and intuitive basis to experience in relation to the fundamental realities of the world.

Relativity theory, in particular, conditions the whole of proper science, and theology must learn from it. Relativity enables science to pass beyond the realm of the observable to the proper relation of things in themselves. Field theory shows that reality is hidden from observation, thus we need to develop 'axiomatic penetration' to discover the rational, logical structure of how the world is. The premises of such a field theory are known only *a posteriori* in conjunction with the work of scientific inquiry and verification. There is an inherent rationality in the nature of things which forces itself upon us, if we are only willing to listen and hear. Thus relativity seeks to end abstraction and to relate conceptual systems with physical processes. It has invented and developed tools suited to that purpose, for example four-dimensional geometry and complementarity in

quantum mechanics. It also seeks to grasp reality by moving
from what we know to what we do not know by means of a
'leap of thought', which reconstructs what we know at the same
time as allowing being to disclose itself to us.

The main feature of science now rests on the view that there
is one basic method of knowing which is appropriate in every
science. It is to be conditioned by the nature of the object. This
means that we have to separate very clearly things in themselves from our way of knowing them, and rid our knowledge
of subjective factors to allow the object to control our thought
and language. We are to be obedient to the object by coming
under its compulsion, and by seeking to allow our minds to fall
under the pattern of the object. We approach people in different
ways from the approaches we adopt to things, for they are
different objects. We approach microscopic reality differently
from the way we approach a cultural setting, for the nature of
the object conditions the approach we are to adopt towards it.
Genuine science is characterized by attachment to the object. It
is not detached from the object.

Science not only believes that the object of its enquiry is
intelligible, but, more generally, science believes in the accessi-
bility of things, in other words, that nature is inherently intelligible, and that the world is inherently rational and therefore
accessible to rational inquiry. Yet we are unable to account for
this rationality, though it is discovered and not invented. We
recognize this rationality and must respect and be obedient to
it. What we know prescribes the mode of rationality we are to
adopt towards it. Without such inherent rationality there would
be no knowledge and no communication.

The situation of the scientist is made problematic because we
ourselves obstruct knowledge. We need to be free from *a priori*
conceptions and philosophical presuppositions, to separate
what we know from our knowing of it, and thus be attached
to the object. This attachment to the object involves a deep
and radical questioning of oneself and one's assumptions. Our
thinking and ideas need to be subject to self-scrutiny and we
need to test everything critically. The scientist seeks to renounce
self to be true to the object. Unfortunately, there will always be
personal factors involved so that we are only in a position of
controlled subjectivity. The aspect of personal judgment is a
necessary part of the assessment of evidence, thus we can never
attain fixed categories or ultimate truth. We can never totally
rid ourselves of subjective factors, nor can we totally capture
reality, for it outruns what we can specify. Here we are unable

to eliminate the *noetic* or rational structure of our human thought and language in our attempt to be true to the *ontic* structure of things. In other words, our forms of knowing affect what is known; what we know, in the end, is not what is there in its pure state, but is overlaid with factors from our minds.

At the same time, the scientist is seeking to clarify the way the world is by means of learning new facts, by reducing the multiple and complex to simplicity and unity; by developing linguistic and cognitive tools appropriate to the new data, and, most of all, by transforming himself and his own outlook, so that he is more rational, more objective, and therefore more in the truth. Having done this, he must then try to communicate to others what he knows, and this involves getting the other person to see the same reality and to be subject to the same rationality.

This view of science is relevant to the theologian in that he must set aside wrong-headed ideas of what science is and seek to conduct his theological thinking as a proper science, clarifying the rational structure in his thought. Always he must be faithful to the object of his study, in all the differences that has from other objects, and in the appropriate science for that object. The theologian must develop a theological science appropriate to God.

Theological science
Theology is a positive science seeking to investigate its own particular object, God. The church needs to be renewed and reformed by grasping the objective rationality of God. Theology seeks therefore to help man to refer his thoughts properly to God and so develops modes of rationality and verification which are appropriate to this. Theologians must seek to adapt reason to God's revelation in Christ and faith is the appropriate response to the nature of God. The problem for the world is not God, but humanity, and thus it is only in terms of God coming to deal with us and freeing us from individualism, that we properly discover who we are. It is thus we are given the capacity to act rationally.

Theological science shares its methodology with the other sciences, in that the crucial factor is integrity as regards the object. Science assumes that the object is open to inquiry and open to rational understanding. Thus theology shares with science the stress on objectivity, rationality, the object thrusting itself upon us, that is the given, the inner intelligibility of that given, and the discipline and rigour of method. Their problem is a common one. It is the struggle with ourselves properly to refer our thoughts to reality, and to restrain ourselves from investing the object with subjective factors.

There are, however, crucial differences between theology and other sciences centring on the nature of the object which theology investigates. As the object is different, so the modes of reference, verification and rationality which are appropriate to the object must also be different. Thomas Torrance warns against the overlap of views or theories from other sciences into territory which is the express domain of the theologian. Science cannot fill any gaps in theological understanding, because the object of theology is so unique and different. Indeed, the problem is that the theologian risks stretching ordinary concepts to breaking-point, as he or she uses them to point to the divine object. Theology, because God is the object of study, is able to show other sciences what real objectivity is, for God is ultimate objectivity and rationality.

Theology can also learn from other sciences. Its specific methods must match those of science in general. Theologians must learn to test theology on its proper grounds and clarify the whole pattern of relations. Their approach must be subtle, flexible, dynamic and precise. They must use the interrogative form of inquiry with critical application, seeking logical simplicity and coherent unity. This process of clarification and explanation is to be developed because theology is an open inquiry, *i.e.* open to its object. Theologians must therefore develop new systems, logics and linguistic tools, better to shape our minds to the truth. The test of such devices is their fertility in illuminating reality. Theological science, thus grounded and co-ordinated, will help our minds to grasp what is beyond mere concepts and to express what faith really is for today.

CRITIQUE

The obvious attraction of Thomas Torrance's view is that it seems to solve many problems. Unfortunately, his own account is not immune from criticism. He fails to clarify his notion of rationality, especially in relation to the central issues of justification, evidence and criticism. He talks of the rationality of the universe, things, nature, the world, existence, theology, scientists, creation, and of God, as if 'rationality' in each case were one and the same sort of thing. Torrance claims that his view leads to objectivity; yet he also admits that the subjective cannot be eliminated. Thus the cure for subjectivity seems as afflicted by the subjective as everything else. Torrance claims that to be rational means that we allow the object to prescribe the mode of rationality we are to adopt towards it. Yet his own account seems to suggest only one approach and that a universal one. In one sense, Torrance seems to be stating the obvious, *i.e.* desks and people are different and require different approaches. However, he claims a more substantial content to his view. In addition, there arise problems over the sense of 'objects', the nature of intuition, what is meant by 'modes', and the failure of Torrance's view to exclude any area which claimed to be a science, and to have an unique approach to its particular object, *e.g.* astrology. Torrance's view seems to be immune from criticism on his own account, but there is something odd about the refusal to allow the critic any ground on which to stand.

However, Torrance does offer a view of theology in the light of science. This is a fruitful area for consideration, even if he does seem to tie theology so closely to Einstein's view of physics, that if that view collapses, so too will theology.

CONCLUSION

While recognizing that there remain genuine problems in the relationship between science and religion, there is no longer any serious attempt to make science the ultimate explanation of everything. Certain philosophies still make such claims, but these fit uneasily with the tone of modern science. Scientists today recognize that science and particular sciences are offering interpretative frameworks for reality and telling us how we may grasp and use that reality. Science is increasingly pragmatic. It is also increasingly honest about its presuppositions and its limitations.

Religion in general and theology in particular may be more confident and less defensive, when it comes to science, as long as science is given its proper place. Where the theologian may well emulate the scientist is in the care to ensure that his theology, be it of creation, of eternity, or of the nature of God, is expressed in coherent and consistent terms, matches with the reality specified by theology, and actually does what it claims to do in terms of transforming people and situations. There can be no escape from the litmus test of success. A theology which does not produce a difference, in a moral sense, is inadequate to the claims of Christianity. Such a vibrant, living Christianity has nothing to fear from good science and everything to gain from emulating it.

Key words

science. An ordered and systematic way of knowing, and expression of that approach.

objectivity. What is really the case regardless of personal interpretation.

subjectivity. (a) a person knowing something as a person; (b) a purely personal approach based on one's own opinions or attitudes.

creationism. The approach to the origin of the world and universe which stresses the fact and nature of God's bringing the world into being.

beginning. The start or origin.

revelation. The unveiling of truths which cannot be reached by reason alone. It is used to refer to God's unveiling of himself and his will through nature, history, the prophets, the Decalogue, Christ and the Scriptures.

intelligibility. Ability to be understood, and to make sure of what there is.

hypothesis. A theory put forward for testing, to establish the validity of that theory.

fundamental realities. What is the case beyond or behind appearances; that which makes things what they are.

method. An approach which has order and purpose.

time. Successive states or experiences; various ways of regarding these; the realm of the changeable, impermanent, and of limited duration.

eternity. The realm of what is unchanging, everlasting and permanent.

theology. The study of the nature of God.

Reading

I. G. Barbour, *Myths, Models and Paradigms* (SCM Press, 1974)

Del Ratzsch, *The Philosophy of Science* (IVP, 1986).

Colin A. Russell, *Cross-currents: interactions between science and faith* (IVP, 1985).

T. F. Torrance, *Theological Science* (OUP, 1978).

10   Do people need God to be good?

'Morality' in modern moral philosophy – A pen-sketch of Christian morality in relation to the Bible – A supernatural morality – Heaven, hell and morality – Behaviour and belief – Religion and morality

In the past, religion and morality appeared to walk hand in hand. A religious man was a moral man and a moral man a religious man. In recent times, the separation of morality from religion has called in question the dependence of morality on religion. Some have even turned the traditional approach on its head. R. B. Braithwaite, as we shall examine in detail later, has argued that religion is really all about morality. Religious stories are simply encouragements and reinforcements of a moral way of life. The Christian may accept that particular moralities are possible without a religious base, but would deny that religion is possible without morality and that religion can be reduced to morality. But what do we mean by 'morality'?

'MORALITY' IN MODERN MORAL PHILOSOPHY

Morality is about right and wrong behaviour. Every moral system gives some account of ideals, defining what is good and right. It speaks of the nature of people, of rules to be followed defining what ought and ought not to be done, of the motives that help and hinder our moral choices, and of the role of the consequences of our actions in making moral decisions and living a moral life. Different moral systems reflect different understandings of the nature of mankind, the course or basis of morality, and the way moral decisions are and ought to be made. In modern moral philosophy, the lines of division may be seen to be drawn up on two sides. This is obviously a rough and ready distinction. A key way of expressing the difference behind these broad approaches is between *objective* and *subjective* views of morality.

An objective view begins with a description of moral reality. The *descriptivist* believes that morality is expressed in the way things and people are. You can describe what you ought and ought not to do by examining the nature of the world and humankind. Some things are good for people and are right. Other things are bad for people and are wrong. Morality is thus a reading off from the world around us. If we do what is good for us, we flourish. If we do wrong, we harm ourselves. If this were the case, morality would be objective and independent of man's judgment. There is, it is claimed, a moral law in the very fabric of reality so that all moral disputes can, in principle, be solved by checking the principles involved with reality.

The *prescriptivist*, on the other hand, believes that morality is the product of humankind. People prescribe what is moral both for themselves and for others. The basis of this description may vary enormously. Hedonists and utilitarians believe that *pleasure* is the basis of moral prescription. Thus people prescribe what gives pleasure, either to themselves (the hedonist) or to the greatest number (the utilitarian). Emotivists believe that morality is essentially a matter of *feeling*. We prescribe moral rules for ourselves and others on the basis of what affects us strongly. Passing a moral judgment is really expressing what we feel and encouraging others to feel the same thing too. Whatever the basis of the prescription, the prescriptivist believes that morality is essentially a subjective thing, where people express what they want or need; morality is simply a reflection of those desires.

There is one other important distinction in moral philosophy which must be noted. It concerns the form of moral judgment rather than the content. It is the distinction between *deontology* and *teleology*. The deontologist is concerned with what is right in itself. The mark of deontology is keeping rules for the rules' sake and doing what is right because it is right. The teleologist, in contrast, is concerned with the end result of keeping or breaking the rules. Consequences are what matter in teleology. 'Right' is what leads to good consequences, and 'wrong' is what results in bad consequences. Rules may be broken if breaking them leads to better consequences than keeping them.

A PEN-SKETCH OF CHRISTIAN MORALITY IN RELATION TO THE BIBLE

In contrast to this brief description of modern moral philosophy, the relationship between religion and morality in Christian thought needs now to be examined. For the Christian, morality begins with God. Christian morality is a reflection of the nature of God. The ideals defining right and wrong, badness and goodness, stem from God. The rules which specify what ought and ought not to be done are revealed by God. The motive involved in morality is the wish to reflect the nature of God. The consequences which follow a moral action are ultimately under the control of God. When stated as baldly as this, the Christian view of the relationship of morality and religion is to see everything in the light of God. This is essentially correct and in keeping with the biblical account of morality.

For the Old and New Testament writers, morality depends on God. God is the fixed point before man and all creation. Man is created by God and made in his image. Man is thus seen as dependent on God, made for relationship with God and answerable to him. The early picture is one of harmony between God, the man and the woman, but then the man and the woman are presented choosing evil. They disobey God's commands and do what seems right to themselves. Disorder and broken relationships follow between God and themselves, each other and the created realm. The rest of the Scriptures is the account of God's dealings with men and women and the restoration of harmony and relationship.

The Old Testament pictures a God who reveals moral rules. In the Pentateuch, from Adam through to Moses, God forbids certain things and allows others. The climax is the giving of the Decalogue – the Ten Words, or the Ten Commandments. The context of the law-giving is crucial. It is the context of a covenant relationship in which both parties bind themselves to each other and accept responsibility to keep their side of the covenant relationship. God is the one who reveals the law. To live according to the law leads to a life of blessing and prosperity. To break God's law is to come under his curse. In one sense, the rest of the Old Testament account is the history of a people alternately obeying and rebelling against the God who had chosen them. At the same time, there seems an increasing awareness of the God who reveals the moral law, expressed in the Wisdom literature and the prophetic writings. The Wisdom literature has been called 'rules from heaven for life on earth', and is full of practical, down-to-earth wisdom and common sense. Good living leads to good consequences. Even the book of Job deals with that theme, except it is in an apologetic analysis of why good living has not resulted in happiness, prosperity and blessing. Being right with God usually means prosperity, but if it is a choice between prosperity and being right with God, then the latter is always to be followed.

In reading the prophets, the shift in emphasis from the ceremonial and religious law to what is more recognizable as a social morality is marked. Loving God has always meant loving one's neighbour, but flesh and blood are put on that concept in the strident demands of the prophets. God's demands are not simply for us to be in a right relationship with him but also to be in right relationships with all mankind. This aspect of revelation is summed up in the coming of Jesus Christ, described by the New Testament writers both as a prophet and the new Law-giver. In the teaching of Jesus yet higher standards of morality seem set, certainly in terms of motivation. 'You have heard that it was said, "You shall not commit adultery." But I say to you that every one who looks at a woman lustfully has already committed adultery with her in his heart' (Matthew 5:27–28). Apart from the Sermon on the Mount, there is no systematic moral teaching on the part of Jesus, and while the same is true of the rest of the New Testament, there is in the letters to the churches a great deal of space devoted to moral issues.

Briefly, the essence of New Testament morality is conformity to the example of Jesus by the power of the Holy Spirit. There are some lists of 'do's and don'ts', but there is also the recognition of some moral diversity, and the necessity of finding a way of coping with that diversity. Romans 14 and 15 seem to have this much in mind. There is no gap between theology and ethics in Paul's thinking. To believe certain things means to live in a certain way. That way of life transforms the here and now and leads to eternal life in the presence of God himself.

It is not our task here to describe the biblical content of Christian ethics, but what is crucial is to see how philosophy has called in question some of the basic assumptions of Christian morality.

A SUPERNATURAL MORALITY

The God described by Christianity is a transcendent being who is supernatural. He is independent of the natural, created order.

This is the God who reveals morality to mankind. This immediately raises certain problems. How can an omniscient, omnipotent, transcendent God be described as 'moral' in any sense of the word? The essence of morality seems to be choosing between good and evil. If God is all-perfect, he has no struggle at all to do good. He does it naturally. So, is he really moral? This sounds suspiciously like drawing a line in a certain place and then complaining because something is on the other side of the line drawn. Always doing what is right does not mean that I am beyond morality. It simply means that I am perfectly moral. Logically, I may still do what is wrong, though actually I may never do so. Logically, God can do whatever he likes. If his nature is perfect, he will always choose to do what is right. However, such expressions reveal the anthropomorphic way we talk of God. We cannot meaningfully apply human standards of morality to God. He does not exist in time, choose, act or reflect in the same way as human beings. Rather, the Christian expresses morality as stemming from God. God defines what is moral, and to complain about the misapplication of 'moral' to God is like asking whether logic is logical or beauty beautiful. Such conceptual difficulty shows that we have come to the limit of what can be said and to the level of fundamental assumptions, beyond which, by definition, we cannot go. As J. O. Urmson put it, following Archimedes, we all need a point by which to lever the world. We all must stand somewhere in order to look and evaluate all else.

The sceptic returns to the theme of the supernatural with the complaint that a supernatural God can know nothing of the immanent, natural order of things. In Christian terms, a holy God can brook no contact with sinful mankind. Such an attack overlooks the doctrine of God's creation of humanity in his own image. God makes mankind and, accordingly, knows them better than they know themselves. He creates men and women in the likeness of God and he creates them for a purpose. Such a God does not dwell only in the realm of the splendid isolation of transcendence. He is intimately involved with his creation. This involvement is reinforced and completed in the doctrine of the incarnation, where the transcendent God becomes human flesh in the immanent world of time and space. If the creator God knew nothing of man's moral dilemmas, then there could be no real understanding of what man faces in moral decision-making. However, the clear evidence of the New Testament is of Jesus struggling with, and being subject to, temptation; yet overcoming and being victorious.

Nevertheless, it is proper to ask what is the relationship between the moral standards derived from the realm of the supernatural and the realm of the natural. Christian tradition has responded to this question by the doctrine of natural law. God has put in the nature of things and in human nature a moral law. Such a morality may be seen by all reasonable men. It is an objective, rational morality. Properly to understand its source, there must be faith, but all people everywhere, regardless of belief, may have some grasp of the morality itself. It may be by a voice of conscience within, or by using the mind to discover what is obviously right and wrong. This sounds very close to the notions of descriptivism. It need not be exactly the same, for different descriptivists may quarrel about the source and origin of natural law. Nevertheless, in the emphasis on objectivity and rationality, there is a close parallel.

Two levels of objection to natural law are forthcoming. The first is to call in question whether or not there is such a basic moral law to be found in nature. Moral diversity is stressed by the relativist who denies that there are any absolute moral rules. He or she argues that what is right and wrong varies from time to time, place to place, and person to person. If he or she is correct, then there can be no one, universal, natural law. The second level of critique is to enquire why, even if there were such a moral law in nature, it is necessary to seek any justification for that moral law beyond the law itself. That is to say that there is no need to postulate a God who is the originator of the natural law. Occam's razor suggests that entities should not be multiplied. Simple explanations are to be preferred to complex ones. The responses to these objections are twofold. We must try to show a basic unity in moral judgments and in criteria on a universal basis. It is interesting to see that no matter what the code of morality there does seem to be a common core of morals throughout history and culture. It centres on truthtelling, the value of life, parent-child relationships, sexual partnerships and economic organization. There does seem to be some kind of universal, core morality. The basis of such a morality, it is argued, is only properly understood by reference to Christianity. It is in God that we find the source of morality in nature.

This debate becomes more specific. The sceptic points to the fact that there are plenty of good people outside the church and Christianity, and plenty of bad people within the Christian fold. The believer responds that, if God has made mankind in his image, then, despite sin, it is no great surprise to find vestiges of goodness in non-believing people. That they were created by God ensures that it is possible for some trace of the divine handiwork to remain. Other Christians are more forceful in rejecting the claim that there can be any goodness outside Christianity, though this seems to depend on particular exclusive definitions of 'goodness'. The presence of bad people within the church is acceptable. The church is the home of sinners. A T-shirt slogan expresses the point: 'Please be patient. God hasn't finished with me yet.' More seriously, it is no necessary reflection on the truth or falsity of Christianity that some exponents of the faith do not attain the standards set within the faith.

Recent Christian writing has tended to reject the notion of natural law partly as a reflection of different attitudes to scientific laws and methods, and partly because of the challenge of relativism. Some have recently tried to revive a variation on the natural law theme, arguing that it is possible to discuss absolute moral laws as reflections of the creating and sustaining work of God. Such a moral law might form a court of appeal for all people, even those outside the faith, and serve as a basis for law-making and social morality within a nation and between nations.

Regardless of whether natural law revised or unrevised is accepted, the Christian is still proclaiming a revealed basis for morality. Morality is not something people think up and decide for themselves. It is given and revealed by God. The sceptic challenges such claims for revelation. How do you know? How can you be sure? What tests are there? We have looked at revelation and its grounds earlier, but the acceptance of God's revelation of morality will rest on grounds other than those of morality itself.

To put the point provocatively, we might ask on what basis God makes the moral rules and laws, and how we might judge them. Abraham is told to sacrifice his son Isaac. God demands an action from Abraham which seems on the face of it immoral. Is it right for Abraham simply to obey God, because God has commanded it? Is it not proper for Abraham to ask if God is 'right' in commanding him to do this? The moral philosopher by raising these questions is asking whether we have some notion of goodness and right which we apply to God as a kind of test, so that only if God passes the test can we affirm that God is good. The moral philosopher tends to believe that the truly moral person should always ask, 'Ought I to do this?' whenever he or she is commanded to do something. This is certainly the case, if the standard of morality is derived from somewhere else than the command of God. However, it is hard to see what grounds for moral judgment Abraham or the Christian may bring to the commands or demands of God. This is all the more difficult, given the fallen state of our human judgment in terms of our understanding of right and wrong and our ability to put that into practice.

For Abraham, the command to sacrifice Isaac must have seemed to go against common sense, parental responsibility, and even the earlier promise of God that through Isaac all nations would be blessed. Nevertheless, Abraham obeyed God and came to the place and point of sacrifice. We are then told that this was a test of whether the son and heir of Abraham had become an idol and replaced God. The story climaxes in God's provision of a substitute sacrifice and a renewal of God's covenant with Abraham. It is hard to see that Abraham had any basis to pass a moral judgment on God, given that he was sure that this was the command of God. This last qualification is vital. When confronted with the living reality of God and his call, there is no room for doubt and question. For the Christian, the crucial question rests on the acceptance of the validity of the revelation of God. That revelation sets the moral standards. The Christian morality stems from that revelation. Other moral standards may be possible, but have no basis in the revelation of God and are inappropriate to that revelation, as far as the Christian is concerned. Here again, we are brought to the fundamental assumptions and to the point from which the rest of the world is grasped and judged. That point cannot be questioned except by the substitution of another ultimate standard.

The final area of debate concerning the concept of a supernatural source of morality centres on man's freedom. Was Abraham really faced with a choice? If he had no choice, could his actions be counted as 'moral'? The essence of morality is thus interpreted as making free choices and accepting the responsibility for those choices. If God made us, does not he make us choose certain things? Scripture and experience show us that we are not forced to choose. We are pictured as free to choose good or evil. Indeed, God is pictured setting before us that choice of evil and goodness. The nature of God's creation is that we are free, responsible persons, who must face the consequences of our choices. The sceptic leaps to the Christian doctrine of grace and suggests that God's unmerited favour removes the consequences of bad behaviour. Man is let off scot-free. This is not quite the case. The consequences of sinful action are still dealt with under the doctrine of grace. God himself in Christ suffers the consequences of sin, according to the Scriptures. At the same time, man is not scot-free under the doctrine of grace. In response to the grace of God, man's freedom becomes a freedom to serve and obey God.

HEAVEN, HELL AND MORALITY

The caricature of Christianity suggests that it is simply 'pie in the sky when you die'. The emphasis on the consequences of the life lived in the here and now, in the there and then of heaven and hell, raises questions about the nature of Christian morality. Heaven is often presented as a reward for a good life lived, and hell the punishment for an evil life. Some have questioned whether behaviour motivated by the desire to avoid punishment or to gain a reward is truly moral. This suggests that true morality is a matter of doing what is right because it is right and not because of any consequences. There is a proper concern to avoid the self-interest which seeks to protect the self at all costs. Morality certainly does not consist of self-interest. Indeed it is often a useful way of highlighting the morality of a particular action to show that it does not serve one's self-interest.

However, there is a danger of over-reaction to the concept of fear of punishment or the selfish seeking for reward. To over-react is to deny that heaven and hell have any part in Christian morality. Christian teaching is clear that a life lived in accordance with God's will results in eternal life in what is called heaven. This in no way implies that the only motive for living that good life is a desire for a beatific state. Indeed, having that motive may mean that there is neither a good life lived, nor a heavenly reward gained. Likewise it is possible to live a good life and avoid the evil described as hell, without that avoidance being the significant factor in living the life. Heaven and hell are presented as the natural and inevitable consequences of a particular style of living. We get what we deserve and reap what we sow. That is the way things are. We do not do the good and avoid the evil in order to achieve the consequences. We do those things because they are right to do. The consequences follow as night follows day. This should not frighten the Christian moralist into refusing to talk of heaven and hell. The philosopher, however, rightly draws attention to the insidious role of fear and self-interest in reinforcing behaviour patterns which happen to result in certain kinds of consequences.

BEHAVIOUR AND BELIEF

A similar line of response may be given to the charge that religion is simply a means of reinforcing morality. R. B. Braithwaite argues that the point of religious stories and myths is to encourage and reinforce a particular quality of moral life. Braithwaite's thesis is a positive attempt to distil an essence of religion which is acceptable to empiricists. Marxists take a less generous view, when they argue that religion is the opiate of the people. Religion breeds and supports a morality which keeps the underprivileged in check by promising improvement in the hereafter, and allows the rich to sleep easy at nights knowing that the after-life is what counts. Such promises lead to unquestioning acceptance of an intolerable here and now.

Both Braithwaite and the Marxists have grasped that belief and behaviour go closely together. It is obviously true that Christian belief is supposed to issue in Christian moral behaviour. The link between belief and behaviour is neither the essence of Christianity nor purely a negative, conservative feature. Christianity claims to be true as well as to result in a good life. Christianity, while it has often been used to support unjust regimes, may also be a critic of regimes. The prophetic aspect of Christian teaching shows that Christian teaching and morality may act as a challenge to a society and its morality. This is particularly complicated in western Europe, where Christianity has affected the development of social and personal morality. With the loss of confidence in belief, there remains a hang-over of morality. But is this genuine, full-blooded Christian morality? Christian moral behaviour should challenge non-believers to take seriously the claims of Christian teaching. Behaviour, in this case, would lead to the possibility of belief. For the Christian, it is vital that there is a match between behaviour and belief, that behaviour is the genuine fruit of Christian belief, and that Christian morality fulfils its proper role of challenge to the world and society outside the Christian faith.

This process of matching behaviour and belief occurs in the context of the religious community. It makes reference to Scripture, tradition and to the knowledge and experience of God.

RELIGION AND MORALITY

While moral behaviour may challenge individuals and society, there seems little hope of proving the existence of God from the existence of morality. Morality may exist independently of the concept of God. Moral rules may simply be there, or be the products of human feelings, rather than the will of a divine law-giver. As the gap from the physical world to the divine reality is too great to bear the burden of proof, so the gap between the human and the divine spoils attempts at proof of divine existence as the basis of morality. While morality may not act as a proof of God's existence, it does require some explanation in terms of origin and basis. The involvement of God with the Christian account of morality offers a consistent statement of a life-style, which is a possible alternative to other moral systems. The key question then becomes one of judgment between competing systems and philosophies.

We have seen how the philosophy of relativism suggests that there is just a diversity of moral views and competing systems and that this diversity should be accepted and thus lead to tolerant acceptance of difference. The descriptivist and the Christian might usefully join forces in stressing the objective, absolute character of morality, which refutes relativism. They might also point out the absolute character of the relativist claim that 'everything is relative' and the illegitimacy of the move from the relativist descriptive account to the absolutizing of tolerance as the supreme virtue.

Christian morality brings together the thread of the deonto-logical and the teleological. It is concerned with what is right and wrong in itself and with the ultimate consequences of good and evil actions. Christianity claims an objective basis for morality. The validity of Christian morality depends on the truth or falsity of Christianity itself and its belief system. Revelation is the keystone of the testing of the truth or otherwise of Christian belief. Christian morality stands or falls on the basis of revelation.

Key words

morality. The doctrine and practice of duties and obligations of individuals in society.

right. What is regarded as morally correct and conforms to a standard; the opposite of what is wrong.

good. A positive value having desirable qualities.

descriptivism. An approach to philosophy which stresses that moral values are objective features of the world, and may be described as moral facts.

prescriptivism. An approach to philosophy which stresses that moral values are arrived at by prescribing what counts as good or bad for ourselves and for other people.

revealed morality. The view that

standards of right and wrong, good and bad, stem from outside, and are independent of human thinking. These are shown to us by God in various ways.

natural law. The notion that there is in the nature of things, of people and of the world a moral law, which it is correct to obey.

image of God. The idea that God, in creating humankind, has left his mark and stamp on every·person. The content of the image may be interpreted as conscience, freedom, rationality and/or moral freedom.

moral judgment. The ability and exercise of deciding what we ought to do and what is right, wrong, good and bad.

choice. The freedom and ability to select between options, especially good, bad, right or wrong.

reward and punishment. The notions of giving positively and negatively what someone deserves on the basis of what they have done or chosen.

belief. Trust, confidence, acceptance of something as true.

objective morality. The notion that standards of rightness, wrongness, goodness and badness are not simply matters of personal opinions, but are factual realities.

Reading

D. Cook, *The Moral Maze* (SPCK, 1983).

Arthur F. Holmes, *Ethics: approaching moral decisions* (IVP, 1984).

T. Maclagan, *Theological Frontier of Ethics* (Allen and Unwin, 1961).

Oliver O'Donovan, *Resurrection and Moral Order: an outline for evangelical ethics* (IVP, 1986).

11   Prove it!

How do we know that God exists? Is it possible to prove it? Almost everyone says, 'If you could only prove God to me, then I'd believe it.' But is this really possible and is it the proper task for the Christian believer today? Many have tried, and we shall examine the claims to prove God, noting especially the different starting-points and the steps in the arguments.

THE ONTOLOGICAL ARGUMENT

The most fascinating attempt at proof orginates from the work of Abbot Anselm. His monks wished to discover whether it was possible to prove that God existed. Anselm produced a version of the argument from being – the ontological argument, which took the form of a prayer. This was all part of his stress on faith seeking understanding, which is examined later. The prayer and proof began with the concept of God. What is God like? Anselm responded that God is that than which nothing greater can be conceived. We shall call this concept *TTWNGCBC* for short. Anselm went on to argue that something which exists in the mind alone is not so great as something which exists both in the mind and in reality. Having a slap-up meal is far better than just thinking about it. If God, and thus the *TTWNGCBC*, existed in the mind alone, we could form the idea of an even greater being. Such a being would be one which not only existed in the mind, but existed also in reality. Thus the *TTWNGCBC* which was in the mind alone was not in fact that than which nothing greater can be conceived. The *TTWNGCBC* which is true to its name and description must exist both in the mind and in reality or else it would not be the *TTWNGCBC*. That is to say that God *must* exist.

In the second form of the argument (though there is debate whether this is simply a variation on a theme) Anselm argued that existence must apply to God in a special way. When we talk about God's existence we mean something quite different from all other forms of existence. God alone has a uniquely necessary existence. God has to be. Anselm held that if we try to imagine the non-existence of God, we end up with something which is inconceivable and self-contradictory. There cannot be a God who does not exist. To be God, God must exist. In other words, God necessarily exists.

The argument is deceptively simple. It begins with an idea we all have and then moves to the reality of the being to whom the idea refers. Even the fool has this idea. When, in Psalm 14, it is recorded that the fool says in his heart that there is no God, the 'God' referred to is *TTWNGCBC*. If the fool were to examine the idea properly, then he would come to see that God must exist.

This type of approach is still the subject of much discussion. There are even modern attempts to reinstate the argument both as a proof of God's existence and to support belief in God. The debate began almost as soon as Anselm produced the proof. Gaunilo, another monk, replied to Anselm 'on behalf of the fool'. His response was as simple and direct as Anselm's case. Gaunilo argued that he had the idea of a perfect island which is *TTWNGCBC*. It was greater to exist in reality than in the mind alone. This must mean that if the island were truly *TTWNGCBC*, then it must exist. Therefore, the most perfect island existed, or else it would not be the most perfect island. The problem, for Gaunilo, was that the perfect island did not exist. If the perfect island did not exist, then there was no necessity for God to exist either.

Anselm was swift to rebut this attack. He claimed that the argument worked only in one particular case. It worked only for the concept of God. It was only of God that one could say that he was *TTWNGCBC*. God's existence was of a different kind from that of perfect islands and, indeed, of anything else. He had necessary existence. Only of God may it be said that it is greater to exist than not to exist.

HISTORICAL SUPPORT FOR ANSELM

There are three main lines of defence and support that have been offered to help Anselm. Descartes, Leibniz and Spinoza all offered variations on Anselm's theme. Descartes' presentations are the best known. He introduced both a form of the ontological argument and also a causal argument based on the same definition of God as the all-perfect. Descartes argued that existence is a property of a predicate. It describes what belongs to something. Existence is something that a thing may or may not have. There are some predicates that an object *necessarily* has or else it would not be that particular object at all. A triangle must have three enclosed sides with its angles adding up to 180 degrees. In the same way, for God to be God, the supremely perfect being, it is necessary that he has existence. Otherwise he would not be the supremely perfect being. He would lack the perfection of existence. We may express what Descartes meant by looking at two lists:

God 1	God 2
Omnipotent	Omnipotent
Omniscient	Omniscient
Eternal	Eternal
All-loving	All-Loving
Just	Just
Merciful	Merciful
+ Existence	− Existence

God 1 and God 2 are exactly the same except in one crucial respect: God 1 exists, while God 2 does not. If we accept that God is all-perfect, then we must ask which of these two Gods is more perfect. It is obvious that God 1 is more perfect than God 2, because he exists. It is better to exist than not to exist. It is better to have a real pound note than an imaginary one. The argument seeks to show that God must exist.

Descartes' other argument is that we all have the idea of a supremely perfect being. His question is, whence did this arise? He held to the old notion of Aristotle that the cause must be greater than the effect. What, then, caused the idea of the all-perfect? It could not be myself, my parents or my society, for all of these are imperfect. One cannot get the perfect from the imperfect. The only thing that could have caused the idea of the all-perfect is something which is more perfect than that idea of all-perfection. That must be the reality of the all-perfect. Thus

Descartes argued that God really must exist or else we would never have been able to form the idea of God.

These are the sorts of lines that Spinoza and Leibniz followed. In contrast, Karl Barth used the work of Anselm to bolster his own view of the nature of faith. The title of Barth's book expressed his position – *Fides Quaerens Intellectum* (faith seeking understanding). Barth believed that Anselm was not intending to offer a 'proof' for unbelievers. Rather Anselm was expressing how believers come to a rational understanding of God. They begin with a faith in God. They then begin to examine the nature of the God in whom they believe. They are thus led to see that this God is that than which nothing greater can be conceived. From this concept believers see that God necessarily exists. This was not so much a proof, as a clarification of what, in fact, they held already. Barth was insistent that reason cannot bring a person to faith. Reason's role, then, is simply to explicate what faith already holds dear. Barth argued that Anselm was doing just that.

In more recent times the ontological argument has enjoyed a come-back. Norman Malcolm, Charles Hartshorne and Alvin Plantinga have tried, in their own different ways, to express the argument in order to show what Anselm really meant. Their reformulations rest on the idea of necessary being. They argue that there is no ground for rejecting the concept of necessary being as nonsensical. It is not obviously a self-contradictory notion. If there is a God, he must necessarily exist. Otherwise, he would not be God at all.

THE CASE AGAINST

Gaunilo led the attack by querying whether 'God' was any different as a concept from the idea of a perfect island. Anselm replied by stating the uniqueness of the concept of God. This is both the strength and weakness of the argument. If there were lots of necessary beings, then the argument might be easier to accept, but it would ruin the claim to have proved God. For Anselm, God is the only necessary being, thus he is unique. The problem is that God's uniqueness is preserved, but at the price of making what seems to be a special case. What makes it special?

Immanuel Kant and Bertrand Russell have been the two chief protagonists in the debate. Kant first of all picked up the notion that it was self-contradictory to describe God as non-existent. If I describe the subject 'God', can I then reject the predicate 'exists', given the definition of God as *TTWNGCBC*? Kant neatly sidestepped the question by noting that an analytic truth (one true by definition) did imply that if one accepted the subject of a sentence, then one was bound to accept the object and predicate. However, there was no reason to accept the subject and object or predicate together. Kant maintained that it was possible and perfectly correct to reject the whole subject-object and subject-predicate relation that 'God exists'. If this is correct, then Anselm has not proved that there is a God. Rather he has shown that if you accept God as defined, then he necessarily exists according to the definition. This is a very far cry from any proof of an existing reality. In other words, Kant is suggesting that Anselm is not really putting together two different ideas in an argument and moving from an idea or concept to a reality. Instead, Kant surmises that Anselm is presenting a package deal in which the terms 'God' and 'existence' are not really separate, but united in the package 'God necessarily exists'. Kant is arguing that it is possible to reject the package lock, stock and barrel and that Anselm has failed to prove that God really exists from the kind of concept of God we are supposed to share.

The second attack on the 'proof' was even more fundamental. Kant denied that existence is a predicate at all. 'Being' is not a predicate. It is not a concept of something which can be added to the concept of a thing. Existence is not a quality like other qualities. It is not a quality of things at all. This means that Anselm is cheating when he talks about 'God' and then explores what it means to add or subtract 'existence' to and from God. Existence cannot be added to or subtracted from anything. To talk of a thing at all is to talk of it as existing. So to talk of 'God' is to talk of him existing. Anselm's argument is not really an argument at all, for it simply repeats its initial assumption.

Bertrand Russell picked up this notion and drove it home, basing his case on his famous 'theory of descriptions'. He argued that to describe something is quite different from affirming its existence. When we affirm that something exists, we are affirming that there are objects answering to the concept as it is described. To put it in a technical way, the concept is *instantiated*. When I describe a table as mahogany, polished, oval and having four legs, I do not add to that description by saying 'and it also exists'. Existence is not a description of an object. It is not a predicate or quality that things may or may not have. Russell's own famous example is that of the present King of France. If I say that the present King of France is bald,

I am describing a concept or idea which in fact is *not* instantiated, *i.e.* the reality does not exist. There is no present King of France and therefore I cannot say whether or not he is bald. As Kant suggested, it is possible to reject both the subject – the present King of France – and the predicate – baldness (is bald). Indeed it is not only possible, but it is absolutely essential. Here is the force of Russell's critique of Anselm's proof. We must reject the whole thing, according to Russell, for Anselm has confused description with the affirmation of existence. A simple lesson in logic would have avoided that confusion.

WHAT VALUE IS THE ONTOLOGICAL ARGUMENT?

There can be no doubt that the ontological argument fascinates. The idea of the *TTWNGCBC* is both mysterious and yet tantalizing. It seems like such a good definition. It looks so self-evidently true, until we begin to ask what the actual content of such a definition is and where it came from. Is it true that we all have that idea of God? Or is it more accurate to say that there are as many ideas of God as there are people to have the ideas? If we do accept that there is a common concept that we share, it might still be that the concept is the result of prior Christian faith on the part of those who have educated us into the belief.

Does the concept even make sense on its own terms? Has Anselm cheated when he begins with 'that than' or in some versions with 'the being'? This looks suspiciously like the smuggling in of the very thing that he wishes to prove. Even if we proceed with the definition as it stands, we then come to the phrase 'than which nothing greater'. This is set in the negative form. Think of something and it will not be good enough. One may be tempted to say, then, that any idea of God is bound to be a human one and therefore not good enough to do justice to the reality of God. It is the use of the *comparative* in the phrase which is suspicious. To what does 'greater' refer? For a comparative to work there need to be two distinct entities to be compared. Are there really two such entities here? Moreover, what is the force of 'great'? Why need we take that to mean 'perfect'? The whole idea is far from clear.

The final phrase brings us to what seems to many to be the nub of the problem – 'can be conceived'. Is it really possible to move from the concept to the reality? What is the relationship between the content of a concept and the content of the object of which it is the concept? Certainly in no other instance is it usual or possible to move from the idea to the reality. Mental hospital wards are full of people who imagine that it is a possibility.

In reflecting on the relation between 'existence' and the concept of 'greater', I wondered what might happen if we reversed the proof. If I have a concept of a devil who is *that than which nothing worse can be conceived,* following Anselm, I realize that it is worse not to exist than to exist. Therefore, if there is a devil, who does exist, he is *not* that than which nothing worse can be conceived. I can conceive of a worse devil, *i.e.* one who is a devil and does not exist. *Ergo,* there cannot be a devil in reality. This seems to be just as logically correct as the positive version from Anselm; yet we do not feel that it is convincing. Anselm has fastened upon a concept which seems so nearly correct, but yet is not fully satisfying.

The key question is to know what the relation is between conceptual reality and existence. We may simply be creating problems where there are none. We know that there are different ways in which we talk about things as if they were real. We talk about theoretical concepts which are purely abstract. We talk freely about legend, fiction and fairy-tale. These forms of talk sound as if they refer to reality, but we know that there is a basic and crucial difference between what is actually in existence and what we assume in order to make sense of science or to tell a good story. Hobbits, gryphons and electrons have no real existence compared with tables, chairs and Presidents of France. The crunch comes when we are asked to put 'God' in one category or the other. Our immediate response would seem to be, 'It all depends what you believe.' Indeed, to the believer it is obvious that there is a God and that he is the most real thing of all. In contrast, the unbeliever regards this as harmless (or occasionally harmful) superstition. It seems to point back to faith seeking understanding.

There seems little prospect of satisfaction in examining the concept of necessary being, for there are so many different kinds of necessity and it is far from obvious which form is appropriate for the divine. Some, like Tillich, argue that the very fact that man tries to formulate this kind of proof is some intimation of the infinite and the immortal breaking through into our finite and mortal existence. It is less clear that Anselm or his successors have succeeded in bridging the gap from earth to heaven and produced a forceful proof of the reality of God. The ontological argument is not the answer to that problem.

THE FIVE WAYS

Thomas Aquinas was not over-impressed by Anselm's efforts and offered a series of different arguments in his *Summa Theologica*. Aquinas believed that it was possible to prove to someone who did not know God that there was a God. This was done by beginning with an empirical feature of the world. Each of Aquinas' five ways to God begins from the world and moves to try to prove the existence of God. These five ways were to be tools for the missionary as he tried to convert the heathen who did not know God, but did live in the real world.

There is much debate over the five ways. Some hold that they are all simply variations on the one theme and there is thus only one way. Others feel that there are five distinct ways. Still others feel that Aquinas is building up a graded series of proofs until he reaches the strongest one – his fifth way. But who can read Aquinas' mind?

The first three ways are remarkably similar. They all start from known features of the world – motion, causation and being. All of these arguments depend implicitly on Aristotle's view of science. Aquinas argued that we come across something in motion. We then look to see what caused it to move. The thing that moved it was itself in motion. The motion was transferred from the one to the other. We then try to trace back along the line of moved movers which bring other things into motion. This would be an infinite regress unless there were at the very outset something or someone which was itself an *unmoved* mover. If there were no such unmoved mover, there would be nothing in motion. Obviously there are things in motion. Therefore, there must be an unmoved mover. This is what all men call 'God'.

The second way is exactly the same except that, for *motion*, Aquinas substitutes *cause*. He then traces back along the line of caused causes to find the uncaused cause, which is what all men call 'God'.

The third way needs a little more explanation. Aquinas looks at the world and sees contingent beings. (Contingent beings are beings that can exist [be] or can *not* exist [be]. These are beings which come into existence and pass out of existence having a beginning and an end.) Aquinas believed that what comes into existence does so because something, which is already in existence, brings it into existence. Here again, Aquinas follows the infinite regress argument. He concludes that there must have been something which had the power to be without having the power *not to be*. In other words, there needs to be some *necessary being* to be able to call contingent beings into existence. This necessary being *cannot* not be. If there were no such necessary being, there would be no reason for anything to be. Obviously, there are things now, which are not necessary, *i.e.* they can *not* be. These things must ultimately have come from that which *cannot* not be, *i.e.* God himself.

In ways four and five, Thomas Aquinas offers arguments based on degrees of value or goodness, and features of design in the world. He says that we experience things in the world which are noble, true, good and valuable. These things must take their reality from things which are more true, noble, good and valuable. To avoid an infinite regress, there must be something which is the most true, noble, good and valuable. This is what all men call 'God'. Thus Aquinas presents his fourth way.

The fifth way is the famous teleological argument, or way from design. This way sees that things in the world are adapted to a particular end. We can ask what things are for. They are given that purpose or end by the thing or person who designs them. This process of design flows backwards to that which is the source of all design. This is the one who gave the world its initial design and purpose. This is what all men call 'God'.

HUME, KANT AND THE VALIDITY OF THE FIVE WAYS

David Hume, Immanuel Kant and, in modern times, Anthony Kenny have offered detailed critiques of Aquinas' arguments. It is wise to read them carefully. For our purposes, it is helpful to consider the general line of criticism which can be made against the five ways.

Each of the ways involves two distinct strands. Each proof takes as its starting-point the world of phenomenal things, *i.e.* the finite and mortal. It ends up with some statement about the infinite and immortal. There is a move from the finite, moved, caused, contingent to the unlimited, infinite, uncaused, unmoved and necessary. Each of the arguments begins with things that we can experience and grasp. The emphasis is on experience. Yet, somehow or other, we end up at a level of which we have no direct experience. Indeed, some would say that we cannot even grasp the nature of the concepts involved. We have no human experience of the unlimited, infinite, uncaused and necessary. If we did, we would not need an argument which began with other features of the world to convince us of the reality of the divine. Another way of expressing the point at issue is to note that we may begin with such terms as 'cause', 'motion' and 'being' which make perfectly good sense at the level of particular causes, movements or beings. We then find that the use of these concepts is stretched to deal with the cause of all things, the mover of all things, that which makes all things to be, the source of all moral and aesthetic values, and the designer of the whole cosmos. Does it make sense to talk of some totality caused, moved or whatever? Even if it does make sense, can we arrive at that point from the discrete and separate items of our experience?

In short, these last few arguments suggest that Aquinas bridges the gap between this world and God and the immanent and the transcendent in an unfair way. If the last term of each proof is a part of the immanent world, which was the starting-point, then it is not clear that this is of any help whatsoever in understanding the immanent world as a whole. If there is some step *beyond* the immanent, to the level of the transcendent, then there may well be insight as to the point, purpose and nature of the immanent, but there is then no genuine point of contact between the immanent and the transcendent. Aquinas has indulged in a great leap, while appearing to lead us along an intact line.

The second step is to recognize that all his arguments depend on the notion of an infinite regress to lead us to accept the need for an uncaused cause, unmoved mover, *etc.* Aquinas presents us with a dilemma. Either you accept an unmoved mover, uncaused cause, or necessary being, or else you have an infinite regress of movers, causes and beings. But what is the problem with an infinite regress? Aquinas looks as if he is making a logical point rather than an empirical one. He seems to be saying that no matter what cause, motion or being you come up against, it will not stop the infinite regress. This needs empirical proof as it is an empirical question. He never tells us why the regress must be infinite. In fact, there are many explanations of phenomena which we accept, knowing full well that they are not and do not claim to be total and final explanations. We accept *proximate* explanations, recognizing that understanding the next few and last few steps may be the best that we can do in the circumstances. This does not mean that this groundwork is insecure or unreal. It is rather a sober estimate of our own abilities. Is it possible and proper for us to ask for the kind of ultimate explanation, which Aquinas is purporting to offer? Even if we had such a one, would we be able to recognize that we did have it and were entitled to do so?

Many have argued that Aquinas' argument may well have seemed valid at the time of his writing, but that changes and developments in modern science have shown the falsity of his case. This is serious for the followers of Aquinas, who are called Thomists. Aquinas' argument depends on observation of features of the world. If the basis of that observation is different from the basis of Aristotelian physics, then the arguments have changed fundamentally. Nowadays, motion, causation and existence cannot be understood on the model of Aristotle's science. There is no necessity for the mover to be itself in motion. Motion is not passed from thing to thing in the simple, direct way imagined by Aquinas. So too, causes are not always greater than effects, for a small pushing of a button may unleash a nuclear holocaust. David Hume went further in his critique of causation, for he argued that 'cause' is not a feature of things in themselves but rather it is a way we interpret the relationships between things. If Aquinas is presenting a scientific argument, then he is in trouble today. Even if the argument is a metaphysical or purely philosophical one, then the very metaphysics is still derived from Aristotle and must be questionable in light of advances in science and knowledge.

The final step in the argument, where Aquinas comes to God, has been much disputed. At the very best Aquinas has managed to prove only that there is an uncaused cause, unmoved mover, necessary being, source of all value and a perfect designer. He has not shown that they are all the *same* thing. Nor has he proved that these are what all men call 'God', for people's ideas of God are many and varied. The gap between an unmoved mover, a first cause, a necessary being and the God of Christianity seems great. But if we allow Aquinas some success in establishing his case, then it is still doubtful whether this will bring the heathen to a belief in Christianity. In short, we must query whether he is entitled to make that last step in the process of argumentation. Why should there be just *one* such cause, mover, designer or necessary being? Why not a team?

This brings us back full circle to the gap mentioned earlier. The last step takes us from the realm of human experience to a transcendent realm of the infinite. There must remain doubt as to the validity of the leap and the success of the argument. What lies behind these arguments from the cosmos (hence the name *cosmological*) is the notion that the world has some meaning and can be understood. However, there need be no reason to assume that the universe or anything in it has some meaning or even that it can be understood in some final and total way. This is not to call in question the very existence of science, as some have done when such a point is made. Rather it is to offer and accept a realistic view of human ability and of the difficulty of absolute knowledge of temporal things, let alone eternal things.

There are still supporters of the cosmological argument today. They are people such as Eric Mascall, Father Copelston and the neo-Thomists. They have tended to concentrate on the themes of necessity and causality. They have tried to rebut the criticisms of the cosmological arguments, especially of the third way. They have explored the sense of necessary being which belongs to God alone. God cannot not be and he is the only ontologically self-sufficient reality. Everything else is contingent and could be other or different from what it is or even could not exist or be at all. Such finite, temporal reality which comes into being and passes out of being requires some ontological, necessary ground in order to exist at all. Kant's critique of the cosmological argument suggested that it cheated by smuggling in a reliance on the ontological argument. This point may be seen at its strongest in the third way. This criticism drives the modern Thomist back to consider whether or not we can conceive of God's existence in any way. Their response is that, for God, non-existence is impossible.

If this impossibility is a logical impossibility, it would seem to give little detail about the empirical world. This led Thomists to examine the nature of factual necessity, possibility and impossibility. It is argued that we do need some totally satisfactory explanation of everything that is, and that 'God' can be regarded as a necessary and sufficient explanation. To establish 'God' as the ground of causal necessity required the Thomist to show not only that everything has a cause, but also to show good reason that God is not part of the 'everything' which has a cause. Such 'good reason' must be more than a definitional move, if the cosmological argument is to remain genuinely empirical. The Thomist must also show that there is and can be no infinite series of causes, and that no line of overlapping, finite, contingent realities would be sufficient to explain the causal sequence.

There have been two theological responses to the cosmological type of approach. One, favoured by process theologians, is to interpret the world and its relation to God along the lines of the processes of the world and of history. The danger here is of a reduction and rejection of any real transcendence in God in favour of total immanence. 'God' may be seen as 'process' without remainder. The other extreme follows the lines of Don Cupitt and Maurice Wiles, who are critical of reducing God to the level of the immanent and stress the transcendence and otherness of God so as to banish 'God' from the world and any dealings with or dependency from it (see chapter 4). God cannot be God and be involved in the material world. These theologically contrasting views arise from a variety of sources, but all have something to say about the cosmological relation between God and the world. Theologians are far from agreement about God's relationships with the world and what may be built on that relationship.

WILLIAM PALEY AND THE WATCH

The fifth way of Aquinas is a form of what is known as the teleological argument, or argument from design or purpose. Its best-known example has been immortalized by William Paley. He began by examining the human eye. Here was an example of design where each part of the eye played its own part in producing sight. The purpose of the eye was to see. To explain how the various parts are adapted to the end of seeing, we require the postulate of a supernatural designer. Paley pictured a savage on a desert island discovering a watch. The savage has no previous experience of watches. Paley argued that the savage will know that this instrument did not happen by chance, but must be the result of the work of an intelligent mind. The watch implies the maker of the watch, even if you have not seen one before. Indeed, even if the watch does not work, it still reveals itself as the handiwork of a designer. Though there may be parts we do not understand, the watch still points to its maker.

Paley argued that it is the same with the natural world. It is manifestly designed. The order and symmetry of everything, from the human brain to the planets above, deny that they are the products of chance. To suggest that the order in the world or the universe is accidental is like suggesting that the *Oxford English Dictionary* was formed by knocking over a pile of *Scrabble* pieces. Thus there must be a designer and orderer of the universe. This is God.

We have already seen Hume and Kant's critique of this kind of argument. The problems begin with the knowledge that, even if there is an order, it might simply be the way things are and require no explanation beyond the order itself. Moreover, the order might be just our reading into things what we want and need to cope with the world. If we know what humans can make, we may not necessarily know what God can make, for we have no other experience of God at work to be able to recognize his handiwork when we see it. Some have queried the whole model of designed artefact as a way of looking at the world. Perhaps the world or universe is more like a vegetable or organism, which does not require a designer to explain its shape and form. Of course, even if successful, the teleological argument does not show that the designer is the same as the all-loving God of Christianity. Features of design do not tell us the important things about the designer.

There are elements of evil in the world and these count against the idea of a good and loving God, who is responsible for the design of everything. The reality of evil in the world implies either that God is responsible for the evil, in which case God is not good, or else that God is not responsible for evil. In this case there must be some other cause of things (*i.e.* evil) in the world, so God is not the only designer or cause. Evil itself may also call in question the idea of purpose, for evil seems both to deny purpose and to serve no purpose. If there are elements in our world which have no purpose, then there may be no need or possibility of design or for a designer.

It is vital, if we are to respond to these different criticisms, to be clear at which level of design and purpose we are operating. Some concentrate on the evidence of design at the microscopic level, where the adaptation of eyes and ears, flowers and bees and the like are difficult to deny. The problem arises when we try to *explain* that adaptation and design. The second level of design deals with the universe as a whole. It is not so much concerned with the individual as with the universal. Everything is seen as fitting together in a remarkable way as a whole. It is the whole which requires explanation. Again the problem comes when we seek to explain that level of design. To argue that 'God' is the designer of either the micro- or macro-level is one hypothesis, but it is not the only one. The explanation might be chance, the ways things are, or merely a function of the way people interpret the world, rather than something inherent in things themselves. For some, the point of the teleological argument is not so much to offer a final proof. It is rather to demand some understanding of the whole of reality and some explanation for the apparent rationality of the world and the things in it. In this way, teleological arguments point to the answer of the Christian concept of God for their question of the ultimate reason, ground and origin of the world and all that is in it. These arguments are often a useful part of the apologetic armoury and help to raise the issues of the meaning and purpose of life and of the world.

THE MORAL ARGUMENT

The awareness of morality in the world has been held as a proof of the existence of God. There are a number of versions of such a proof. The first suggests that there are objective moral laws in the nature of things. If there are such laws, then there must be a law-giver. This law-giver would need to be above the moral struggle. We experience conscience as the voice of that divine law-giver addressing us directly. We feel responsible, ashamed, guilty and worthy of punishment. These feelings imply one to whom we are responsible, who makes us feel ashamed and guilty, and who decrees that we are to be punished for evil. The cause of these emotions and moral sentiments is not in the visible world. It stems from the supernatural and divine realm of God. The essence of this argument is that we cannot explain morality in purely natural or social terms.

The second argument is the claim that everyone, who recognizes that morality makes overriding claims on a life, is implicitly believing in some basis for this morality, which is beyond the human. This is the God pictured in religion.

Kant offered an account of morality which pointed to the key notions of God, freedom and immortality. It was a 'pointing to', for there could be no proof, as such. Rather God, freedom and immortality were necessary postulates, if morality were to make any real sense. Kant argued that the heart of morality is to do the right thing for its own sake – to do duty for duty's sake. We do not do what is right primarily because good consequences will follow. We do what is right, because it is right. Duty rests on the notion of setting and recognizing laws. The free man recognizes that there are moral imperatives or commands to be obeyed because they are right in themselves. These categorical imperatives demand that I act morally whether I want to or not, regardless of the likely outcome of my action. We are ourselves law-givers in this situation by the exercise of our rational, autonomous human will. These notions of laws and law-giving imply that there is reward and punishment in return for our regard or lack of it for the law. The ideas of reward and punishment imply that there is freedom to choose good or evil. There is no point in blaming people for doing what they did, unless they could have done differently. If we demand that people 'ought' to do something, this implies that they *can* do it. Indeed, it implies also that they are free *not* to do it. Such freedom is basic to the notions of reward and punishment. These ideas, in turn, imply a just desert to be received. Study of the world soon shows that virtue and evil do not always have their proper reward in the here and now. There must be immortality and life beyond the grave which allow time for the rewarding of virtue and the punishment of evil.

In summary, Kant is suggesting that to make any adequate sense of morality, we must assume the existence of God, the reality of freedom, and the necessity of immortality. He is not really claiming that this is an objective proof of God's existence, but instead that only on the basis of these postulates can we make sense of morality. We must postulate the reality of God, of freedom and of immortality.

The problem with the moral proofs of God's existence begin with the presence of so many other explanations and descriptions of morality. Each must be rejected in favour of a view which adds the problems of transcendence and immanence to what looks like an entirely human affair. God is not necessary to explain all morality. These proofs also appear to suggest that morality comes from a divine realm; whereas it may rather be that morality is purely a human tool for keeping social order and varies from place to place and time to time. Economics, biology, psychology or much else may rule human life. Besides, even if the moral proofs and morality itself point in the direction of God, this does not *prove* that God exists or that God has all the characteristics claimed for him in the Christian concept of God.

THE ARGUMENT FROM RELIGIOUS EXPERIENCE

There are as many versions of this 'proof' as there are people and religious experiences. Miracles, answers to prayer, inner mystical experiences of fear, dread, wonder and the numinous are used as a basis to argue for a transcendent cause of those experiences. If I hear the voice of God, there must be a God speaking to me. If I see a heavenly vision, there must be a heavenly realm for me to see. If I pray to God to do something and that something happens, then there must be a God who answers prayer. These lines of argument seem in practice to work well for individual believers. They constitute a proof *for me*. It is less clear that religious experiences constitute proof *for others*.

The Christian may respond that, if there are enough people who have similar sorts of experiences and describe them in the same sorts of way, then that constitutes proof. Such a variety of people in different places and at different times have experienced God, that it is unreasonable to suggest that they are all deluded. Even if there are problems about the universality of such proof, no matter what anyone says in response to this argument, the Christians claim that their own experience is real and that no-one can take that away from them.

However, problems remain. The simple fact that we have an experience does not guarantee the interpretation of that experience. My description may be faulty. Religious experiences are certainly genuinely human experiences, but they may not necessarily be experiences of God. This may also be true of the cumulation of believers' experiences. It would be necessary to prove that they all do have an experience, or that sufficient of them had an experience and that the experience was essentially the same thing. But what does this mean and how could it be tested? Indeed, the objection goes further, for it claims that this kind of argument for God's existence makes the reality of God depend on whether or not we happen to feel something. Either God is simply the projection of our subjective states of mind, or he is dependent on these subjective states. Of course, the easy response to this is that if we had no experience of God, which was not our experience, then we could know nothing of God. There are two senses of 'subjective' at work here again (see p.13). My experience is subjective in the sense that it is my own experience, but it is not thus only based on feelings with no objective basis. However, there are many other psychological and physical explanations for many experiences people have and the testing and verification of religious experiences is extremely difficult.

COMMON CONSENT, SCIENCE AND PROCESS

There are a number of briefer arguments whose essence is very similar. They are as follows:

Common consent
Throughout all the ages of history, people have looked towards heaven and worshipped a God. Such universal presence of worship and belief proves that there must be an object of

worship. God exists. The problem is that everyone may have a belief and practice which is universal, but they could all still be wrong.

Science
Scientific study depends on order and rationality in the nature of things. Unless things fitted together, there could be no science. There is science and things do fit together. That fitting must come from somewhere. So God is necessary for science to happen. This is a variation on the teleological argument and is subject to the same criticisms.

Process
Biology reveals an evolution in the nature of things. This evolution expresses purpose. Everything works towards that purpose. It must have come from somewhere. God gave the world its purpose. Again this is a teleological type of argument and is subject to the response that there may simply be process and purpose in things themselves. There need be nothing beyond the process.

RECENT MOVES IN THE PROOFS OF GOD

In recent times there have been attempts to reformulate some of the traditional arguments, notably the ontological, cosmological and teleological. There has also been a different kind of move. Many philosophers of religion have been moving away from the idea of logical proof, whether of the inductive or deductive forms or the conceptual or empirical type. There are a number of parables which are often presented in the context of explaining what faith is and how we talk about God. In a sense, these may be seen as modern 'proofs' of God, or to be more accurate, what we must do in the place of traditional attempts to prove God's existence. We must tell stories which show the nature and ground of belief in God. The first and trend-setting parable or story was presented by John Wisdom.

Wisdom's garden
John Wisdom offers a parable of two men travelling through a jungle and coming upon a clearing. One remarks that this is a lovely garden and points to the plants, the order and the signs of care for the garden. He knows that there must be a gardener who cares for this garden. His friend, however, is sceptical. There is neither a garden nor a gardener. He points to the

disorder, the weeds, and the similarity of this place to the rest of the jungle. This is just how things grow naturally. There is no gardener. They argue and decide on a test. They will wait for the gardener to appear. They sit and wait, but no gardener comes. The pro-gardener suggests that the gardener is invisible and undetectable by electric wires, radar screens and the like. He believes in the gardener. His friend is totally sceptical and equally certain that there is no gardener.

Wisdom is not seeking to prove the existence or otherwise of God. He is reflecting on the nature of the exercise we engage in when we try to prove or disprove God's existence. He suggests that there are *no matters of fact* which separate the believer from the unbeliever. Both look at the same world and indeed see the same things. The believer can even accept disorder as well as order and the unbeliever order as well as disorder. The difference between the two is in their different interpretations. Thus the question of proof becomes a question of different and competing interpretations and how we decide between them. Wisdom realizes how difficult this is, for our interpretations are not ways of looking at the world which we easily pick up and discard. They are our only ways of interpreting the world, at least while we hold them.

Many felt that Wisdom had made a significant contribution to understanding how we approach the issue of the proof or disproof of God's existence and much else. They were less happy with the picture of a garden and of a gardener, for Christian belief is not about coming across a world, but being in that world and part of it. This line of critique led to alternative pictures.

Mitchell's stranger

Basil Mitchell suggested that a better alternative was a story from the Resistance movement. A partisan meets a stranger in a café. The stranger convinces him that he is in fact the secret leader of the Resistance and is working for the overthrow of the enemy. To do this work, there are times when he must appear to be supporting the enemy and working against the Resistance. In fact, all the time, he is working *for* the Resistance cause. The partisan is convinced and asks the stranger to help. The stranger promises that he will send help when he can, but it will not always be possible and sometimes the requests will be denied.

The partisan returns to his Resistance group, which is sceptical about the stranger. Occasionally the stranger is seen in company with the enemy. The partisan is told this, but explains that this is all part of the stranger's plan. Sometimes, in desperation, the partisan sends to the stranger for help. Sometimes help comes and sometimes it does not.

Mitchell, like Wisdom, recognizes the importance of the interpretative framework. He substitutes for Wisdom's impersonal picture a personal account of belief. On the basis of an original meeting, the believer is convinced because he has entered a personal relationship. That belief recognizes the ambiguity of the world and of the evidence for the divine and his relationship with the world. Nevertheless, the believer continues to believe *because* of a trusting relationship.

This draws closer to the traditional Christian view of God, but it is inadequate in its account of the nature of belief. This kind of 'proof' may suggest a 'one-off' meeting rather than a continuous relationship and stresses the personal element to the exclusion of the community as the basis and reference of faith.

Hare's blik
R. M. Hare offers an account of an Oxford don who believes that all other Oxford dons are trying to poison him. Nothing will be accepted as evidence against his belief. If he takes tea from a don and it is not poisoned, he suggests that this simply proves the subtlety of the dons in their fiendish plot to poison him. He refuses to be lulled into a false sense of security by all the examples of goodness and love which dons might produce. Hare calls this belief a 'blik'. He argues that nothing can count against a blik. Similarly for Christian believers there is nothing that can count against their belief. It is total and absolute.

The problem with such an account is that things *do* count against the Christian view and are recognized as problematic for faith. The parable also fails to give a basis for differentiating a faith that is soundly based from madness or faith with no sound basis.

Hick's road
John Hick moves back a step from such heavy reliance on presuppositional and interpretative frameworks. He believes that there is a proof for God and for the validity of the Christian faith as a whole. This proof he calls 'eschatological verification' (see pp.69f.). Two men are walking down the same road. One believes that this road leads to the celestial city. The other believes that the road goes nowhere. It is just a road. The one

159

points out signposts on the way. The other tells him not to be misled by false hopes. Hick argues that, in the end, when they arrive at the end of the road, there is a proof. There is either a celestial city or there is not. If there is, the believer will be proved right. If there is no city, the unbeliever will have been right. Verification is possible, but only in the *eschaton* (the end).

This seems an attractive suggestion, but there are flaws. The major problem is the sense of 'verification' that is possible in the end and what kind of proof such a 'proof' would be for the here and now. To talk of verification is misleading, for it is only proof, if the believer is correct. If there is a celestial city, life after death, and God, then we shall know it. However, if there is no city, no life after death, and no God, then there will be no-one there to know that there was and is no city. There is and can be no disproof, for there is no-one there to know the falsity of the belief. Besides, even if there were proof there and then, it is hard to see what use such proof is for the here and now. It does not constitute a proof now. It would at best offer the hope of a proof, but not the reality.

THE CUMULATIVE CASE

To complete this Cook's tour of the proofs of God, there is one other line of proof to be considered. It is the *cumulative* case. Such an argument accepts that *no one* proof is successful. However, things are different if you add all the proofs together. They make an overwhelming, cumulative case. Antony Flew makes short work of this suggestion. Ten leaky buckets added together do not make a full bucket, which has no leak. No amount of bad arguments will add up to one good one. The cumulative case may just as easily show how totally wrong people are about God.

CONCLUSION

Our examination of the proofs of God has suggested that there is no one proof or group of proofs that will satisfy the sceptic. This is hardly surprising in light of what was said about faith and reason. This does not mean that the person who seeks to disprove God's existence carries the day. His problems are just as severe. In one sense, it is much easier to pick holes than to state a positive case. This does not mean that there is no point to such 'proofs'. They may help us understand God and ourselves rather better than before. They may serve as guides for proper and improper ways of talking about God and expressing our faith. They may bring us clearly to realize that the essence of Christianity is not proof, but faith. They may show that the existence of God is a possibility without ensuring that it is a reality.

The emphasis on interpretation and presuppositional frameworks pushes us in a positive direction. People *do* change not only their minds, but also their basic beliefs. People are converted from and to Christianity. Why this happens may be a useful insight into faith. That this happens means that there is a role for the presentation and defence of the Christian framework of interpretation. There is also a role for an attack on the presuppositions of other philosophies which in turn attack Christianity. They too are interpretations and such philosophies have presuppositions likewise. The Christian must seek to uncover all presuppositions and clarify all interpretative frameworks, so that the faith adopted by anyone may be seen to be based on proper, legitimate grounds. What we demand from others must be clearly shown in our own case. The proof of the pudding is in the eating. There is a pragmatic test for God's existence in the transformed life of the believer. This does not necessarily prove that God exists beyond all possible doubt, but it does demand that the Christian interpretation be taken seriously by non-Christians. Jesus used miracles as signs of the kingdom of God. These miracles showed that God was at work. The Christian is a sign of God at work. He or she may be a poor, inadequate sign and may fall short of showing *that* and *what* God is, but they may still be a sign for others.

Key words

proof. The process of ascertaining the truth or facts.

God. The Supreme Being; in Anselm's terms 'that than which nothing greater can be conceived'.

ontological argument. Built on Anselm's argument, which seeks to prove the reality of God from the concept or definition of God.

existence/being. What is, and what is in being.

necessity. What is unavoidable or has to be.

contingency. What can or could be different or other than it is. What can *not* be.

idea. Notions, concepts or beliefs as opposed to what is actually in existence.

perfection. Being complete, supreme; excellence.

predication. A description or ascription of something.

cause. What produces an effect,

or the bringing about by agency, power or influence.

quality. A characteristic, or what belongs to something, which helps to make it what it is.

motion. Movement. Used in Aquinas' argument, based on the fact and process of things moving each other.

design. Plan, order or purpose. Used by Aquinas as an argument based on the purpose and end of things in the world.

infinite regress. An endless series or process of interrelated features dependent for their nature or being on the prior feature.

transcendence. Referring to God standing over, against, independent of and above the world.

cosmological. Refers to the argument to prove God's existence based on the idea that the cosmos is not self-explanatory, and requires God as the ground of the explanation.

process. The way or order in which anything happens or is done, often applied to the world or history as a whole.

evil. Wickedness, the opposite of good, that which causes displeasure and pain.

morality. The doctrine and practice of duties and obligations of individuals in society.

religious experience. The feelings, emotions and personal involvement with the object of faith and worship.

stories. The accounts given to explain the nature of something in a lively way.

cumulative proof. The attempt to establish something by adding together various arguments or pieces of evidence.

presuppositions. What we assume or take for granted.

Reading

C. Stephen Evans, *Philosophy of Religion: thinking about faith* (IVP, 1985).

John Hick, *Arguments for the Existence of God* (Macmillan, 1971).

A. J. P. Kenny, *The Five Ways* (Routledge, 1969).

Richard Swinburne, *The Existence of God* (OUP, 1979).

Keith E. Yandell, *Christianity and Philosophy* (IVP, 1984).

12   Talk of God

'Everything that can be said can be said clearly,' said Ludwig
Wittgenstein in his *Tractatus* (1919).

The discussion of religious language in the twentieth century
has been dominated by the empiricist challenge and responses
to it. The empiricist philosophers believe that all language is
divided into two parts – matters of fact and definitions. The
definitions are *a priori* true, and are recognized as true without
reference to experience. Matters of fact are known as true or
false only in light of experience of the real world. They are
known only *a posteriori*. Definitional truths like those of mathematics and logic, it is claimed, tell us nothing about the real
world. In contrast, matters of fact are highly informative. If all
language is to be fitted into one of these two categories, which
is the appropriate slot for religious language?

THE PRINCIPLE OF VERIFIABILITY

To help decide the difficult cases, empiricists designed a simple
test, the *principle of verifiability*. Empiricists saw this as a tool to
get rid of metaphysics rather than primarily an attack on
religion. Metaphysics was seen as idle speculation about the
fundamental nature of reality, as if we could somehow or other
get behind appearances to some esoteric world of absolute
reality. Empiricists believed that there was nothing to be known
in such a metaphysical realm and no way of knowing it. In its

original form, the principle suggested 'a statement is meaningful if and only if we are able to verify it by sense experience'. This meant that whenever one was confronted with a statement, the way to check whether it said anything meaningful or not was to test whether it was an appropriate sense experience. 'Her hat is red' and 'His hearing is going' were easy to check. But 'God is spirit, and those who worship him must worship in spirit and truth' (John 4.24) was problematic. Could this be checked by some test of sight, hearing, sound, taste or smell? None of these seemed appropriate. This implied that the statement was therefore meaningless or else true by definition. The trouble with definitional truths is that they are simply relations of ideas and tell us nothing about reality. Religious believers claim to be saying something which not only has meaning, but is also true. They claim that their statements correspond with reality. The principle of verifiability calls this in question.

It is important to repeat here the difficulties raised for the empiricist principle. It called other statements in question. Ethical, aesthetic, metaphysical as well as religious statements failed to pass the empirical test of meaning. That was not an overwhelming problem, for the empiricist, following David Hume, believed that these kinds of statements were all simply expressions of feeling and taste and not matters of fact. A more serious exclusion was the effective ruling out of descriptions of historical events and the statement of scientific laws. It was not possible to verify by sense-experience *now* that 'Caesar crossed the Rubicon' nor that '*All* water boils at 100°C at normal pressure'. We cannot go back, nor can we cover every possible example of water boiling. Accordingly, these statements are either true by definition, which does not seem to be the case, or else they are meaningless.

This problem of excluding what the empiricist wished to retain was exacerbated by the question of the status of the principle of verifiability itself. Is it as a statement itself meaningful? How could it be verified by sense experience? It seemed that there was no experience which could verify the meaningfulness of the principle, so it was either true by definition (and there seemed no reason to assume that) or it was literally meaningless on its own terms.

In the light of these various criticisms, a slight emendation of the principle was made: 'A statement is meaningful, if and only if we know, *in principle.* how to verify it by sense experience.' This means that it is not necessary to be able to do the sense-experience test immediately. What matters is that we know *what kind of sense-testing* would or should be done and the fact that there *are* such relevant tests. This move saves historical statements and scientific laws from exclusion, though not the principle itself, or ethical, religious, aesthetic and metaphysical language.

One other move to save the thrust of the principle was to stress its role as a principle of falsification. The scientist 'proves' the 'truth' of his or her hypotheses by attempting to falsify the theory put forward. Evidence is presented to try to disprove the view. If no evidence can be found, then it is not a factual matter at all. If sufficient evidence cannot be found *against* a view, then it is accepted as true for the moment. This had the virtue of being more scientific in tone, but was accompanied by a weaker claim to have certain and indisputable knowledge. This claim of certainty is near the heart of the empiricist case.

THE EMPIRICIST CHALLENGE

It must be clear that empiricists are not simply presenting one test for meaning. They are offering a distinctive view of the nature of the world, knowledge and human experience. Empiricism offers a comprehensive framework for interpreting the world in which we live. This starts with a basic view of the central importance of sense-experience. As we have already seen, recent empiricists have centred their attention on the nature of meaning. There are, however, some who have tried to discover some form of basic unit of sense-experience or some mathematical or scientific representation of such a unit. One major suggestion for this unit was that there were 'sense-data', which were the irreducible 'bits' of experience. These are simple units of experience put together by us to make the complexes we call objects. A field of grass is really a blur of green, a fibrous feeling, and a whiff of freshness added together. These units of experience, whether sense-data or not, were pictured by the words and sentences used. Thus, language is meant, in this view, to correspond to reality. Our words are to picture accurately the way things are. We are also concerned to go beyond what something means, to ask whether or not it is true.

Within empiricism this has expression in the correspondence theory of truth and the picture theory of language. The correspondence is supposed to be between language and reality, so that the role of language is to picture reality like a mirror. The radio commentator uses his words to picture the scene he is commentating on to the listeners. The picture is intended to convey reality. How may this correspondence be tested? It was back to the principle of verification. Meaningfulness is established, it was argued, when the words accurately reflect the sense-experience. The major source of unease with the correspondence theory is that one must have a third point at which to stand to observe the language expression and the reality, but it is not clear what the relation of this third point is to either language or reality. Can it be any different from experiencing reality? This point is most clearly seen, when people try to check their experience of a sense-datum. The problem is that if I look again at some object, I will not be checking the original sense-datum, but rather having a new or other sense-datum. Thus, whenever I have a sense-experience, I have a sense-datum, but no way of checking it, either by another experience or by remembering, both of these activities producing yet more sense-data. There is no external point to stand to check on a sense-datum. Nor indeed is there a point from which to 'see' or 'experience' the reality sensed by any other means than sense-data. If all my experiencing is via sense-data, I have no independent access to reality apart from sense-data. There is thus nothing to use to check either the reality or the relation of sense-data to reality.

The picture theory of language was much more subtle than to suggest a one-to-one correspondence. Nevertheless, there must still be some means of checking the relationship between the picture and the thing or reality pictured. A former professor of mine summed up this objection to the empiricist picture theory of language in a neat way. 'You cannot picture *in* a picture, *how* a picture, pictures *what* is pictured.' In other words, you require a third term or point of reference, and so the point of reflection retreats along a line of infinite regress, for each point needs a new point by which to check the relation of the old point to language and reality. The essence of the empiricist complaint against religious language is that the believer cheats. He cheats by using words from one area of life, where their sense is plain, in another realm where the sense is totally unclear. Antony Flew complains about the way believers talk about God in terms of human characteristics, ' . . . that because they are so distinctively personal, they cannot without losing all their original meaning be thus uprooted from their peculiarly human habitat and transferred to a context so totally different. If it has to be that much different and that much more so, it cannot be the same at all.'

Flew recognizes that the believer is not so naive as to use the descriptions on a one-to-one correspondence basis. Rather the terms are qualified. 'God is a father, but not in the physical sense. He is not the shape or size of most fathers. He does not beget children as fathers normally do. He doesn't have a wife.' Flew calls this kind of argument 'the death of a thousand qualifications'. The quality or characteristic is *qualified* to such an extent that it is qualified out of existence. The final description of the quality is so different from the starting-point, that it is no longer the same quality – or even a quality in any normal sense of the word.

The traditional response to this kind of criticism of religious language is the claim that we talk to God by *analogy* with human experience and knowledge. In one sense, this is simply to state the obvious. To talk of anything or anyone is to use human language derived from human experience.

ANALOGY

There are various accounts given of the nature of analogy as it is used in religious language. There are two main types of analogy much used in theological discussion. The first is *analogy of proportionality*. As its name suggests, analogies of proportion are used to state that the attributes of God are in the same way proportional to his nature as the attributes of human beings (and other creatures) are proportional to their nature. The main difficulty with this approach is not so much in the analogy, but in being able to start the analogy. How does one know of the attribute in the first place? This objection may have a response to it. That is to suggest that all language is an expression of prior experience and thus analogy is no worse off than other language forms. The empiricist retort must be that for ordinary experience language problems can be overcome by going back to experience. The empiricist is sceptical as to whether God can be experienced at all, far less talked about. A further problem with analogies of proportion is the necessity to specify exactly the relationship of the two things claimed to be proportional. Obviously, human attributes are not exactly equivalent to divine attributes. The question is, 'How different is different?' In what way are they *like* divine attributes? Do we not need to know this *before* any analogy or proportion will work?

Another form of analogy is that of *attribution*. For this approach to work one required a primary term in the analogy. If one is drawing an analogy between God and man, then there must be some priority. If we are talking of wisdom, then man's wisdom is a reflection of God's wisdom. God's wisdom is thus the primary term in the analogy. However, for this to work, again one needs some prior, direct knowledge of God's wisdom which is *not by analogy*. If one tries to use some other primary term – like creation – then it is difficult to see how this helps us 'arrive' at God. It starts from within the created order and 'stretches' to a point beyond or above that order.

It is clear that the problems of analogy as an appropriate way of talking about God reduce, in the end, to problems over how we know and experience God, and thus are able to talk about God and our experience. Where the analogy method is in danger of breaking down is in the claim that there is a sense in which God is *like* anything human at all. All descriptions of God are seen as attempts to stretch human concepts on the basis of likeness to the level of the transcendent and divine. The question remains whether such an exercise is possible, given the differences between 'God' and all things human.

It is slightly odd that empiricists should lay such stress on all things human when they really mean 'sense-experience'. Herein lies a weakness in the empiricist tradition. The concept of 'human' is not the complex, many-sided description of all that a 'person' denotes to most of us. Rather, in some empiricists, this is interpreted in a neutral, object-like way. This is part of claiming a radical disjunction between matters of fact and matters of taste and feeling. It is not so much that the empiricist denies these feelings and tastes. He refuses to allow that there is any objective basis and certainty to be found in these realms. They are not, in his terms, empirically based. Thus the empiricist is fascinated by some elements and parts of human experience almost to the exclusion of other aspects of personal life, being and, indeed, of the whole human knowledge and experience. The empiricist banishes objectivity, truth and objective meaning from the ethical, aesthetic, moral and religious realms. These are not simply vital parts of human life. They are no more, and no less, areas of uncertainty and doubt than the so-called scientific, empirical areas of life. Subjectivity, if it is a problem, is a problem for all our knowing and experiencing. To limit experience to 'sense-experience' and to set that as the standard by which all else is to be judged, may be readily debated. The trouble with concentrating on individual, discrete parts or details of anything is that one easily loses a sense of the whole.

RELIGIOUS LANGUAGE AS . . .

Some empiricists, while believing that there was no way that religious language could express any matter of fact about the world, still held that there was some purpose in religious language. H. Randall suggested that religious language was a way of expressing emotion and of spurring to action. Braithwaite held that the real purpose of the stories told and language used by believers was to reinforce a particular moral way of life. The purpose of religious language was to inculcate and reinforce a moral way of behaving. Accordingly, to ask whether such language was true or false was beside the point. The real meaning of religious language was to be judged by its moral effect.

These approaches, which stress some ulterior motive and purpose in the use of religious language, are helpful because there are obviously a number of different purposes actually served by religious language. However, to suggest that expressing emotion or reinforcing morality are its *sole* and *main* purposes is to subvert the normal understanding of believers about the function of their language. When they express themselves about the nature of God, they believe that they are describing reality and making, not only meaningful, but also true statements, because the language matches the reality. The essence of religious language cannot be reduced to one purpose which it happens (or even is intended) to serve.

DON'T ASK FOR THE MEANING, ASK FOR THE USE

The very narrowness of this traditional empiricist approach led even some of its exponents to revise their views. Instead of this search for the chimera of meaning based on sense-experience, there arose a stress on examining the actual way in which language was used. The empiricist had reduced the variety of language to a search for reference to some sense-experience. The problem was trying to find some basic element of sense-experience to which all else could be reduced. Furthermore, even if they were to be successful in finding such a basic unit, did the reduction do full justice to the nature of knowledge, humanity and reality? Those who rejected such a narrow view thought that the empiricist search for meaning was looking for fool's gold. Ordinary language was the proper source of study, for meaning was to be found in the context of how language is used. If one wanted to understand the meaning of language, the place to look was in the settings and in the company of the language users. This sounds rather like an exercise in sociology. The philosopher of religion sits and watches (or rather listens to) believers talking and tries to work out what they mean by the way they use the terms. He is not concerned with the truth or falsity of language, but with the way it is used and the functions it performs for those who use it. The main trouble with such a view of language is that it makes language use sound like a spectator sport. We not only use language in contexts, we *live* in those contexts too, for they are part of our lives and of us.

Wittgenstein coined an idea to express what was meant. It was 'language game'. He believed that there were different language games and that the meaning of anything was always relative to the game that was being played. There could be no justification beyond or behind the fact that the game was played. Games were not true or false. If you wanted to discover meaning, then it could be found only in the context of a particular language game. In this way, believers at worship are playing a language game. If you want to understand what it means to say 'The Lord is here', you must look at the structure, setting and rules of that particular worship game.

This last phrase reveals part of the difficulty with the idea of 'language games'. Where does one game end and another begin? Indeed, the very flavour of the word 'game' makes life sound flippant and suggests that we have a choice whether we play or do not play games. In fact, life is not a game, not made up of a series of games, if by 'game' is meant something other than reality. Of course, Wittgenstein was not suggesting flippancy, but rather that rules govern language and language games and that the understanding of these rules cannot be divorced from the ways that these rules are used in practice.

There were, however, attractions about the idea of a game for the believer. Each game was immune from criticism from every other game. Thus the 'religious game' became safe from the attacks of the 'philosophy game'. Sadly, the price of such immunity was removal of any possible absolute and universal claims from religion. The real cost of immunity was fatuity. For the religious believer the making of absolute and universal claims concerning God is not a take-it-or-leave-it matter. It is the very heart of religious belief. The logical conclusion of this kind of view of the nature of language was expressed in W.V.O. Quine's *Ontological Relativity*. This will help us see where such views may lead, if carried through to their extreme.

Quine stated that 'to be is to be the value of a variable'. A story will illustrate. In my study lives Rory. Rory is invisible to everyone except 5' 7" Scotsmen, who have attended University for eight years. Rory teaches me all the philosophy I know. If ever I am asked a philosophical question and do not know the answer, I trundle up to my study and ask Rory. He always gives me the correct answer. Many inquisitive students have tried to capture Rory, but they lack even the qualifications to see him. Some have dared to imply that Rory does not exist. How could I prove that he did exist? I cannot show him to people, unless I can find someone who fits the 'seeing requirements'. I am totally consistent in my talk about Rory and in my behaviour, when asked philosophical questions. As far as I am concerned, Rory exists. What Quine would say is that Rory 'exists' within my universe of discourse. My talking about him as existing gives him existence. He 'is' in the sense that he is part of my life, and part of my way of thinking and speaking of myself and my students. Rory's existence is relative to the world I inhabit and function in and with.

It is not difficult to see how this might apply to religious language. God 'is' in the sense that he 'exists' in the world of the religious believers' thinking, talking and practice. What there is, is a function of what and how we know, and what we say. The danger is that this might seem all that there is to say about God's existence and thus remove any more absolute or universal claim to truth and reality. Both these claims to truth and reality seem implicit in the language and thought of the believer.

THE IMPORTANCE OF RELIGIOUS LANGUAGE

Our language is an important part of what it means to be human. We use language to communicate what matters to us. This basic role that language plays in life in general is interestingly reflected in Christian theology. Theologians talk of the 'Word of God' referring to God speaking and revealing himself through prophets, events, the Bible, and through Jesus Christ. The phrase the 'Word of God' implies a need to hear and respond to what is said. Many would describe the Bible as an account of God speaking to mankind and the responses of people both positive and negative to that revelation. In the coming of Jesus, we see that the Word of God is an incarnate word, expressed in human terms and thus comprehensible by us all. There is no getting away from the fact that Christianity is totally committed to religious language, to talk of God, and to a God who talks and communicates with us.

It is obvious that many people do talk meaningfully about God. This is an expression of what they already know and feel about a reality they have experienced. They are putting into words what has happened and is happening to them. Knowledge of God appears to precede the speaking of him with any full appreciation of what is actually being said. Certainly, there seems to be a close relationship between language about God and knowing God. Indeed, there seems little to be said about God, if he is unknown and unknowable. In this sense, believers are at an advantage in understanding talk of God. There must then be a sympathetic attempt to understand what is actually meant by the believer, if the unbeliever is properly to comment on the truth, validity and meaningfulness of religious language. Such a sympathetic approach must not confine religious language in too narrow a strait-jacket. There are subtleties in all language use and the area of theology is no exception. The meaning and logic of theological utterances need to be examined both for coherence – do they make sense taken as a whole? – and for correspondence – do they reflect reality in some proper way?

THE CONFUSION OF MEANING AND TRUTH

One of the key ways of avoiding the confusion set by the empiricist line of approach is to recognize that meaning and understanding are different from verification and the apprehension of truth. When confronted by a sentence there are two fundamentally different questions to be asked. Does it make sense? Is it true?

The first question is concerned with the intelligibility or the *sense* of the sentence. The second question is concerned with the relationship between the sentence and reality. It deals with the *reference* of the sentence to reality. The empiricist has seriously misled us all by confusing meaning and verification. To ask what something means is very different from asking whether or not it is true. Religious statements do make sense. They are meaningful both to believers and to unbelievers. People understand what is being said. What is in dispute is whether or not the sentences refer to the realities claimed.

THE VARIETY OF LANGUAGE USE

Another weak point in the empiricist attack on religious language is its interpretation of language solely at the level of stating facts and its use of this interpretation as the standard by which to judge the meaningfulness of all language uses. In fact, we use language in a whole variety of ways. We tell stories, give commands, express emotions and intentions. We describe, prescribe and perform things in and through our language use. Any proper attempt to understand religious languages must be sensitive to the whole gamut of linguistic tools and skills.

We do not use the language of personal relationships in the realm of the physical sciences. Likewise, we should be hesitant in using linguistic criteria from some other aspect of life in the religious realm. We cannot expect other criteria necessarily to work in a different setting. There are many internal criteria which can be fully grasped only by those within the religious setting. James Stewart, a famous Scottish preacher, made this point forcefully in describing the difference between the believer and the unbeliever. He used the picture of the stained glass windows of a cathedral. To the outsider, the glass is dirty, smudged and pigeon-spattered. To the believer inside, as the light streams through the windows, the true pattern and splendour are revealed. To grasp the truth and meaning of religious utterances properly, you need to be inside the religious realm. The view from the outside is always distorted. Certainly, it is the believers themselves, in the context of the religious community, who act as their own checks and balances, allowing what may and may not be said. The community has always exercised a role of judgment over what may properly and appropriately be expressed and what must be rejected. This is not to reduce Christianity simply to a way of looking at things. Its claim is that it is a more adequate way of looking, because it matches up to reality. To test that claim both the reality and the language must be experienced and understood.

In essence, it is not only too narrow a view of language that the empiricist tries to force on us all. It is also too narrow a view of experience. Existentialism and phenomenology have begun to correct that imbalance by their emphasis on alternative ways of looking at and expressing reality. This reinforces what many know already from their experiences of art, music and drama. One of the joys of approaching an impressionist painting is that we can see it not only from different angles, but also at different distances and with different levels of attention to the details of colour and the brush strokes. We are able to describe these experiences and say what is proper talk about them. Any full description of our experience will cover all those kinds of detail, as well as our emotional, artistic, aesthetic and critical judgments. There are many different levels and aspects of 'looking' at a painting and justice must be done to them all.

The experiences stressed by the existentialists may lead to moments of revelation, insight and disclosure of something previously not grasped and not articulated. Religious experiences and the language used to express them offer such moments of revelation, insight and disclosure which require sensitive appreciation and sympathetic entering into experiences. Words are often simply pointers towards the reality of these experiences. The psalmist, contemplating man's existence beside the glory of the heavens and the mighty power of God, put into words an experience we can share and enter into. This is something far more than a simple recital of certain words.

KNOWING MORE THAN WE CAN SAY

The user of religious language never claims that his language has totally captured, far less exhausted, the religious reality he has experienced. Reality is more than we can say and know. The reality of God is greater than our capacity to express it in words. We may know more than we can say. This is not some kind of special pleading. Rather it is a common feature of life. The pianist may be able to play a tune in perfect harmony, but be unable to express that skill in words. Indeed, if he or she tried to break down the movements into individual notes and phrases, the skill might evaporate. The skilful rugby player may make a perfect move, but be totally unable to explain in words how he knew what to do. Words fail all too often.

There is an element of mystery in the religious realm. We would expect nothing else, given the conditions of sight of the believer. He or she sees 'in a mirror dimly'. He or she knows only in part. What is known is a transcendent God, who is known in the context of this world and its limiting conditions. This is why we need to develop symbolic ways of talking about God and his reality. We need to create and use models which disclose something of the reality we are talking about. Such models and symbols are tools to help us to see new meaning beyond what we presently understand. Indeed, in this respect modern science does what religion has always done through parable and story. Science constructs models and symbols to assist in understanding reality at all its levels and in all its forms. The task of the believer and theologian is the same. It is to create models and to express through symbols the reality beyond and behind mere words. It is to do this in such a way as to encourage those who have not experienced this reality to do so for themselves.

Key words

matters of definition. What is true simply by virtue of the meaning of the term.

matters of fact. What is the case discovered by experience of the world and reality.

verifiability. Able to be tested for truth.

meaning. The sense and import of words and sentences. What is intended to be conveyed, understood or signified, usually by actions or language.

truth. What is the case in contrast to falsity or mere opinion.

falsification. The process of seeking to refute or disprove, often as a way of reaching certainty.

correspondence theory. The view that statements are true when they correspond to the world.

picture theory. The notion that language operates by giving us a 'picture' of reality.

language and reality. The relationship between what we say and what there is, especially how we are to describe what is there.

analogy. An agreement of likeness between things which helps us understand the one thing by reference to the other.

language as use. The view that language is to be studied in terms of how we use it, and how it functions in a society or group.

language game. A way of resolving conceptual problems into differences between the ways people use language in particular contexts called 'games'.

disclosure. An uncovering, or revealing.

Reading

I. G. Barbour, *Myths, Models and Paradigms* (SCM Press, 1974).

Selwyn Bevan, *Symbolism and Belief* (Collins, 1962).

F. Ferre, *Language, Logic and God* (Greenwood Press, 1977).

I. T. Ramsey, *Religious Language: models and mystery* (SCM Press, 1973).

Keith E. Yandell, *Christianity and Philosophy* (IVP, 1984).

13   The heart has its reasons: religious experience

The ambiguity of religious experience – Explanations of religious experience – Seeing as – The verification of religious experience – The challenge of religious experience

We live in an age where the heart seems more influential than the head. Religious people describe their faith more in terms of what they feel and experience than in tightly logical or rational terms. When people are drawn into Christianity, it seems that emotion plays as large a part as reason. Indeed the force of the empiricist attack on religion is that religion is purely a matter of emotion and nothing else. To see the faces of believers in the setting of worship is to see a sense of genuine feeling and involvement on their part. None of this is surprising. Emotion is part of what makes us fully human. The realm of feeling separates humanity from the world of machines or inert reality.

If religion is about the fundamentals of the reality of a personal God, who deals with the totality of human life, then the experiential content of Christianity is crucial and expected. It is, however, a small step from this to an apologetic and evangelism which emphasize the necessity of a particular religious experience and may seek to create a setting and atmosphere where such experiences are likely to occur. Such a false emphasis on emotion must not obscure the essential place of feelings in religion. Nor must such an emphasis blind us to the variety of reactions to the emotional in life. Some are fascinated by such experience and drawn to seek it for themselves. Others are appalled by the 'emotionalism' of it all, and dismiss the whole of religion as nothing more than emotional claptrap. Both these views suggest a faulty understanding of the relationship between what we feel and what we think.

THE AMBIGUITY OF RELIGIOUS EXPERIENCE

There is no doubt that people have what they regard as religious experiences. What is more difficult is the variety of experiences which come under the heading of 'religious experience'. Dreams, visions, ecstatic utterances, silent contemplation, and much more, fall into the category of religious experience. This variety might be a reflection of the way the phrase is used. However, there is a genuine ambiguity not least in relation to the terms used to describe religious experiences as well as the claims made about them. There are a number of competing theories about the essence of such religious experience.

For Friedrich Schleiermacher, genuine religious experience was a feeling of absolute dependence. It was an awareness of helplessness before the divine. It was typified for him by the pattern of meeting God recorded in the Old Testament, where the person involved falls on his face before God and believes that he will die. For Rudolf Otto, as we have seen in chapter 2, religious experience is the realm of the numinous, the *mysterium tremendum*, the *fascinans* and the sense of creatureliness. For William Temple and John Hick the essence of religious experience is the total experience of religious people. It is the way in which religious people respond to and interpret reality and human existence. For them the religious interpretation is not one set of experiences, but rather a way of regarding the world. For Martin Buber and H. H. Farmer, personal encounter expressed in the 'I-Thou' encounter is the heart of religious experience. We meet a personal God in a direct experience of another, who calls us in question and into a relationship. For Ninian Smart, with his interest in religions in general, it is some reference to a transcendent state of being which is marked by prophetic and contemplative experience. These experiences point away from themselves and this world to a higher realm of otherness.

It is all too easy to read such accounts as totally diverse descriptions. However, there are certain common threads and features which may be identified. There is obviously some clear distinction between religious experience and other realms of experience, such as the moral and aesthetic. At the very least, this is the case because 'religious' experience occurs in the setting of, or in relation to, a set of religious ideas, concepts, practices and realities with some kind of reference to a religious community. If a stronger claim is made for the difference of religious experience from other experiences, it is usually along the lines of the uniqueness of the object of religious experience, *i.e.* God, in the Christian setting. Religious experience is thus held to be *sui generis* unique. It is like nothing else and can be understood only on its own terms. In this light, religious experience is a kind of *intuition*, which is self-authenticating. You know one when you have had one. You cannot be mistaken about having such an experience, for it is a direct knowing. However, before such a retreat to absolute uniqueness, there are other facets of religious experience which are generally accepted and agreed.

We may analyse religious experience into both objective and subjective elements. The two elements in the experience may be referred to as what is experienced, and my experience of what is experienced. The object of experience is what causes the experience. Herein lies a difficulty. The critic of religious experience claims that the cause is the subject, who has the experience, or else some other object, but *not* a religious reality. As far as the unbeliever is concerned, there is no religious reality, so religious experience must have some other cause and explanation. In claiming that religious experience is entirely subjective, there is usually some account given of the emotional state, psychological condition, gullibility and the like of the believer. We shall consider this further under the heading of 'explanation' below. The religious person rejects all such reductions of religious experience to the merely subjective. Naturally, there is, and must be, recognition of an essential subjective aspect not only to religious experience, but to every experience. Such a subjective aspect is what makes my experience both *mine* and *experience.* This in no way detracts from the possibility of some objective basis for it. The problem is how we may be sure that there is some object there to be experienced, apart from the experience of the object itself. When I look at a blue book, how do I know that there is really a blue object there? Obviously, my subjective experience is of a blue book, but I might be wrong. Note how the method of doubt begins to be applied. So often the sceptical attack on Christianity and theology rests on the application of the method of doubt. Some may feel impatient with such doubt, especially when it is applied to experiences of blue books. But if we take the doubt seriously, we recognize that no amount of looking again will guarantee that there really is a blue book. All these looks might be entirely subjective experiences. In the end, the blueness of the book seems to be given an objective basis, showing that the blueness is independent of my seeing it only by a general acceptance on the part of others that the book is blue. Such an acceptance on the part of the 'community which comes in contact with that blue book' rests ultimately, if the sceptic pushes his doubt all the way, on a scientific measurement under specifiable conditions in terms of light.

The sceptic concerning religious reality immediately seizes upon the gap between the solution of doubt about blueness and any possible solution of doubt concerning the reality of the religious object. God cannot be tested in the same way. The believer's response must be that God cannot, of course, be checked in the same way as physical reality. No-one should expect the same check. It is possible to go further than this in defence, however. There may be a parallel to the 'community which comes in contact with the blue book' in the 'community which comes in contact with God'. Any argument about such a community only claiming a contact may be matched by the reflection that the same claim element holds for the 'blue book community'.

The crux of the problem of the objective basis for religious experience is now seen to be a question of what fundamental 'scientific' basis may be offered as an account of religious reality. Such an account depends on what is meant by 'science' and the presuppositions which make any science or area of knowledge a study worthy of that name. We have already discussed this in detail in chapter 9, but what is crucial here is to see that there is no essential difference between the scientific and religious enterprises in their need to give some persuasive account of their objective basis. How they show that objective basis need not be the same, but that they must give some adequate account, is clear.

The problem over the subjective-objective content of religious experience is highlighted by the claim that some contact is made with a transcendent level of reality. Part of what makes religious experience 'religious' is the reference to, and involvement with, an aspect of the divine, the 'other', the 'holy', or the transcendent. This 'religious' element is something more than the material and physical; it refers to a spiritual reality. This transcends or goes beyond purely human experience, that is, experience which is based and formed purely by human features. The kind of reality to which transcendence refers is impossible to encapsulate or conceptualize in terms of immanent reality (reality in terms of the here and now alone). This causes doubt as to the very possibility of expressing anything at all about that reality. If religion is to do with the inexpressible, then the hope for a rational account of religion is slim. It is important that the inexpressibility of religion is carefully stated. Simply put, it means that as far as religion is concerned not everything can be said about it. This is very far from suggesting that nothing can be said. There is no need for embarrassment about stating that we cannot say everything about the inexpressible. If we really meant total inexpressibility, we would be reduced to silence. Somewhere in between the two extremes of total silence and total explanation is the realm of the numinous and mysterious which we examined in chapter 2.

The question of the rationality of religious experience remains a proper area for reflection. When Isaiah saw the Lord, high and lifted up, he was still able to use words to express that reality. The early chapters of Ezekiel express a more flexible attempt to encapsulate the reality of religious experience by the use of metaphor and picture. It is the use of such metaphorical and pictorial language which then comes under attack with reference to religious experience. Those, like Martin Buber, who claim that the best way to describe the essence of religious experience is in terms of personal encounter between the I and Thou, are criticized. This description, it is argued, rests on the analogy of meeting people. We all know what it is to meet a person. What is less clear is that meeting God is in any sense parallel to meeting a person. The gap in the analogy means that talk of personal encounter with God must be carefully treated.

There are two elements to this unease over talk of a personal encounter. One is over the personal nature of God and the other is over the objective reality of God in any sense. That God is a person must be established and justified by more than simple reference to religious experiences. When the 'God is dead' movement captured the headlines in the United States of America, Billy Graham, the evangelist, was asked to comment. His reply was, 'No. He is not. I talked to him this morning.' Such a response, however, is not the only basis for asserting the reality of a personal God. Personal experience is certainly relevant, but must be coupled with an account and description of the object of religious experience which is coherent, makes sense and corresponds with a reality which may be tested in other ways than by oneself and one's own experience. Some rational account must be given of the content of religious experience. The difficulty is that the content of the experience may be too indefinite to give a clear and overwhelming knowledge of the God of Christianity.

Religious experiences then are claimed to have both subjective and objective elements, and to refer to some transcendent reality. To substantiate this claim they need to be associated with some wider description of the basis of religious experience than the terms of the religious experience itself. To make the attempt to give such an account involves examining the explanation and verification of religious experience.

EXPLANATIONS OF RELIGIOUS EXPERIENCE

There is no shortage of attempts to explain the essence of religious experience. Believer and sceptic alike offer some account of religious experience. There is a *natural* explanation in terms of some aspect of nature and physical reality. The believer and unbeliever may look at a sunset. The one sees the brushstrokes of the divine. The other sees, at worst, particles of matter in motion or light refracted through pollution, or at best, the glory of the natural world. The believer might call his experience a 'religious' one. The unbeliever's response is to explain the experience *totally* in neutral terms. There is *only* what both have seen and nothing more. In this way, religious experience is reduced to some other level of explanation.

A more subtle explanation, both of religious experience and the different accounts offered by religious and non-religious people of their own experience, is to concentrate on the expectations people bring to experience and the presuppositions at work, both in having an experience, and equally in the way it is related. In this way, religious experiences are explained by some psychological state or attitude which marks off believers from unbelievers. This may be seen not simply as some psychological 'problem state', but as a result of tradition, education, upbringing or indoctrination. On the day of Pentecost, the Jerusalem crowd were amazed to hear uneducated men preach the gospel in a variety of languages matching the diversity of scattered Judaism. Some offered the explanation that the men were drunk. The disciples had a different account to offer of their strange experience. They turned to the prophet Joel, who said, 'And in the last days it shall be, God declares, that I will pour out my Spirit upon all flesh, and your sons and your daughters shall prophesy, and your young men shall see visions, and your old men shall dream dreams . . .' (Acts 2:17). The movement of God's Spirit is the ground of the explanation, but it is expressed in relation to prophecy and teaching which were familiar to the audience. There is a continuity with the past, which Peter was building on, when he addressed the crowd to explain what was happening.

This makes it clear that there are at least two different things which may come under the heading of 'psychological' explanations. The first emphasizes a weakness, suggestibility, or influenced state on the part of the believer. If they were in their right minds, they would not say what they said or experience what they experienced. Behind this account is the notion that Christianity is a kind of drug taken by gullible people who induce belief in others or have it induced in themselves because of some need or inadequacy. Any experiences they claim to have may be explained in terms of their needs, usually expressed in particular psychological states, or in the way these needs are met.

The other level of explanation, which is confused with the negative psychological sense of the last paragraph, is an account which suggests that people experience what they expect or want to experience. Interpretation depends on our presuppositions. Thus the sunset observed by the believer is interpreted as the handiwork of God. The same sunset observed by an unbeliever is interpreted as a sunset with as much or as little aesthetic overtone as that particular person brings to the experience. In other words, religious experience is a matter of subjective taste and depends on your presuppositional framework. As has already been suggested, this stress on subjectivity is a truism inasmuch as it says that for an experience to be my experience, I must feel something and experience it for myself. However, this attempt to reduce religious experience to the purely subjective fails to do justice to the complex nature of religious experience in both its subjective *and* objective elements.

This reductionism must be treated with great respect and examined carefully. The reduction rests not so much on the application of philosophical method to religious experience, but rather from the setting up of a standard from some other philosophy or ideology. Thus there are two clear elements in reductionism. There is the proposal of a particular standard and the evidence for that standard in terms of a philosophy of life. Secondly there is the reduction of alternative accounts by the application of the standard. This is how the Marxist, Freudian and many sociological accounts of religion operate. They argue for a Marxist or Freudian philosophy and then seek to explain religion in terms of and in the light of the new standards of that philosophy. The believer must query whether such an application of such standards is justifiable. He must ask both whether the Marxist or the Freudian account is correct in itself, as well as doubting whether such accounts can properly be used to dismiss Christianity. The believer must uncover the presuppositional framework and test its adequacy or otherwise. These presuppositional beliefs and bases must be made clear. Then a choice must be made between the different presuppositions by making comparisons to test adequacy and truth. The Christian may quite happily accept that religious experiences meet the psychological needs of people, without accepting that they *only* meet needs and are purely a function of psychological needs. The objective basis must be clarified if the believer is to escape the reduction. The unbeliever offers a natural account and demands to know why it is essential to add a supernatural level. The believer must show that the reduced explanation fails to do justice to the reality of the religious experience.

SEEING AS

Some religious believers seem to accept the reduction and to make a case based on it. John Hick tries to explain religious experience in terms of 'seeing as'. When Moses led the Israelites across the Red Sea, or fed the people with quails in the wilderness, what really happened? According to Hick's approach, what happened in the first instance was that a low tide created a channel and a high tide wiped out the Egyptians. In the second instance, migrating quails which fly over the Sinai peninsula fell with exhaustion, as they sometimes do. In both examples, a purely naturalistic explanation has been given, which accurately describes part of the event. But Hick goes on to say that this naturalistic view does not adequately describe what it meant for the threatened Israelites to experience these natural phenomena. The Israelites *saw* these natural events *as* God providing for their needs in response to their requests. The religious believer experiences events, which have some naturalistic basis, but sees these events in relation to the divine. The significance of the events, according to Hick, is in their timing and relation to a set of religious beliefs. Thus all of life is interpreted in relation to the divine. Individual experiences are characterized as *seeing as* from the divine perspective.

In one sense, this is the very opposite of reduction. It claims that experience is a function of a whole package of presuppositions and beliefs. You buy the whole package and not one part of it. To understand each part, you must put it in the context of the whole. There is much truth in this, as long as it is not used to escape from the necessity of producing some account of objective reality. To say that God painted the sunset is not simply a picturesque way of talking. It is a claim for a certain pattern of relationship between the transcendent Lord of creation and the world he has made. The evidence for such claims must be presented and substantiated. Christianity is not simply *one* way of seeing reality. For the Christian it is *the* true and accurate account of the nature of reality as a whole.

This necessity for evidence and explanation makes the task of justifying religious experience extremely difficult, especially if the experience is claimed to be totally ineffable and inexpressible. Justification cannot be totally beyond our knowledge, meaning, verification and evidence. What is beyond words and telling cannot be communicated, far less judged and justified. Thus the revelation of the divine must disclose something objective which may be understood, tested and reacted to in terms of humanity and its experience.

THE VERIFICATION OF RELIGIOUS EXPERIENCE

The main search for a justification of religious experience has concentrated on the question of verification. Is it possible to test whether there has been a genuine experience of God? The empiricist argues that claims for religious experience fail the test of empirical reality, for they are not susceptible to sense experience. This seems like a classic case of reductionism. Unless religious experience reduces to the empiricist's terms, it will be rejected. If it does, then it ceases to be religious in any real sense. If the believer seeks to reject such a sense experience test, then it is essential that some other kind of testing is described, if the claim to 'truth' of any kind is to be taken seriously. The tests for the genuineness of a religious experience might take the following form. There might be a test in terms of *cause*. Was the origin and basis of the experience some divine object? The problem with this test is how the divine object can be known except by experience. Thus, one experience or set of experiences is used to judge and safeguard the validity of another experience. This is similar to the 'blue book' example, though the question of the possibility of some more ultimate, scientific description of the divine object still remains.

The second kind of test might be one based on the *internal features* of the experience. There might be some kind of checklist of features, such as feelings of awe, being overwhelmed, words failing, happy glows and the like, which, taken together, characterize an experience as religious or not. This is fine for the person who regularly has religious experiences, but for the outsider it is no help at all. How could one be sure one has had a real experience, if one does not know the genuine feeling from the bogus?

One popular test suggested as a verification of religious experience is the *difference* the experience makes. Religious experiences should show religious results in the life and behaviour of the believer. This is undoubtedly true, but will not serve as the uniquely descriptive basis for validity. These results may have been caused by other things. They might have happened anyway, without the religious experience. Moreover, even if no results followed, the experience itself might still have been real, but other things have prevented the proper consequences. If we are to avoid the trap of seeking a verification of religious experience in terms foreign to the reality of religion, we must examine the kinds and levels of tests which the Christian community itself uses. Not every claim to religious experience is accepted by the community. Criteria are used. Verification is appropriate. Sometimes it is proper to reject the reductionist's demand for justification on the grounds that he or she has no right to ask for justification or that the terms and standards of justification required are unfair and inadequate to the reality of religious experience. To escape from the reductionist demand is not, however, to be absolved from all verification.

From the days when the people of God passed judgment on the truth or falsity of a prophet, religious communities have conducted some kind of test for the validity of religious experiences. Such experiences within the Christian community must *'fit'* with its history and tradition. They must be tested by and grounded in Scripture. True religious experiences of God are in keeping with the character of God. The consequences and results flowing from such experiences must also be in keeping with the nature of God. For the Christian community, the threat comes from religious experience with a demonic rather than a divine cause. The fruits of such experience in word and deed are proof enough of their origin.

What is being suggested is that the only kind of meaningful verification of religious experience occurs in the context of the religious community with reference to the totality of that community's world-view and life. After allowance for the variation between individuals and cultures, and the possibility of innovation, has been made, the essence of verification is a 'fit' with Christian teaching and life. These themselves, like true religious experience, accord or 'fit' with the divine. There is thus not only an internal coherence in the religious experience and the account given of it, but there is also an external correspondence between the experience and the character and nature of the God who is experienced.

THE CHALLENGE OF RELIGIOUS EXPERIENCE

There are many religions and many different religious experiences. Some have attempted to draw parallels between different religions and the religious experiences within these religious traditions, seeking some common core of 'religious experience'. If the last section is correct, then such a task is of no help in the verification of religious experiences, for it overlooks that which gives the uniqueness to an experience. It rejects not only each specific religion's description of their divine origin and basis, but also the normative role played by the religious community and its tradition, scripture and life-style. Behind the search for some such essence of 'religious experience' is a desire to use that essence as some kind of proof of the reality of the divine.

This attempt to use religious experience as a proof of God's existence has also characterized some Christian apologetics. It seems, however, logically impossible to infer God's existence from the mere fact that people have religious experiences. One classic danger here is of a kind of proof by numbers, where the number of believers having an experience is supposed to validate the reality of what is experienced. The majority is not always right and may not be of much help in judging the truth or falsity of Christianity.

The biblical writers did not seek to use religious experiences as a proof of anything. They simply described them. Religious experiences comforted people and challenged them. The biblical writers were unafraid to use metaphors and pictures. In Genesis, God walks in the garden and talks with man. Personal encounter is a natural parallel. The experience of God is also often set in historical terms. 'In the year that King Uzziah died I saw the Lord . . .' (Isaiah 6:1). There is no total loss of sense and no dislocation with reality. Yet often the experience of God is an experience of 'otherness' and 'holiness' creating fear, dread and awe. Men such as Isaiah, Gideon and Job expected that they would die, for they had seen God. Often these religious experiences are marked, too, by the transformation they bring. Perhaps they mark the start of a prophet's career, a change of direction in life, or a facing up to the reality of personal sin in new self-knowledge. The biblical writers are also unashamed to proclaim the ultimate mystery in religious experience. For them, religious experience is not ineffable, neither is it so unique that no parallels may be drawn with other human experiences. Nevertheless, there is an element of eye not having seen, ear not having heard, of seeing through a dim glass, of the not yet, still to be fully grasped and revealed.

Religious experience is not the same as the description of religious experience. It is better 'felt' than 'telt', as the Scottish proverb puts it. Yet there is a rationality and objectivity connected with it. Religious experience is an expression of what is fundamental for the believer and forms part of the presuppositional framework by which the religious life is lived. The major problem is the avoidance of the apophaticism of silence and inexpressibility. It is also the avoidance of the nonsense of expressing what cannot be reduced to words alone or else reducing to a false simplicity what can be adequately characterized only on its own terms.

Key words

experience. Knowledge acquired through the senses or through what we feel.

feeling. Physical sensation or mental perception.

emotionalism. The cultivation of superficial emotions. The tendency to yield to or exalt feelings.

absolute dependence. A total and unconditional reliance for everything on something or someone (usually God).

numinous. The felt presence of the divine. The feelings of the worshipper in the presence of God.

personal encounter. The meeting directly of individuals who are genuinely persons.

transcendence. Referring to God standing over against, independent of, and above the world.

religious community. The society and group in which a religion is practised and judged.

uniqueness. Unparalleled or the only one of its kind.

intuition. A clear and distinct perception by the mind. A direct act of knowing that something is true, *e.g.* when 'the penny drops'.

subjective. (a) A judgment belonging to an individual person. (b) A purely personal opinion or attitude.

objective. That which belongs to or comes from the object known. What is really the case regardless of personal interpretation.

inexpressibility. Unable to be put into words or concepts.

metaphor. A figure of speech referring to a resemblance things have to each other. A picturesque way of referring to things.

explanation. A making plain or intelligible.

reductionism. An approach to issues and problems which tries to make the complicated seem simple by reducing it to the key themes or points.

interpretation. A way of understanding or looking at reality.

seeing as. To perceive the world in a particular way and to interpret things in the light of that.

verification. Proof or confirmation.

proof of God. The attempt to establish the truth and reality of God's existence and nature.

Reading

Archibald Alexander, *Thoughts on Religious Experience* (Banner of Truth, 1968).

P. Donovan, *Interpreting Religious Experience* (Sheldon Press, 1979).

J. Edwards, *The Religious Affections* (Yale University Press, 1959).

H. D. Lewis, *Our Experience of God* (Collins, 1970).

Keith E. Yandell, *Christianity and Philosophy* (IVP, 1984).

14 Philosophy – so what's the point?

*Philosophy rules OK? – Rationalism: reason first – Introducing Fred
– Descartes and the idea of God – Empiricism: experience first –
Ideas and sensations – The search for meaning – A third way? –
Descriptive metaphysics – Summary*

For many Christians, a verse from Colossians is the beginning
and ending of their dealings with philosophy. 'See to it that no
one makes a prey of you by philosophy and empty deceit . . .'
(Colossians 2:8). Sadly they fail to read the qualification which
is integral to Paul's point. 'See to it that no one makes a prey
of you by philosophy and empty deceit, according to human
traditions, according to the elemental spirits of the universe,
and *not according to Christ*' (my italics). It is not the love of
wisdom which is the problem for the Christian, but rather some
particular philosophies and what lies behind them. Nevertheless, in a real sense, Paul's struggle with the various philosophies at Colossae has often been repeated through the ages.
What had Jerusalem and its Jewish religion to do with Athens
and Greek philosophy?

Much of the New Testament has come to us because of the
challenge of particular philosophies to the early church's
mission and understanding of truth. The truth 'made manifest
to the saints' (Colossians 1:26) was delivered because of
dialogue, controversy and struggle with philosophies inimical
to the essence of Christianity. It has been the same throughout
church history, for the church defined what was believed and
taught against the background of the ideas and philosophies of
the surrounding age and civilization.

These kinds of philosophical challenges are quite easily recognized and dealt with. There is, however, a more subtle effect
which philosophy may have on religion. In seeking to combat

a particular philosophy the theologian needs tools. Sometimes these tools have been derived from alternative philosophies which may not only have been not Christian but have actually run counter to biblical Christianity. It is easy for us to see in reading Augustine and Aquinas the strong influences of Plato, Aristotle and their followers. It was not so easy for Aquinas and Augustine to realize that influence, or the long-term impact that it would have on Christianity, evangelism and apologetics.

Many centuries later, when the church struggled with the philosophy of Darwinism, it was hard for the church to realize its own dependence on other views of science and reality – philosophies which were nothing to do with Christianity itself, but were the product of scientific study before the nineteenth century. The same kind of thing is true today as Christianity confronts or engages in dialogue with the philosophies of Marxism and existentialism. The framework of reference used by the Christian is all too often the product of the secular world and its education than a biblically based or 'Christian' philosophy, if such be possible.

If you have followed the argument so far, you will have begun to realize that the word 'philosophy' is ambiguous. It may refer to particular ideologies or philosophies. It may also refer to all the processes of reasoning and thinking by those who propound individual ideologies and philosophies. In this sense, philosophy is concerned with the logical presentation, examination and criticism of ideas. I believe it is possible to distinguish between particular philosophies and philosophical method in general. Philosophies such as Marxism and Christianity offer a specific framework of thought, belief and usually some recipe for action. In contrast, philosophical method is the way of approaching these systems of thought using rational and logical methods. It is this latter sense which has been important for our study and which brings us to the crucial question of what relationship there is or should be between philosophy (philosophical method) and theology.

PHILOSOPHY RULES OK?

For modern men and women the answer is very simple. Philosophy is the standard by which theology is to be judged. By this is meant not simply the use of a particular philosophy as the criterion of judgment, but that certain standards of reason, logic and truth must be used as yardsticks by which religion stands or falls. For some people, as we have seen, sense experience is the test that should be applied to everything as the standard of meaning, truth and reasonableness. According to their view this means that whenever anyone says anything, we ought to ask, 'Can I check this out by reference to a particular sense-experience?' What cannot be checked or tested by sense-experience is meaningless, has no truth value and does not fall under the control of reason. When you try to put this test into action, however, you find that certain statements run into trouble. Statements about what we feel, believe, and give moral approbation to do not obviously have a cash value in sense-experience. If we support the philosophy which applies such a test, then we are left saying that statements about feelings, religion and morality are not about reality or truth. They are just expressions of what is going on inside us or of our deep-felt needs.

This modern view is the exact opposite of the traditional approach of Christianity in which theology ruled philosophy. The two disciplines were seen to go hand in hand, but theology set the agenda which philosophy had to follow. Philosophy's job was to provide ways of thinking, arguing and communicating, which enabled the church to know what she believed and the world to understand the gospel the church proclaimed. Philosophy was a means of arriving at better theology, mission, apologetics and evangelism. The break between the traditional and modern views of philosophy's relation to theology occurred with the rise of modern philosophy. That rise may be summed up in the development of two particular philosophies – rationalism and empiricism.

RATIONALISM: REASON FIRST

The history of rationalism goes back to Plato and before, but its modern life began with René Descartes. A gentleman soldier, taught by the Jesuits, he travelled Europe fighting, as well as writing in the fields of mathematics, physics, mechanics, optics and philosophy. He was dissatisfied with the current state of knowledge in his studies, for there was doubt in every discipline. So Descartes decided to set aside all he knew and to try to build up his knowledge on a new basis. Descartes was trying to discover whether there was any one thing which he knew beyond all possible doubt. Were there any truths which could not be doubted? Was it possible to be absolutely certain about anything? The French philosopher applied a set of tests to all the things that previously he had assumed to be true. In this process of casting doubt on all accepted wisdom, he followed four rules:

1. *Accept only what is self-evident* (by this he meant what is plain and obvious to every reasonable person).
2. *Divide the problems into as many parts as possible and necessary.*
3. *Move from the simple to the difficult and complex.*
4. *Make sure of complete enumerations and general reviews.*

Descartes' aim in following these rules, and indeed in embarking on the whole enterprise, was to arrive at certainty. To reach certainty, Descartes used the method of doubt. He was, however, no sceptic seeking doubt for doubt's sake. The sceptic tries to destroy knowledge by using doubt. Descartes used doubt as a tool to arrive at certainty. It was doubt for certainty's sake. When a couple are considering how to spend an evening out together, they make up their minds by eliminating some of the possibilities. The hope is that by casting doubt on some of those possibilities they will eventually arrive at the one way of spending the evening about which they both agree and over which there is no doubt. This is in fact the way that science proceeds. When a scientist propounds a theory, he or she supports it by trying to *disprove* it. It is not always possible to produce positive proof, so instead he or she seeks to show that there is nothing to count against the theory. This is done by trying to make things count against it and examining all the contrary evidence. If, at the end of that procedure, the theory is still intact, then it is accepted as true. To put it bluntly, you have proved it until further notice.

Descartes began to apply his method of doubt by asking what were the sources of knowledge which people took for granted. He argued that what we know came from three different sources: from the experts, from the senses and from reason. He examined each one in turn. When he looked at what experts said was the case, he saw that they contradicted each other. We can still see what Descartes was getting at today. If we ask the experts how the world began, some will tell us that it all began with a 'big bang'. Others argue that a gentle process led to its evolution. Still others stress that God created it. The experts disagree and contradict each other. Descartes did not examine whether these disagreements were genuinely as serious as they appeared to be. His point was simply that if we look for absolute certainty in the direction of the experts, we shall be disappointed, for they contradict each other. The problem is compounded for us, for, not being experts ourselves, we do not know which expert is correct and which one is wrong. Thus Descartes arrived at the conclusion that there was no certain knowledge from the experts which was beyond all possible doubt.

Descartes next turned to the senses and presented various examples of what seem to be illusions. If I look at a statue from nearby, it seems large. If I look at the same statue from a distance, it seems small. It cannot be both, so my senses disagree with each other. This must mean that at some point my senses are deceiving me. Descartes also looked at towers which seem round from nearby and square from a distance and vice versa. He examined the case of parallel lines (like an avenue of trees, or a straight road), which from nearby seem to be clearly apart, but looked at in the distance seem to come to a point of intersection. He also noted what is called the 'phantom limb' phenomenon. If someone has a limb amputated, then he or she still describes pain taking place in the limb which has been amputated, even though there is nothing there to 'have' the pain.

Our response to the first of these arguments is that Descartes has forgotten about perspective. However, the point that he is trying to make is simply that, if we rely on the senses alone without reflection and consideration, focusing only on the very moment of sensation, then our senses may not be relied upon. In other words, our senses deceive us. Descartes then examined the particular moment of sensation and found that there is nothing in or about the sensation itself that tells us that this particular sensation is reliable and another sensation is unreliable. Sensations do not come with handy labels of 'true' or 'false'. They simply occur. If Descartes could find no difference in the sensations alone from the occasions when his senses deceived him and those occasions when his senses did not deceive him, it was *possible* that he might be deceived all the time, or at least deceived when he thought he was not and vice versa.

It is vital to note that Descartes was not saying that we *are* actually deceived all the time, but rather that we *might* be deceived all the time. Descartes' search was for knowledge which could be known with no possible doubt. For him, sense-experience provided only knowledge where doubt was still possible. Thus it did not provide certain knowledge. To reinforce his point, Descartes used the argument of dreams. He suggested that, when we dream, the sensations we experience in the dream are indistinguishable at the time from the sensations we experience while awake. He is arguing that from the sensations alone we can have no certainty about whether we are awake or dreaming. According to Descartes, it is therefore possible that we are always dreaming. Descartes believed that he had shown that no reliance could be placed on knowledge gained from the senses. It was always possible to doubt the information they supplied. In this way Descartes dismissed the experts and the senses as sources of certain knowledge. This left the knowledge which comes from reason.

INTRODUCING FRED

Descartes suggested that there might be a wicked demon who affected the knowledge we gained from using our reason. In my lectures I call the demon 'Fred'. In this age of unemployment, I suggest that Fred is fortunate in having two jobs. The first is to make sure that we always get things wrong. If we are asked to do a sum in our heads or to think of a capital of a country, then Fred makes sure we get the wrong answer. He affects all that we think in an unseen and undetected way. The result is that whatever I think and whenever I use my reasoning powers Fred makes sure I arrive at the wrong answer. But that is only part of his job. Descartes goes further and suggests that the demon also makes sure that we think we have got the right answer. Again undetected, Fred acts upon us in such a way that we assume we have got the correct answer by reason, but in fact have reached the wrong conclusion, thanks to his initial interference. We can make the most of Descartes' point by replying as most folk would: 'What nonsense! Of course there is no such thing as a wicked demon doing such awful things.' This only reveals the subtlety of Fred (and of Descartes), for when we use our reason to arrive at the conclusion that there is no wicked demon, we arrive at the conclusion Fred would have led us to if he did exist. When we protest that we do indeed know absolutely that there is no wicked demon, then Descartes is entitled to reply that the certainty is itself the work of the demon who not only makes me get things wrong, but also makes me think that I have got them right.

Descartes is indulging in a 'what if' exercise. What if there were such a demon, how would it affect the knowledge gained from reason and by thinking? It would mean that we could never be one hundred per cent sure of any process of reasoning. When we thought we had arrived at an answer, it would be wrong, but we would think it correct. Descartes' point is that we could never be sure whether or not there was such a wicked demon. Accordingly, the knowledge gained from reason is not beyond all *possible* doubt. This is nothing to do with actual doubt, but is rather an exercise in establishing what, if anything, is beyond all possible doubt.

Descartes viewed this application of the method of doubt to the experts, the senses and reason, as sources of certainty as a necessary demolition job. Having established the negative side, he then turned to the positive. In light of the loss of apparent certainty, was there anything left which was beyond all possible doubt? Descartes believed that two things were absolutely certain. These were the existence of the self (*Cogito ergo sum* – I think, therefore I am) and the existence of God. Descartes used a variety of approaches to substantiate these points. I shall paraphrase some of the lines of thought he used to try to show the kind of way that he argued and the results.

If I say 'I think, therefore I am', then that judgment is a product of thought and reason. The direct challenge to all thoughts and reason comes from the wicked demon. I must therefore ask whether I am deceived when I think and therefore exist. Let us try to express how the deception might work. 'I do not think, therefore I am.' Or else it might be, 'I do not think, therefore I am not.' Or perhaps it is, 'I think, therefore I am not.' Or again, 'I am deceived that I think, therefore I am.' Descartes suggested that, regardless of whether all my thoughts were wrong, or even if I were to be deceived all the time, then I who thought (even if I thought wrongly), or I who was deceived, must still be something. What then am I? I am a thinking thing, even if all my thoughts are wrong and deceived. This means that, as often as I think, I have existence as a thinking thing, regardless of anything the wicked demon may do. He may deceive me as to *what* I think, but he cannot deceive me about the *fact that* I think. Here, for Descartes, was bedrock certainty, which was beyond all possible doubt: 'I think, therefore I am.'

DESCARTES AND THE IDEA OF GOD

The problem was that an individual was alone on this view and had existence only as often as he thought. Descartes therefore looked to see if there was any other absolute certainty. He believed that this certainty could be found in the statement 'God exists'. Descartes tried to prove that God existed by different variations of the same argument (see chapter 11). To allow his argument to work he needed to assume the validity of Aristotelian physics. In a nutshell, Aristotle's physics centred on the theme that the cause is always greater than the effect. You cannot get a greater thing from a lesser. Descartes then looked for the cause of the idea of the all-perfect God. He believed that everyone had the idea of God. Even the atheist knew exactly what it was that he or she did not believe in and that was the idea of an all-perfect God.

Descartes asked what caused this idea of an all-perfect God. He argued that it could not come from ourselves, from our parents or from our society, for we are all imperfect creatures. Our imperfections are all too obvious when we consider how easily we are deceived by the wicked demon, by sense-experience and what the experts tell us. Being imperfect, we could not *cause* the idea of the all-perfect, remembering that the cause must be greater than the effect. In the end, Descartes believed that the only thing great enough to cause the idea of the all-perfect was the reality of the all-perfect. The only thing better than the idea of all-perfection is all-perfection itself. If the all-perfect did not exist, we could have no *idea* of the all-perfect at all.

It seems obvious that Descartes himself was not totally convinced by this line of argument, for he produced another argument to prove God's existence. It was that God's existence is a necessary part of what it means to be God. If God did not exist, he would not be God. To be genuinely all-perfect must mean to exist or else there would be an imperfection or lack of something good, *i.e.* that of existing. Descartes was suggesting, following Anselm and his ontological argument (an argument which argues from a concept or idea to a reality), that God's existence was a necessary existence. God had to be. God could not *not* be. God has to exist, or else he is not God.

Descartes believed that it was possible to prove that God existed. This, however, still left the problem of the attack on the value of all thinking by the wicked demon. If God and the wicked demon were to have a battle, it was obvious that God must win. If he did not win, then he would not be all-powerful and all-perfect. In other words, he would not be God. This meant that the wicked demon could never get the better of God. So the wicked demon was totally ineffective against God. Thus God ensured that, when we think 'God exists', we get the correct answer. Descartes believed the the proposition 'God exists' was absolutely certain.

Descartes had now, in his mind, two pillars of certainty to become the basis of knowledge. The certainty of 'I think, therefore I am' and of 'God exists' helped Descartes to furnish the universe with knowledge from other sources. Because God was good, he would not allow us to be deceived all the time, so he prevented us from being totally deceived in our senses, or by the wicked demon, or when we looked to the experts for help. God's goodness was the guarantee of knowledge, for he could not make anything which was totally bad or wrong all the time.

Descartes' emphasis was on the power of reason. He is the modern father of rationalism, which stresses this power and makes it the standard by which all else is to be judged. Inevitably this meant that theology and religion would be tested by the standard of reason. Rationalism meant that the search for a true religion must be conducted within the limits of reason alone.

EMPIRICISM: EXPERIENCE FIRST

In contrast to, and often seen as a reaction to rationalism, with its emphasis on reason, came the renewal of empiricism. This philosophy had roots going back to the ancient Greeks, but John Locke, Bishop Berkeley and David Hume were the modern fathers of empiricist philosophy. They all stressed that the senses rather than reason provide us with certain knowledge. They argued that the basis of all knowledge came from experience. To make their case they tended to make two separate lists. One was a list of the nature of the relation of ideas. The other was a list of the nature of matters of fact.

Relation of ideas	*Matters of fact*
belong to the realm of logic and mathematics	belong to ordinary sense-experience
are necessary truths	are contingent truths
are true by definition	are known only by experience
are *a priori*	are *a posteriori*

Reason was the realm of the relation of ideas. It could produce only truths of logic. If I tell you that all bachelors are unmarried men, it does not tell you anything you did not know already. It is simply true by definition. Such truths are not really part of the real world. We assumed their truth before we started out on the process of argumentation. Literally they were known *a priori* – before we commenced we accepted them as true. These

197

truths were necessarily true and could not be false, without anyone who tried to suggest their falsity falling into a contradiction. Sadly, the empiricists argued, these kinds of truths tell us nothing about the world as it stands. They may be true, but they are unhelpful.

In contrast stand matters of fact. Experience – and by that the empiricist meant sense-experience – produced matters of fact. These facts were genuine facts which were discovered in the having, and by the having, of sense-experiences. They were *a posteriori*. People knew that they were the case only after the event, after the experience. They did not know before they started what answer the senses would provide. The facts which were known in this way were contingent facts. They could be different. There was no necessary reason why they were as they were. In this way, knowledge was always subject to the need for sense-experience. That experience was used to check out what was said and claimed on the basis of sense-experience.

IDEAS AND SENSATIONS

Empiricists recognized that common sense revealed that we have ideas and concepts as well as sense-experiences. But from where did these ideas and concepts arise? The empiricists answered that the basis of ideas was either having sensations, or reflecting on them, or the relation of ideas (*i.e.* simply definitions telling us nothing new or real). David Hume expressed it by distinguishing between impressions and ideas. Impressions were the actual content of the mind in the moment of perceiving. They were lively and vivid. Ideas were less vivid and were the result of imagination. Hume then divided up ideas into the simple and the complex. The simple idea was a copy of the corresponding impression. Complex ideas were amalgams of simple ideas and could therefore be analysed into simple ideas and then back to impressions. These impressions were the basis and foundation of all useful knowledge. This meant for Hume that there was nothing in the mind which was not previously in the senses. The basis behind all ideas was sense-experience.

The advantage of this kind of view was that it gave a unified account of all the knowledge we have. More importantly, it also gave an answer to the sceptic. The empiricist argued that we gain certainty not by the use of reason, but rather by sense-experience. This has led modern empiricists to push the search for certainty even further back by trying to isolate a basic unity of sense-experience. The favoured unit has been the 'sense-datum'. There is a flash of blue and red across the sky. The onlookers gasp, 'Is it a bird? Is it a 'plane? No, it's Superman!' The raw unit of what is experienced here is a reddish-blue blur. The empiricist argues that we cannot be mistaken about this basic unit. It is in adding levels of interpretation that error is liable to arise. If we get back to the essential core, then we may have absolute certainty.

This kind of philosophical approach does, however, produce problems. Hume, for example, found it difficult to justify the existence of things like 'the self' or the 'external world'. These were simply defined as bundles of impressions and ideas, without it being clear what constituted a 'bundle', how many impressions were needed to make a 'bundle', or what kind of 'glue' held the various 'bundles' together.

THE SEARCH FOR MEANING

Recent empiricists have been far less concerned with the actual material of knowledge, and much more with the basis of knowledge. Their interest has focused on a search for meaning. For some, meaning was to be found in ostensive definition. This consists of giving a name or term to something, together with a way of pointing at the object so that no other understanding of the meaning is possible. They felt that this was the way that we learn languages. I point to a dog and say to the French class, 'Le chien.' It is clear that the general concern behind this approach is to find some basic ground for certainty. Sense-experience is still seen as the ultimate basis of knowledge.

The practical effect of empiricist philosophy on theology and religion may be seen in the development of the principle of verifiability. In an attempt to grapple with the relationship between meaning and sense-experience a group of like-minded empiricist philosophers (called the Vienna Circle because they centred on Vienna University) created the principle as a test of truth and meaning. There have been important shifts in the expression of the principle itself, as may be seen from a careful reading of A. J. Ayer's revised edition of his work *Language, Truth and Logic* which brought the ideas to Britain. He began in his original edition with a baldly stated version. The principle of verifiability states that 'a statement is meaningful if and only if I can verify it by sense-experience'. This test for meaning is directly related to sense-experience. If I say that a ball is red, then it is possible to test the meaningfulness of the statement by sense-experience. Because I can verify it by sense-experience it is accordingly a meaningful statement. If, however, I suggest that 'time is relative' and then try to verify that statement by sense-experience, I soon discover that none of my senses will help me. Thus the statement is meaningless according to the empiricist. Likewise, if the poet writes, 'Beauty is truth, truth beauty', then this is meaningless, for it cannot be tested by sense-experience. The category of statements rejected by the principle of verifiability grew to include metaphysical statements, such as 'time is relative', and aesthetic, moral and religious claims and judgments. However, the principle's power of exclusion did not stop there, for it also excluded statements like scientific laws, historical statements, and even the very statement of the principle of verifiability itself. This meant that, according to the principle, the principle itself was meaningless!

It became necessary to adapt the principle. The simplest way was to qualify the original form. 'A statement is meaningful if, and only if, *I know in principle* how to verify it by sense-experience.' Others felt that this was simply trying to save a lost cause and a more radical change was required. Karl Popper suggested that instead of verifiability we should rather seek a principle of falsifiability. In other words, following Descartes, we should try to disprove what is stated by reference to sense-experience. A meaningful statement thus is one which we know can be overthrown by a particular set of sense-experiences. Knowing what would count against the statement means that it has meaning as long as what counts against it is based in sense-experience.

None of the reformulations were without problem, but nevertheless their challenge to metaphysics, morality, aesthetics and theology remains. This standard of sense-experience is still being applied by many philosophers as a test of meaning. These philosophers argue that if theological language cannot be grounded in matters of fact and sense-experience, then it is literally meaningless.

Together, the double forces of rationalism and empiricism and their consequences have reversed the traditional roles of philosophy and theology. Once the master, theology is now seen as the slave and victim of philosophy and subject to any and every test philosophy may produce. But need this be so?

A THIRD WAY?

There is an alternative both to theology's mastery of philosophy and philosophy's mastery of theology. This depends on us regarding philosophy as a methodological tool. Philosophy, in this sense, has the task of clarifying concepts. Its task is the analysis of meaning and the content of utterances. Thus it would have the job of analysing the content of theology and of theological utterances. The aim behind this would be to clarify the inherent logic, meaning and standards of sense, truth and reasonableness used in theology itself.

This concentration on the actual usage of theological language requires an understanding of, and a sympathy with, the community in which theology is practised. This is no different from an understanding of mathematics or science. In Euclidean geometry, the basic theorems and propositions of Euclid are assumed as given and true. Only then is it possible to apply these principles to particular problems and to scrutinize the process. In the realm of a specific scientific enterprise, like medicine for example, there is a community of practioners who accept certain given standards of procedure, method and proof, both in diagnosis and prescriptive care. These standards make the practice of medicine possible. Naturally, these standards may come up for scrutiny. Such scrutiny depends, however, on some serious inadequacy in the standards and also the availability of some better alternative set of standards to replace the questioned set. Likewise the assumptions of theology are normally counted as given and accepted as true. Nevertheless, it is always possible to reflect on how the practice and theory of theology match up to what is given. It is possible to raise questions about the given, basic criteria, but only where those criteria are deeply inadequate and some alternative framework of approach is present.

The way in which we are using the word 'philosophy' is as a means of reflection on theology itself on theology's own terms. We are not using the word to include alternative sets of 'philosophies' which might threaten, challenge or support theology. The aim of my book has been only to try to show this adopted sense of 'philosophy' at work. Our task has been to clarify the theological concept. At times, we have had to identify a particular philosophy where it attempts to challenge or support theology. Then we have described the content of that philosophical position.

You can see now that if we ask, 'What is the relationship

between philosophy and theology?' the response must be, 'It all depends on what you mean by philosophy.' The relationship between Christian theology and different philosophies may be instructive, but making these comparisons is not the same kind of activity as clarifying the concepts of Christian theology. This involves clarifying the basic data of theology, the methods and concepts used, and the community in which theology lives, functions and is pursued. It means trying to grasp the relationship between understanding and belief, faith and reason.

DESCRIPTIVE METAPHYSICS

For many philosophers and theologians the picture of faith and reason will not go far enough. They would argue that philosophy and theology cannot escape the task of 'telling it like it is'. Both are in the business of truth and seeking to point to reality. Thus they must try to show the way the world is and what it is. For the Christian this must be the point where philosophy and theology meet and conceptual clarification cannot be enough. The reality of God and his creation, his sustaining, redeeming and sovereign work in and of the world must be described accurately and as completely as possible.

Inevitably we shall have done a little of this in the book.

SUMMARY

Our aim has been to overcome fear by showing how we think about faith by asking questions, and by suggesting some kinds of responses to these questions. Some people will complain that there are not enough, or even that there are no answers given. Their task is to use what has been given to construct their answers to the specific questions they and other people ask. Philosophy is for us all. Thinking properly about faith is every Christian's responsibility. It is not an optional extra. If we believe that all truth is God's truth, and that he made us in his image with minds which can think through the nature of reality, we have nothing to fear from using that capacity to glorify God. Loving God is always loving him with our minds, as well as with everything else. So think, for God's sake.

Key words

philosophy. Literally the love of or search for wisdom. The academic discipline which tries to understand and explain everything.

reason. The human mind

operating to explain and think through things.

experience. Knowledge acquired through the senses or through what we feel.

doubt. To question or hold as questionable. May be used as a way of establishing certainty.

ideas. The notions, thoughts, opinions which the mind forms.

meaning. The sense and import of words and sentences. What is intended to be conveyed, understood or signified, usually by actions or language.

Reading

Colin Brown, *Philosophy and the Christian Faith* (Tyndale Press, 1969).

C. Stephen Evans, *Philosophy of Religion: thinking about faith* (IVP, 1985).

H. D. Lewis, *The Philosophy of Religion* (English Universities Press, 1965).

T. H. McPherson, *Philosophy of Religious Belief* (Hutchinson, 1974).

Keith E. Yandell, *Christianity and Philosophy* (IVP, 1984).

A whistle-stop who's who

Abraham (? 20th cent. BC). The traditional father of the Jewish nation, who was called to offer Isaac his son as a sacrifice. Abraham also prayed that God would spare the city of Sodom, if ten righteous people were to be found there.

Achilles (*c.* 136 BC). A famous Greek warrior used as an example by Zeno of Elea to show that a swift runner may still never overtake a slow tortoise. This is one of the well-known paradoxes of Zeno.

Adam. The first man in the Bible (Genesis 1 – 3).

Anselm (*c.* 1033–1109). A medieval philosopher who became Archbishop of Canterbury. He formulated the ontological argument using the idea that God is 'that than which nothing greater can be conceived'. His general approach to belief is that faith precedes understanding and that faith seeks to understand.

Aquinas (*c.* 1225–74). A medieval philosopher and theologian who developed a bridge between the philosophy of Aristotle and the Christian faith. He presented the famous 'five ways', which are attempts to prove the existence of God.

Archimedes (*c.* 287–212 BC). A Greek scientist famed for discovering scientific laws in the bath. He was a leading mathematician, who developed ideas on levers in mechanics.

Aristotle (384–322 BC). A Greek philosopher who was a student of Plato and became tutor to Alexander the Great. He wrote extensively on every kind of philosophy, blending an understanding of the sciences with reflection about science. His theories on causation, motion, being, value and order underlie many of the traditional proofs of God.

Augustine (354–430). A Bishop of Hippo, who wrote extensively on doctrine, free will, and the church-state relationships. He developed a distinctive approach to the problem of evil and to the notion of free will.

Austin, J. L. (1911–60). An English philosopher who focused on the importance of the language in dealing with philosophical questions. He lays particular stress on the use of 'performatives' in language, where we use words to enact something, *e.g.* 'I promise', 'I now pronounce you man and wife', 'I name this ship . . .'. He emphasizes the role of common sense and ordinary language.

Ayer, A. J. (1910–). A leading exponent of the philosophy of logical positivism or empiricism. He is highly critical of religious concepts and language, based on his support of the principle of verification, and a view of sense-experience which tries to reduce reality to sense-data.

Bamborough, Renford (1921–). Analytical philosopher with an interest in questions of meaning, truth, reality and metaphysics.

Barth, Karl (1886–1968). A Swiss Reformed theologian well known for his work on dogmatic theology. He stresses the difference between God and humanity, and the role of grace giving knowledge of God. He is sceptical of the value of rational and natural theology to lead to knowing God.

Berkeley, George (1685–1753). Irish bishop and philosopher whose work on vision led to an empiricist stress in knowledge. His famous view is that 'to be is to be perceived'.

Braithwaite, R. B. (1900–). An English philosopher of science who applies his work to ethics. He regards the task or function of religious language as to encourage and reinforce certain patterns of moral behaviour.

Buber, Martin (1878–1965). A Jewish philosopher who stresses the role of dialogue in proper relationships between man and man, and God and man. This is expressed in 'I-Thou' rather than 'I-It' relationships.

Bultmann, Rudolf (1884–1971). A German Protestant theologian who follows an existentialist approach to theology. His New Testament work emphasizes the need to 'demythologize' the Bible to read the central message of salvation in the gospel.

Burke, Edmund (1729–97). A statesman and philosophical writer who supported a conservative view of society and tradition against revolution, especially in the form of the French Revolution.

Caesar, Julius (*c.* 102–44 BC). Famous Roman general, turned historian, who conquered much of Europe and threatened to become Emperor. He was assassinated.

Chevalier, Maurice (1888–1972). A French actor and singer.

Christ Jesus (*c.* 4 BC – *c.* AD 33). One of the many titles given to Jesus, God incarnate, Son of God, Son of man, the Messiah.

Copelston, F. C. (1907–). A Jesuit philosopher and theologian who writes in the realm of the history of ideas.

Copernicus, Nicolaus (1473–1543). Polish astronomer who designed the heliocentric theory of the solar system, *i.e.* that the sun, not the earth, is the centre of the solar system.

Cupitt, Don (1934–). A Cambridge philosopher of religion who is highly critical of traditional orthodox Christianity and its concepts of God, Jesus Christ and faith.

Darwin, Charles (1809–82). An English scientist and naturalist who dealt with the origin of species by means of his theory of natural selection. He became involved in a great debate over evolution with leading churchmen of the day.

Descartes, René (1596–1650). A French philosopher who stressed the rationalist approach to philosophy. He uses the method of doubt to reach certainty and finds this in the argument 'I think, therefore I am', and for the existence of God.

Dives. The rich man in the parable (Luke 16:19–31) who ignored the needs of the poor man Lazarus.

Einstein, Albert (1879–1955). A famous theoretical physicist who developed the general theory of relativity.

Elijah (9th cent. BC). An Old Testament prophet well known for his struggle with Ahab and the prophets of Baal.

Euclid (3rd cent. BC). A Greek mathematician notable for a system of geometry which proves theorems on the basis of given definitions and axioms.

Ezekiel (6th cent. BC). An Old Testament prophet famous for his vision of a valley of dry bones.

Farmer, H. H. (1892–). An English theologian and philosopher who has written extensively on religion and revelation.

Flew, A. G. N. (1923–). An English philosopher particularly critical of religion and the notion of God.

Freud, Sigmund (1865–1939). An Austrian psychologist who founded psychoanalysis; he was highly critical of the role of religion, regarding it as an illusion and repressive in its effects.

Galileo (1564–1642). An Italian astronomer and natural philosopher who came into conflict with the church over the heliocentric view of the solar system.

Gaunilo (11th cent.). A Benedictine scholar who argued against Anselm's ontological argument. He wrote 'on behalf of the fool', using the example of a perfect island.

Gideon (12th cent. BC). One of the judges who ruled Israel and rescued her from the Midianites.

Graham, William F. (1918–). A leading American evangelist who has preached to more people than anyone else in history.

Hare, R. M. (1919–). An English moral philosopher who supports the view that morality is about prescribing moral rules for oneself and for others. He developed the idea of 'blik' as an expression of the way that the religious believer interprets the world.

Hartshorne, C. (1897–). An American philosopher who is concerned with the relationship between God and nature and our understandings of reality, and of the ontological argument. He is in the process school of philosophy and theology.

Heraclitus (*c.* 540–475 BC). A Greek philosopher who held that everything was in a state of flux and change. He attacked popular religion.

Hick, John H. (1922–). An English philosopher of religion, now resident in the USA, who has been increasingly critical of traditional Christianity. He has produced major works on the problem of evil, the ontological argument, and life after death.

Homer (? 8th cent. BC). An ancient Greek poet, supposedly the author of the *Iliad* and the *Odyssey*.

Hume, David (1711–76). A Scottish philosopher of the empiricist school, who wrote in a sceptical way, covering morals, religion and metaphysics.

Irenaeus (*c.* 125–202). A Christian bishop who attacked Gnosticism. He develops an approach to the problem of evil by interpreting the fall as a means of growth and development.

Isaac (19th cent. BC). Son of Abraham who was to be offered as a sacrifice by his father (Genesis 22).

Isaiah (8th cent. BC). An Old Testament prophet who came from the kingly line.

Jeremiah (7th cent. BC). An Old Testament prophet often associated with gloom and despair.

Jesus Christ. See Christ.

Job. A key figure in Middle Eastern tales, who endures innocent suffering and seeks to discover why the good suffer.

Joel (8th cent. BC). An Old Testament prophet. One of his prophecies is fulfilled on the Day of Pentecost.

John, Saint (1st cent. AD). The author of the fourth Gospel.

John of the Cross (1542–92). A Spanish mystic in the Carmelite tradition who emphasized the experience of separation, aloneness and despair as the dark night of the soul. This experience was from God and led to a deeper awareness of God.

John the Baptist (*c.* 4 BC – *c.* AD 29). The cousin of Jesus, who prepared the way for Jesus' coming and baptized him in the Jordan (John 1:19–34).

Julian of Norwich (1342–1416). A British mystic, who focused on the sufferings of Christ on the cross.

Kant, Immanuel (1724–1804). A German philosopher whose work in metaphysics, morals, aesthetics and religion has transformed the face of European philosophy. His critical work may be seen as a bridge between rationalism and empiricism. He criticizes traditional proofs of God's existence and uses a form of moral argument to postulate God's existence as part of his understanding of religion within the bounds of reason alone.

Kazantzakis, Nikos (1885–1957). A Greek novelist who wrote *Zorba the Greek, Christ Recrucified* and *The Last Temptation*, among other books.

Keats, John (1795–1821). An English poet.

Kenny, A. J. P. (1931–). The Master of Balliol College, Oxford, who writes extensively in the philosophy of religion and metaphysics. He has moved from a traditional Roman Catholic view to a more agnostic stance. One of his key early works was on the 'five ways' of Thomas Aquinas.

Kierkegaard, Søren (1813–55). A Danish philosopher and theologian who wrote following an existentialist approach. He emphasized personal religion and was highly critical of institutional religion. He is often associated with the idea of a leap of faith by which people come to experience true Christianity.

Lazarus. The poor man in Christ's parable (Luke 16:19–31) who suffered at the rich man's (Dives') gate.

Leibniz, G. W. (1646–1716). A German philosopher of metaphysics and mathematics. His work on perception, reality and logic was paralleled by his treatment of the problem of evil and the argument for God's existence based on perfection.

Lewis, C. S. (1878–1963). A well-known English writer and novelist whose work ranged from study of medieval English literature to apologetic Christian writing, and novels for children.

Locke, John (1632–1704). An English philosopher whose main work was in founding the English school of empiricism. He wrote extensively in political and educational philosophy as well as on religion and human understanding.

MacKay, Donald M. (1922–). An English scientist whose central written work is concerning the nature of intelligence and the relation of people and machines. He is a strong critic of a mechanistic view of the world.

Malcolm, Norman (1911–). An American philosopher who was a pupil of Ludwig Wittgenstein and who has developed an analysis of necessary being in relation to the ontological argument.

Mascall, E. L. (1905–). An English philosopher and cleric.

Matthew, Saint (1st cent. AD). Author of the first Gospel in the New Testament.

Mitchell, Basil G. (1917–). An Oxford philosopher of religion who first propounded the story of 'The Stranger', and has written widely on religion and morality.

Morris, Desmond J. (1928–). An Oxford sociologist who writes in the behaviourist school of psychology and sociology. His best-known book is *The Naked Ape*.

Moses (13th cent. BC). Old Testament law-giver and leader of the Israelites out of Egypt.

Newton, Isaac (1642–1727). An English scientist of mathematics, mechanics and physics who discovered the law of gravitation and expressed various laws of motion.

Nowell-Smith, P. (1914–). A British philosopher and ethicist who has published a well-known article on miracles and various books of ethics.

Occam (Ockham), William of (1290–1349). A medieval scholastic who followed the nominalist approach to philosophy. He stressed the principle of economy: 'Don't multiply entities unless you need to.' This principle was called Occam's razor.

Otto, Rudolf (1869–1937). A German philosopher of religion who explored religious phenomena and introduced some key terms to describe the nature of the phenomena and the feelings they create in humans (*e.g.* numinous, *fascinans, mysterium tremendum*).

Paley, William (1743–1805). An English theologian who worked in the area of rational theology, and produced an important version of the argument from design to prove God's existence.

Pascal, Blaise (1623–62). A French philosopher of mathematics and religion. He rejected rational proofs for God's existence and likened the basis of faith to a wager, where we have everything to gain and nothing to lose by believing that God exists.

Paul, Saint (1st cent. AD). Apostle to the Gentiles and author of many New Testament letters.

Peter, Saint (1st cent. AD). One of the disciples of Jesus. Leader of the early church.

Plantinga, Alvin. A contemporary American philosopher of religion who has written extensively on the proofs of faith.

Plato (*c.* 428–348 BC). A Greek philosopher. A pupil of Socrates and founder of the Academy. His work covered the nature of knowledge, reality, goodness, as well as political and aesthetic philosophy.

Poe, Edgar Allan (1801–49). American author of mystery and detective tales.

Popper, Karl (1902–). An Austrian philosopher of science who developed a theory of truth and meaning based on what is falsifiable.

Poseidon. The Greek god of the sea.

Price, H. H. (1899–). An English philosopher whose main work was on David Hume, and perception. He has been increasingly interested in the paranormal and its significance for human knowledge.

Quine, W. V. O. (1908–). An American logician and philosopher who deals with questions of being, sense, reference and meaning in logical terms.

Ramsey, Ian T. (1915–72). Anglican bishop and author of material on religion and language, science and metaphysics.

Russell, Bertrand (1872–1970). English philosopher famous for his work in mathematics and logic. Part of the empiricist school.

Schleiermacher, Friedrich (1768–1836). A German theologian and philosopher who stressed that the essence of religion is the feeling of absolute dependence. He followed the Irenaean view that suffering is in order to make souls.

Shakespeare, William (1564–1616). A famous English playwright and author of comedies, tragedies and many historical plays.

Smart, Ninian (1927–). A leading British phenomenologist of religion now working in the USA.

Spinoza, B. (1632–77). A Dutch philosopher of Jewish descent, who wrote on the topics of God and ethics. He followed a Cartesian, rationalist approach.

Stewart, James S. (1896–). A former Scottish professor of New Testament whose work covers theology, ethics, preaching and New Testament issues.

Temple, William (1881–1944). Former Archbishop of Canterbury who wrote about the incarnation and social/ethical issues.

Teresa of Avila (1515–82). A Spanish mystic.

Thomas Aquinas. See Aquinas.

Tillich, Paul (1886–1965). Well-known theologian who tried to bring together theology and philosophy as well as culture.

Tolkien, J. R. R. (1892–1973). An English professor and novelist, best known for his trilogy, *The Lord of the Rings*, and its forerunner, *The Hobbit*.

Torrance, T. F. (1913–). A Scottish theologian whose work has focused on the notion of theology as a science.

Urmson, J. O. (1915–). An English philosopher.

Uzziah (8th cent. BC). King during the time of Isaiah.

Wiles, Maurice (1923–). An English theologian who has written extensively on the early church and the doctrines of God and the person of Christ.

Wilson, Colin (1931–). An English philosopher and novelist fascinated by the paranormal.

Wisdom, John (1904–). An English philosopher who has worked on the different levels of interpretation and the problem of other minds. The creator of the parable of the garden.

Wittgenstein, Ludwig (1889–1951). An Austrian philosopher originally a positivist, who then stressed an approach to philosophy through language, using the idea of language-games. His work has been highly influential in modern philosophy.

Zeno of Elea (5th cent. BC). A Greek philosopher famous for his paradoxes.

Index of names

Index of topics